MIRROR MIRROR

KATHRYN WEIBEL received her Ph.D. in English from Michigan State University, where she taught courses on historical and contemporary images of women.

OTHER ANCHOR BOOKS OF INTEREST

Literary Women
Ellen Moers

Black-Eyed Susans: Classic Stories By and About Black Women
Edited by Mary Helen Washington

Another Voice: Feminist Perspectives on Social Life and Social Science
Edited by Marcia Millman and Rosabeth Moss Kanter

Androgyny
June Singer

No More Masks: An Anthology of Poems by Women
Edited by Florence Howe and Ellen Bass

The Oven Birds: American Women on Womanhood, 1820–1920
Edited with an introduction by Gail Parker

MIRROR MIRROR

Images of Women Reflected
in Popular Culture

KATHRYN WEIBEL

ANCHOR BOOKS
Anchor Press / Doubleday
Garden City, New York

1977

The Anchor Press edition is the first publication of *Mirror Mirror: Images of Women Reflected in Popular Culture*

Anchor Press edition: 1977

301.412
W415 m
1977

ISBN: 0-385-11131-2
Library of Congress Catalog Card Number 76–47835

Contents

Introduction   ix

1: Images of Women in Fiction   1

2: Images of Women on Television   47

3: Images of Women in Movies   91

4: Images of Women in Women's Magazines
and Magazine Advertising   135

5: Images of the Fashionable Woman   175

Epilogue   223

Notes   227

Index   241

Introduction

Specifically, as popular culture has portrayed them, American women have been *housewifely, passive, wholesome,* and *pretty.* Through the years, there have been numerous minor variations on these standard images, but a few reactionary periods notwithstanding, there has been little outright deviation from them.

In its broadest terms, the "housewifely" image portrays women in highly constrained or situated roles which are also suggestive of other aspects of the housewife lifestyle. At different times, various aspects of homemaking have been emphasized, including entertaining, sewing, interior decorating, cleaning, and caring for children, but women have always been portrayed as doing these tasks for themselves and their families, as opposed to making a professional career of them.

In some ways, the passive image of women in popular culture is closely related to the housewifely image, since it derives from the philosophy that man should be master of the house. Passivity has appeared as insecurity, lack of aggressiveness, and commonly as victimization, but in general the person making the heroine insecure or victimizing her is a male, usually her husband or boyfriend.

Likewise, the wholesome image of women is related to the others, since women have been portrayed using their assigned role as keepers of the national morality as a means of gaining power over men. In romance, being wholesome has generally meant being chaste, but chastity has, in turn, been used as a means to obtain a marriage proposal. In the several media adaptations of the domestic melodrama, moreover, religion and self-sacrifice have been used as a type of baptism by fire, through which heroines prove their superior moral fiber to the heroes, gaining a marriage proposal or regaining an erring spouse in the process.

"Pretty" merely rounds out the housewifely, passive, and wholesome images. Pretty heroines have been youthful and wholesomely attractive by the standards of the time, but not beautiful—in short, the ideal housewife type. The specific forms that these images have taken, however, can best be introduced and illustrated by citing examples from each of the media reviewed and analyzed in the following chapters.

Remember the "housewifely" image means that women in popular culture have been portrayed in domestic or highly situated roles. Dating back to the early nineteenth century, for example, domestic novels have always comprised a major category among best-selling fiction. Even the many teen-age heroines of domestic novels, from Susan Warner's *The Wide, Wide World* (1850) to *Pollyanna, The Glad Girl* (1913), have been confined to worlds defined by a house, a family, and often housework.

In addition to the heroines of explicitly domestic fiction, female characters in the ever popular romance stories are clearly future housewives, since beyond the marriage, no alternatives are posed for them. Even heroines of the "working girl" romances like those written by Laura Jean Libbey during the 1880s and 1890s, or like the modern Harlequin romances, are really only working at getting a husband.

Just as books have consistently mirrored a housewife lifestyle, so have popular magazines. In the pre-Civil War decades, the leading cultural magazine was a woman's magazine

—*Godey's Lady's Book*. It stressed the leisure pursuits of the housewife, such as fiction, fashion, and fancy stitchwork, since the educated, urban readers of *Godey's* were a prosperous and idle group by standards of the times. With the spread of public education, however, America became a nation of literates, and the leading women's magazines after the 1870s were aimed for the large middle class of housewives who did most of their own housework.

Even today, about half of all women choose to be housewives. During most of the nineteenth century fewer than 10 per cent of nonfarm females worked—the remainder were immigrant girls and other poor women who worked in factories and as domestic servants. Not that staying at home was without its responsibilities for the middle-class woman. Although the same industrialization which reduced the need for female labor provided her with canned and packaged foods, fabrics, lighting devices, and later a sewing machine and other domestic appliances (all used mainly by the hired girl), she was nonetheless expected to supervise the household, dress fashionably, and attend to the moral education of the young. But there was also much time for leisure, and middle-class women became avid readers.

Predictably, as women became a large and conspicuous reading public, clever authors and magazine editors (many of them female) began competing for the market. They presented images close to the lives of their readers, and in the process, laid down stereotypes that subsequent generations of writers, editors, and later, producers of the new electronic media would be wary to chance.

Ironically, "popular" culture, in the sense of art forms mass produced for a mass audience, has always been created by "middle" class practitioners and aimed for the growing middle-class audience that has time and money to enjoy it. This being the case, however, it is not surprising that, for over two hundred years, the image of women in popular culture has been a middle-class image reflective of the role assigned women under the division of labor created by the industrial revolution.

From the first, articles and advertisements in such magazines as *Ladies' Home Journal*, *McCall's*, or *Woman's Home Companion* were geared to help women create clean, healthy, and attractive homes. Since the major maintenance task of the housewife has always been cleaning, the earliest advertisers were soap companies. Brand-name food products, linens, furniture, and floor coverings were also advertised early on. After Edward Bok, the innovating second editor of *Ladies' Home Journal*, introduced women to the interiors of each other's homes, decorating ideas were added to the cooking, cleaning, and sewing services already provided. Over the years, some women's magazines have specialized in one aspect of homemaking, but even magazines aimed for the young working woman, such as *Redbook* or *Cosmopolitan*, assume that home entertaining, decorating, cooking, and so on are important parts of the reader's lifestyle. By contrast, only a few men's magazines assume home responsibilities.

Traditionally, the housewife image was key to magazine fiction as well, although since the turn of the century, fiction in the women's trade magazines has steadily decreased and more service articles have been substituted. The only mass magazines which currently emphasize fiction are the love story magazines of the *True Story* or *True Confessions* variety. But here again, these stories are really domestic melodramas of the type popular with novel readers of the nineteenth century.

When the movies entered their most prosperous decade, the 1920s, they too picked up on the housewife theme. Cecil B. De Mille's domestic dramas presented a very upper-class view of housewifery, with an emphasis on entertaining and fashions. A more melodramatic view of the domestic routine was preferred by Depression women who went regularly to the matinee "weepies." In these stories, the trials of a housewife (or the domestic trials of a working woman) provided the central movements of the plot. Although this type of movie largely disappeared after television stole the afternoon audiences, it was succeeded by a more cheerful, generally musical, postwar version aimed at the whole family. Actresses like Debbie Reynolds, Doris Day, or later, Julie Andrews proved their mettle as supermoms by taking in tow and reforming whole broods of children.

Meanwhile, as movies were turning their attention from weeping housewives to frolicking supermoms, television soap operas were being instated as the next legitimate heirs of the domestic melodrama. But in addition to the soaps, which dominate TV's afternoon hours, other types of programs also portray women as housewives. The morning game shows, for example, are really symbolic shopping sprees for the housewife consumer. And situation comedy has always been a family affair. Most women in the situation comedies are housewives or else working women in name only, since their jobs are seldom portrayed on the program. Even those sitcoms which portray women as single and career oriented, still show them confined to demanding relationships of a family type. The housewife image of women on television is especially impactful, moreover, since few alternative images are provided. Though there are more exceptions in recent years, programs without housewives have tended to be programs without any female regulars at all.

Even in the arena of women's fashions, the expectation that women would remain at home has been a prevailing influence. Although in the United States the men's business suit was fairly well standardized by the 1830s, "fashion" was geared for the idle woman until after the turn of the twentieth century. As middle-class women entered business occupations, all of women's fashion became less conspicuous and more practical. Not until the 1950s, however, did "house-wife" clothing, suburban style, become a fashion all its own.

If popular culture has consistently pictured women as housewives, it has just as relentlessly portrayed them as passive. In fact, the two images are closely tied together, since the expectation that women be passive is rooted in the philosophy that although a woman's *place* is in the home, she is not to be master, even there. The first superselling novel in America, Susanna Rowson's *Charlotte Temple* (1794—first U.S.), set forth the ultimately passive heroine—one who seemed to have no independent substance at all and who was totally victimized (seduced and abandoned) as a result.

The heroines of the nineteenth-century domestic novels were generally victims of poverty, desertion, or the unexpected death of a parent, but their own industry guaranteed their ultimate financial and usually romantic success anyway. However, despite the fact that the domestic novels revealed metaphorically that much was miserable about the housewife's lot, paid employment was justified in the novels only for the really desperate. Passivity and dependence were mandated for all the rest.

And despite the fact that romance is virtually the only adventure that literature allows to females, the romance heroine has standardly been, as critic Joanna Russ puts it, a passive protagonist. Heroines of recent romances are typically insecure in their dealings with everyone, especially the hero. They would never consider making a verbal, much less a physical, advance. Leaving a dangerous or highly unpleasant situation is usually as active as the most aggressive of these heroines get.

Women's magazines have also advised women to cater to their husband's wishes. Readers of *Godey's Lady's Book* and other pre-Civil War women's magazines were told in no uncertain terms that they should regard their husband's word as law. In 1905, *Ladies' Home Journal* readers themselves voted that the word "obey" should be kept in the marriage ceremony. And, notwithstanding the fact that articles in the women's trade magazines have projected the image of a practical housewife, advertising has introduced insecurities about everything from sick children to "yellow wash" to "undie odor." In addition, as late as 1971, studies indicate that fiction in magazines, aimed both for working-class and middle-class women, persists in portraying a majority of females as dependent, ineffectual, unemployed or underemployed, and as unable to achieve economic or social mobility through their own efforts.

Movies have offered the major exceptions to the passive image of women in popular culture. Though in recent years women in the movies have gone from passivity to obscurity, female characters were fairly spunky for over three decades beginning in the 1920s. One thinks, for example, of the adulterous wives in De Mille's domestic dramas; of the overtly sensuous Garbo and Dietrich; of wisecracking West and Harlow; of workers like Clara Bow, Joan Crawford, Jean Arthur and Rosalind Russell; of high society dames like Katharine Hepburn; and of perpetually psychotic Bette Davis. In the post-World War Two decade, heroines by and large pursued woman's oldest adventure—man hunting.

In an almost complete turn-around during the 1960s and 1970s, however, women in movies have been progressively victimized by men and by their own passions. More perversely, they were the victims of mass lady killers in movies like 10 Rillington Place, Frenzy, and Stepford Wives.

But if movies have portrayed women as more and more victimized during the 1960s and 1970s, television soap operas have raised voluntary suffering and needless self-sacrificing to new heights of popularity during the same time period. Whether male or female, characters on the soaps prove their goodness by being constantly worried about someone else's welfare and by becoming victims in order that someone else might be spared.

By comparison, women are often portrayed as aggressive on the evening situation comedies, but this aggressiveness is never placed within a context of achievement. Instead, female (and male) aggression always appears in the context of failure. That's why it's funny, however. The heroine's funny failure may be anything from a mild misinterpretation of someone's actions to a badly mangled attempt to make women's liberation converts at a Christmas party. More alarmingly, though, studies have shown that most of the victims on the evening drama and adventure programs are portrayed by women and minorities. By contrast, of course, almost all of the heroes on these programs are white males.

Well beyond the propaganda value of the passive images of women, however, women were literally physically coerced into passivity by the corsets and confining, body-contorting fashions that were mandatory throughout the nineteenth century for all who could afford them. The ornate and heavy dresses had much in common with the stuffed-looking furniture of the period, since both were designed to suggest luster and comfort within the home. Not until designers and manufacturers aimed specifically to attract middle-income college girls, working girls, and housewives did styles come to reflect a more active life. Gabrielle "Coco" Chanel finally unshackled women completely when she introduced short skirts and simple, uncorseted styles at the end of World War One. After World War Two, however, when women were being urged to leave their wartime jobs to the men and return to homemaking, fashion under the leadership of Christian Dior again called for mildly confining clothes. To complement his many "figure-8" styles, resurrected from nineteenth-century couture, Dior recommended that ladies wear a short corset designed to take two inches off the waist. Even after the waistless look again became popular in the 1950s, however, skirts got so short as to be partially immobilizing. Though tights and pantyhose made women feel covered up in the mini fashions, it was necessary to stand perfectly straight or else sit with legs tightly crossed in order to remain visually decent by conventional standards of the time. But in rejecting both the mini and the midi in favor of the pants suit, women in the 1970s have reasserted their right to choose styles allowing mobility and freedom as opposed to those suggesting confinement and dependence.

Like the housewifely and passive images, the image of women as "wholesome" has roots in the practical reality of the female lifestyle. Women have often been portrayed as religious and as helpful to the point of needless self-sacrifice, but such "wholesomeness" has always been calculated to produce very tangible, earthly rewards. Because of the extreme power inequities between women and men during the nineteenth century, domestic novelists pictured heroines using appeals to God as a means of overriding the authority of husbands. By association with the divinity, women in these novels gained a type of power denied them in their subordinate, domestic position. One indication of the fruits of this power in these novels was the heroine's ability to convert derelicts into religious zealots.

All the heirs of the domestic melodrama, including the movie weepies, the television soap operas, and the *True Story*-type magazine fiction, have followed the format of portraying self-sacrificing or religious heroines. This is because the basic fantasy behind the melodrama formula itself involves a belief in benevolent forces in the universe, most simply stated as a belief in God. Metaphorically, this belief in a benevolent universe is illustrated when evils, and apparent injustices are rectified at the end of a melodrama. The evil seducer is killed, the lost fortune is recovered, the erring husband returns to the fold, the child that died is replaced, and so forth.

Ever since Samuel Richardson wrote *Pamela* in 1740, chastity has also been stressed by popular culture as a particularly important virtue for women. In the main, this is because withholding sex has been recommended as a practical means of obtaining a husband. In particular, chastity has commonly been assumed for heroines of romance fiction. Not infrequently, too, would-be seducers emphasize the heroine's virginity by trying to lure it away from her.

Likewise, chastity was taken as a standard by women's

magazines. Even the more titillating stories in the *True Story*-type magazines portray heroines as paying dearly if they succumb to their sexual passions. After the birth control pill came into widespread use during the 1960s, however, a national woman's magazine, *Cosmopolitan*, was able to adopt a positive posture toward sex outside of marriage without incurring the taint of social irresponsibility.

Chastity was imposed from without on the movie industry. Although the first movies had been often burlesque vaudeville adaptations attended by men, women and children were lured as an audience by the presentation of wholesome young heroines. The movies lost their virginity quickly in the 1920s, though, and what with Garbo, West, and Harlow, images got even sexier up until a surge of protest from such guardians of morality as the Catholic National League of Decency, the Daughters of the American Revolution, and William Randolph Hearst forced the movie industry to adopt the Production Code of 1933. From 1933 up until the late 1950s, when television became the primary family medium, the censors kept close watch over screen sex. During this time, heroines could be assertive, headstrong, or crazy, but they couldn't be overtly sexual. By the time the censors lost interest in monitoring screen sex, however, moviemakers had lost interest in strong women, so stories about unwed mothers, unhappy affairs, brutalized sexpots, and a few sensationalized accounts of lesbianism have appeared in lieu of more aggressive and satisfying portraits of females examining their sexuality.

Although not all television characters are portrayed as chaste by any means, chastity remains the standard for America's most popular medium. Women on the soap operas frequently fall victim to their passions, but they made retribution with disgrace, abandonment, or unwed motherhood—at least temporarily. Until recently, female characters were presumed chaste on the situation comedies, but television has expanded its perspective to embrace more current normal behavior, so now single women may have affairs, though adultery is still taboo. On the evening drama and adventure programs, however, where women are generally transient characters only, females are frequently sexual, even prostitutes.

Rounding out the picture of women in popular culture is the "pretty" image, since "pretty" is really only the wholesome, youthful, housewifely, and passive side of beauty as our culture sees it. Thus the popularity of the expression "Pretty is as pretty does." By contrast, beautiful women, often the rivals of heroines, are usually portrayed by popular culture as, at minimum, vain and, quite often, as outright corrupt.

Again, movies have provided the greatest number of exceptions. But since being "pretty" is associated with being young and wholesome, it should not be surprising that most of the glamourous movie actresses have portrayed overtly sexual roles as well. Again, think of Gloria Swanson in the De Mille domestic dramas, or Garbo, Harlow, Dietrich, or West in their early 1930s roles. After the Production Code went into effect, however, movie heroines got less unusually beautiful, less overtly sensual, and more conventionally "pretty," as with Jean Arthur, Claudette Colbert, and Irene Dunne, for example.

The heroines of the post-World War Two musicals were also conventionally pretty, but they were heaped into the "glamour" category by the flashy displays of their figures. Those like Doris Day and Debbie Reynolds who kept their figures under locks were the daytime versions of the sexpots.

Unable to tolerate intense images of any sort (remember Richard Nixon's image-making problems in the presidential campaign of 1968), the television medium has always portrayed women as more pretty than beautiful. Men are not portrayed as superhandsome by television either, of course. In fact, most men on television are portrayed as middle-aged and fairly ordinary-looking, despite their cool, professional airs. Similarly, advertising in women's magazines must be careful not to offend the broad segment of middle Americans, so it is careful to suggest wholesomeness by portraying women as pretty as opposed to ravishingly beautiful. In this way, too, the reader of the ad has an image to aspire to, without being closed out by the utter impossibility of achieving it.

By writing a survey text jointly focused on women and popular culture, I hope to contribute additional perspective to the study of both subjects. It is apparent, first of all that the current interest in women and women's issues is not an isolated condition produced by the Women's Liberation Movement. Women have eagerly sought reflections of their lives and concerns where these have been available—in the popular media. What have been almost completely absent until recently, however, are critical *assessments* of the motivations and values behind these reflections. Because of the superior political and economic standing men enjoy in this country, relatively more analytical evaluations of their activities exist at all levels. Any student of history knows that it is the story of men. In addition, male academics, dominant in the profession, have generated more serious scholarship on popular forms portraying masculine fantasies, like the crime drama, for instance, than on female-oriented forms, like the love story. More synthesis and evaluation of the type presented in this book are needed just to balance the scales.

Clearly, moreover, this book is about popular culture just as much as it is about women. No one seriously doubts the influence of the popular media. Children mimic TV violence; women commit suicide at the death of a movie idol; a plane is hijacked following a television movie on that theme; girls across the country wear their hair like Olympic ice skating champion Dorothy Hamill. Even more influential, I would argue, are the subtle images endlessly depicting men and women leading "normal" lives. It is hard for a girl growing up with a Donna Reed image of womanhood to consider a career as a doctor. Similarly, boys who see fatherhood portrayed repeatedly as a joke by the media must surely approach the role with distaste.

In part, then, this book is intended to help close the currently incomplete loop between the popular culture image and the individual. In the absence of some type of evaluation of popular culture images, the relationship between the media and the individual is a one-way street. The image bombards the individual. By providing "feedback" or descriptive evaluation of dominant images of women, however, this book aims to help open options for individuals to reject or even change the image.

Every era has its short-range critics of popular culture, of course. There are people who review plays, books, and movies; fashion commentators; editors of magazines; as well as a host of self-styled cultural critics of various sorts. A true process of evaluation, however, requires a historical perspective since we need to know about the origins of popular culture images if we are to judge the validity of the cultural norms they pose for our own present lives.

As opposed to the more analytical framework suggested by a treatment of women in popular culture on an image-by-image basis, therefore, I have chosen to present the dominant images evaluated in this book "story fashion," by giving a brief history of each popular culture medium included and incorporating the images of women into the discussion. I thought it was important at the outset, though, to identify the major images of women that have consistently recurred throughout American popular culture, since they provide a common thread which lends internal unity to each of the chapters and links each to the book as a whole.

More specifically, I have tried to deal with the images of women in popular culture in the context of those who created the images, or the practitioners, and in the broader cultural context of the times. Thus, for example, the image of the deserted wife in Mrs. E. D. E. N. Southworth's domestic novels is discussed in relationship to Mrs. Southworth's own life as a deserted wife and in the context of nineteenth-century marriage norms in general.

Of necessity in a book of this length, the treatment of each medium and of the images portrayed has had to be fairly generalized. And, in truth, the study has also been limited by the availability of primary materials as well (such as the nineteenth-century novels, for example, which are now collectors' items). The book does not aim to be a definitive study of women in popular culture. Rather, I hope it will be a useful and practical guide to dominant trends in the portrayal of women in popular culture, and one which will in the process suggest to each reader some of the exciting areas of research which beckon to those interested in uncovering and evaluating our past history as women.

A number of people contributed toward making this book a reality. I would like to thank Prof. Victor Howard, Director of the American Studies Program at Michigan State University, and Prof. James H. Pickering, formerly Associate Chairman of the Department of English at Michigan State University, for their encouragement to develop the courses that eventually became the major substance of this book. Special thanks go to Prof. Russel B. Nye, Distinguished Professor of English at Michigan State University, for his continued aid and information during the research phases of this project and for reading part of the manuscript. Parts of the draft were also read and critiqued by Marion Welsh Van Winkle, Steven M. Freeman, and Ardith H. Weibel. Finally, my thanks and appreciation to Claudia Ospovat for her creative design and illustration of the costumes shown in the chapters on women's fashions.

MIRROR MIRROR

1.

Images of Women
in Fiction

No one would deny that "women's themes" are big business for the popular media these days, especially for the most highly reviewed and analyzed medium—best-selling fiction. A majority of the new best sellers by and about women are part of the so-called "raised consciousness" school. Books about disillusioned wives and lovers, like Sue Kaufman's *Diary of a Mad Housewife*, Eleanor Bergstein's *Advancing Paul Newman*, Anne Roiphe's *Up the Sandbox*, Jill Robinson's *Bed/Time/Story*, or Alison Lurie's *War Between the Tates* (to name only a few), have found large audiences. Variations on the "growing up female" theme (especially when set in the 1960s), like Ruth Doan McDoughall's *The Cheerleader*, or Alix Kate Shulman's *Memoirs of an Ex-Prom Queen*, have proven to be as popular. Books lacing these standard formulas with liberal doses of sex are most popular—Erica Jong's *Fear of Flying* or Lisa Alther's *Kinflicks*, for example.

In part, of course, the popularity of these books is linked to the influence of the Women's Liberation Movement of the very early 1970s. Not since the last liberation period of the 1920s have the heroines of so many best sellers been so eager to question and discard traditional female roles and behavior. But echoing the outcome of such 1920s novels as

A. S. M. Hutchinson's *This Freedom*, Booth Tarkington's *Claire Ambler*, or Warner Fabian's *Flaming Youth*, endings of the modern novels suggest no new or satisfying alternatives for liberated women. Heroines in the former novels typically gave up independence for marriage or a renewed commitment to family life; heroines of the 1970s novels often give up everything for a state of confusion. Nonetheless, in both cases, their greater awareness of self, evident at novel's end, is intended to indicate a better life ahead. (At minimum, we suspect that the heroines of the autobiographical modern novels will glean a small fortune by writing about their experiences.)

In a larger sense, however, the roots of most of the current "raised consciousness" best sellers lie not in the 1970s Women's Liberation Movement but in a tradition of women and popular culture which dates back at least as far as the middle eighteenth century, when fiction became the staple popular medium. These stories, like the fiction in magazines such as *Redbook* or *Cosmopolitan* or so-called feminist movies like *Klute* or *Alice Doesn't Live Here Anymore*, are really just contemporary variations on the theme that has consistently interested female audiences most—male/female relationships.

To point out that modern, more liberated stories tend to focus on traditional female themes like courtship, marriage, or life within a family is not to say that these themes lack artistic potential. But the work of the best writers on these subjects, though they have devoted audiences, rarely become best sellers. For example, Alice Walker's stories of black women sacrificing selfhood for the respectability of marriage; Joyce Carol Oates's vision of the violence embedded deeply within the nuclear family structure; and Mary Lavin's stories about widowhood are too depressing and pessimistic to appeal to the masses as escapist literature.

Best-selling fiction, on the other hand, like popular movies, regular TV series, popular magazines, and other forms of popular culture, is reassuring and generally optimistic. Popular writers achieve these qualities by sticking to time-tested formulas that people have learned to trust for escape and relaxation. And since Samuel Richardson invented the popular novel in the 1740s, the fictional formulas which have consistently appealed to women have been the romance, or courtship tale, and the domestic melodrama. In both formulas, of course, relationships between the sexes provide the focus.

By contrast, popular formulas aimed for a male audience, like the crime story or the Horatio Alger-style success saga, almost never focus on male/female relationships. "Getting the girl" may be part of the protagonist's dream, but it's more comparable to getting a big house or a pretty dress in women's formulas. The hero's primary fantasy involves overcoming great dangers, competing victoriously with other men, amassing a great fortune, or the like. Such fantasies are symbolic of accomplishments in the world of work whereas the fantasies in "female formulas" symbolize domestic successes.

Recently one reviewer expressed frustration at the proliferation of not-too-hot novels exploiting to good profit Sue Kaufman's *Diary of a Mad Housewife* theme. The authors of these books had narrowed themselves down to a fine formula, she observed: "Woman wakes up in empty trough of marriage and deserts in search of her identity." The reviewer was right of course, and in fact, there are other predictable elements of the so-called "raised consciousness" best sellers as well. Most are written in the first person and have an autobiographical tone that is all too convincing. (Many are first and, we suspect, only novels.) Although the protagonist's thoughts and emotions are described to the minutest detail, other characters tend to be shadowy, especially the males. There is frequently a psychiatrist or other helping figure in the book and, at novel's end, the protagonist is typically in a state of confusion, but she clearly wants a new direction for her life.

The tendency to exploit a provenly popular formula is not

unique to modern female authors of the raised-consciousness school, however. Far from it. Imitating and adapting other popular books have always been standard practices among those aiming for the best-seller charts. For another example, someone writes a book in which a luxury liner is capsized by a tidal wave, eventually killing almost everybody on board. By courage, perseverance, and teamwork, however, a few manage to survive. The book is a best seller, and what is more, a movie version quickly follows it. Essentially a horror/adventure story, though elements of romance figure in as well, the specific ingredients—including unforeseen disaster, lives of many threatened, courageous handling of the situation by "the few," etc.—are soon excerpted by other clever writers who then go on to write books about people struck by disaster in airplanes, hundred-story hotels, on vacation islands, or in their own homes, as the rumbles of an earthquake begin. Before the popularity of these books wanes, the authors have worked out a precise and predictable "formula" guaranteed to give readers (and moviegoers) just what they want.

A few formulas, moreover, have proved themselves so popular that, once invented, they have remained staples of popular literature. Although many critics have recognized and passed judgment on the recurrent popularity of such formulas as the Western, the detective story, or the love story, the best attempt at defining and analyzing literary formulas has been done by John G. Cawelti. Chapters One and Two of his book, *Adventure, Mystery and Romance* (1976), provide an accessible and concise overview of his methodology and some of his conclusions.[1]

In brief, Cawelti theorizes that popular formulas are 1) conventional and predictable in their outcomes, and 2) oriented toward some form of escapism. These conclusions may seem obvious, but Cawelti carries the analysis much further by defining the specific type of escape provided by the various formulas. Above all, he says, readers want to escape from the boundaries of their own limitations, so all formulas pose a hero or heroine who personally overcomes obstacles of some type or who is favored with luck or providence in such a way as to come out victorious over obstacles. The fantasy—Cawelti calls it the "moral fantasy"—embodied in all formulas, then, is the fantasy of overcoming obstacles; the nature of the obstacles and the manner in which they are overcome, however, defines the particular formula. Cawelti assumes that there are five *basic* formulas, each with its own defining moral fantasy. These are 1) adventure, 2) romance, 3) mystery, 4) melodrama, and 5) imaginary beings or states (loosely, science fiction and horror stories). In the case of adventure formulas like the Western or spy story, the moral fantasy involves overcoming internal cowardice as well as external forces such as lawlessness and injustice; the romance formula posits that love is triumphant and permanent, overcoming all obstacles between the lovers; the moral fantasy of the mystery is that problems have desirable and rational solutions (which can be discovered); the moral fantasy of the melodrama is a reassurance that the forces of the universe are benevolent and that good ultimately triumphs over evil, no matter how bad or meaningless things may seem on the surface; with regard to alien beings and states, Cawelti says that the moral fantasy is that the unknowable can be *known* (different from "solved," "changed," or "normalized") and related to in some meaningful fashion.

Traditionally, the most popular fiction has been formula fiction. This was so much the case with the domestic melodrama during the nineteenth century that authors like Herman Melville, Nathaniel Hawthorne, Edgar Allan Poe, and Henry James could scarcely find an audience. In his often quoted appraisal of the situation in 1855, Hawthorne bitterly complained that "America is now wholly given over to a damned mob of scribbling women, and I should have no chance of success while the public taste is occupied with their trash. . . ."[2]

Over the years, two formulas have been especially appealing to women—the romance and the melodrama. Both formulas first took on their modern construction over two hundred years ago when Samuel Richardson invented the dramatically unified novel as we know it today. The basic plot of Richardson's first novel, *Pamela* (1740), will sound familiar to fans of the modern paperback romance: A respectable middle-class girl takes a job on the household staff of an aristocratic older woman. Shortly thereafter, she meets her employer's handsome and sophisticated son. The heroine appears to be attracted to him, but she also suspects him of evil intentions toward her (in this case, seduction). When her suspicions seem confirmed beyond a doubt, she flees. At last, the young aristocrat confesses his love and asks her to marry him.

The plot of Richardson's second and best novel, *Clarissa*, would sound more familiar to followers of the modern soap opera. All Clarissa really wanted out of life was a marriage that would allow her some minimal amount of personal happiness, in addition to the necessary financial security. Since Richardson wished to escape the charge of petty materialism (heaped on him by Henry Fielding after *Pamela*), he did what a modern soap opera writer would never do, however. He let pious Clarissa suffer unjustified disownment by her family, the disapproval of friends, and a sexual assault by the dashing hero, Lovelace, without in the end rewarding her with a happy marriage. Instead, Clarissa died of a broken heart, and religious fundamentalists tearfully accepted Richardson's statement that she would be rewarded in heaven. Significantly, *Clarissa*, which is a very long work, was issued in seven small volumes. The heroine's trials and the moral issues surrounding her fate were discussed much like television soap opera characters and dilemmas are discussed today.

Although there are differences between *Pamela* and *Clarissa* and more recent romances and melodramas, it is the pattern of similarities which is most striking. In addition to the superficial features of the plot, this pattern encompasses similarities in the style of narration, in the structural relationship between characters, and in the setting. Well beyond the surface similarities, however, fiction written for women over the past two and a half centuries has communicated to its readers a set of common images and values relatively unaffected by the passage of time.

Stated most simply, the archetypal heroine of popular women's literature has been wholesome, housewifely, passive, and pretty (and white of course). In relation to the hero, heroines have been younger, less experienced, of lower social or occupational status, less affluent, *but* more virtuous. Simply to scatter these images out of context, however, is not enough, since they have appeared in different guises and to varying intensities at different times. "Wholesome," for instance, meant sexually chaste in the early sentimental romances, whereas it often meant religious zealotry in the nineteenth-century domestic melodramas. By the twentieth-century romances, "wholesome" had been reduced to sensitivity and a knack for children and things domestic. The essential sameness of the images of women in popular fiction, then, is best understood through highlighting the marginal differences between the formulas which were dominant at various times.

Since *Pamela* and *Clarissa* established literary conventions and articulated images and values that have been widely imitated ever since, it should not be surprising that the cultural milieu in which Richardson wrote has, in many respects, remained the same up to the present time. Writing during the early years of England's Industrial Revolution, Richardson set forth a telling portrayal of middle-class lifestyles and values, just as they were beginning to emerge. In particular, Richardson's novels recorded the change in the status of women that accompanied the dawn of the industrial era. Some understanding of this change is crucial to an understanding of the images of women in subsequent popular culture.

In brief, the institution of marriage underwent its own little revolution when England made the transition from a nation of farmers to a nation of shopkeepers. As Ian Watt has shown in *The Rise of the Novel*, events conspired at this time to make marriage at once more important for women yet more difficult to obtain.[3] Marriage became more *important* primarily for status reasons. In the towns and cities, unmarried female dependents, always useful to a farm family, had little to contribute by way of payment for their upkeep once most household necessities could be purchased in shops. Even so, being a superfluous dependent was preferable to taking a low-paid, low-status job in a factory or as a serving girl, and "respectable" employment options did not become available for middle-class women until the late nineteenth century. By contrast, being a wife in the prebirth control era automatically gave one the vital function of being a mother as well.

Marriage became more *difficult* for women to obtain because it became less appealing for many men. To begin with, along with increasing professionalism and specialization came a decreasing need for the home to do double duty as factory. By the same token that middle-class women could purchase most of their household needs in the shops, so could men. Furthermore, for the rising young businessman, a wife and children could be positive economic liabilities.

Richardson's novels, however, urged middle-class women to adopt values and behavior designed to maximize on their chances in the marriage market. The "heroes" of both *Pamela* and *Clarissa* hope to establish a sexual liaison with the respective heroines. Both, however, ultimately propose marriage when it is clear that they will not be able to achieve their goals in any other manner. Clarissa turns down Lovelace's offer of marriage since he has previously assaulted her sexually, but Richardson's message is as clear in this novel as it was in *Pamela*: men won't buy sex with marriage if they can get it free.

Of special significance is the fact that Pamela, who was rewarded by marriage because she did not give in to the sexual advances of her employer's son, was set forth by Richardson as a model of virtue. Richardson subtitled *Pamela*, "A Tale of Virtue Rewarded." As the farce *Shamela*, attributed to Henry Fielding, poignantly illustrates, however, there is a great irony in presenting Pamela as virtuous since the letters she writes to her parents reveal that she is constantly *thinking* about the possibility of being sexually defiled. In fact, Pamela is neither innocent nor particularly virtuous. She is a practical young woman, a shrewd entrepreneur, not unlike Richardson himself.[4]

Samuel Richardson was well acquainted with the problems and temptations facing young women of his class, though he prided himself on the fact that he had always been proper in his own conduct, never setting anyone a bad example. As a boy, Richardson had assisted young women in answering letters to their boyfriends, and later in life, he always maintained a bevy of admiring female friends. By contrast, he was ill at ease in the company of men. Richardson, who had been apprenticed to a printer and gained financial success in that trade, made two expeditious marriages. The first was to his master's daughter; after this wife died, he married the sister of a bookseller. It seems inconceivable, however, that Richardson himself would have married a poor serving girl like Pamela.

Since she was a female prototype of the author himself, however, Richardson was completely sympathetic with the heroine of his first novel, and he remained convinced that Pamela's avoidance of seduction was grounded in Christian virtue. As a result, Richardson became the first of a long line of popular novelists to canonize as supreme virtues the ethical or religious values which are also the most practical tools for social survival.

Although the prescriptions for achieving it have altered somewhat over the years, novels have continued to portray marriage as a good woman's Great Reward and courtship as her Great Adventure. This stands to reason since, even up to the present time, marriage is more advantageous financially and socially for women than for men. (Interestingly, though, studies indicate that marriage may be less *psychologically* satisfying for women.)[5] This is especially true in the case of housewives, whose social status and economic well-being are usually determined entirely by their husbands. But it is also the case for women who work.

It is true that the technological advancements which have characterized the industrial era have directly and indirectly created lifestyle options for middle-class women. In this regard probably the two most beneficial by-products of stepped up industrialism include the demand for female white-collar labor which began during the late nineteenth century, and the development of the technology of birth control.

Despite the options to work and/or not to reproduce, however, most women desire a husband and children, and almost 50 per cent still prefer to be housewives. There are some practical considerations which contribute to this preference, however. Throughout the Western world, the higher-status, higher-paying jobs still go to men. Pursuing a career, therefore, may be to a woman's financial, and often social, disadvantage if it precludes marriage. A teacher or nurse, for example, will not be as financially secure as the wife of a doctor or a lawyer. Thus, the popularity of Richardson's marriage-oriented romance and melodrama formulas continues.

The formula originals, *Pamela* and *Clarissa*, were immensely popular books, both initially and for decades afterward. Solely on the basis of public demand, Richardson wrote a part two to *Pamela*. Rarely read today, this sequel deals with the heroine's married life to Mr. B. and the problems she encountered in her advanced social station. Since *Clarissa* was issued serially, its reading literally became a public event, and Richardson corresponded with many of his readers. When the word got out that Clarissa was to be raped by Lovelace, his fans begged him to change the plot, though of course to no avail.

There was good reason why *Pamela* and *Clarissa* were so successful, even though most of England's population was still illiterate in the eighteenth century. Richardson self-consciously wrote for the country's largest group of readers: middle-class women. Especially in the cities, the growth of economic specialization went hand in hand with increased female leisure. The wives and daughters of industrious and prosperous small businessmen had less work to do. Since social life was also largely segregated by sex, women had a great many evening, as well as daytime, hours for reading. Among the lower classes, servant girls had the best opportunity to acquire the reading habit. That being the case, Pamela no doubt found a large audience of eager imitators among the literate waiting maids.

Richardson's novels also found a ready audience in the American colonies, however. Herbert Brown, who has studied the sentimental novel in America prior to 1860, shows that even critics whose approval of fiction "was never very thoroughgoing" approved of Richardson. Fiction was disapproved of on grounds that it was dishonest or a type of false witness to life, and sentimental fiction was particularly frowned on by some who thought it encouraged an indulgence in the feelings at the expense of rational attention to moral principles. Richardson seemed true and rational to many of these critics, however, who believed that Richardson's "moral messages" were very good for youth to read. Brown reports that an instructor of a girl's school in New Haven, Connecticut, said that Pamela and Clarissa, along with Edward Young's Night Thoughts and a few other books, were significant factors in the development of female character in America before the establishment of seminaries for women (beginning in about the 1840s).[6]

Eager to capitalize on the large and growing audience of female readers, a spate of authors began publishing stories patterned on the Richardson formula. Significantly, a large proportion of these new professionals were women. One third of the roughly two hundred original works of fiction written between 1789 and 1829, were written by women, including most of the best sellers.[7] In fact, writing was the first profession in which women competed on an equal footing with men, achieving financial success in the process. Thus, in an ironic sort of way, the status of independent women in the real world was slowly being advanced at the same time that the image of the passive, marriage-oriented heroine was proliferating.

Susanna Haswell Rowson was a sterling example of this new class of literary professionals. Though British by birth, America was Rowson's country of adoption, and during her active professional life in this country, she ably demonstrated her skills as an actress, playwright, poet, novelist, magazine contributor and editor, and founder and chief instructor at the best ladies' academy in Boston. When a girl of sixteen, Susanna Haswell's father, a British officer and collector of royal customs, had been forced to take his family back to England during the years preceding the Revolutionary War. Susanna saved the day by securing a position as governess in the family of the Duchess of Devonshire and then maneuvering a pension for her father. A few years later, Susanna's industry and her talent for novel writing cushioned the blow when her young husband's hardware business collapsed. Thereafter, she was the principal breadwinner for the family, which included William Rowson's sister, his son, and eventually several adopted daughters.

In view of Rowson's own active, independent, and very successful life, it is ironic that in her highly didactic novels, one of which remained the overall best seller in this country for over half a century, she strongly cautioned her female readers against straying from the conventional mode. In *Charlotte Temple: A Tale of Truth*, a novel which went through more than two hundred American editions, Rowson retells a simplified version of Richardson's seduction melodrama. The author's claim that the tale was based on fact is reinforced by the terse narrative, which is almost completely devoid of picturesque description. Despite the constant editorial sermonizing by the author, the book reads somewhat like a newspaper article.

Perhaps out of a sense of social reality, Rowson's central

message in *Charlotte* is that young women must stifle their "sensibility" (translate "sexuality"), distrust men (especially the flatterers), and remain faithful wards of their parents until a duly legitimate marriage takes place. Ever thereafter, a wise and righteous woman will remain faithful, dutiful, and even content with her married lot, no matter if this devotion illicits only indifference from her spouse.

Like Pamela and Clarissa before her, Charlotte's virtue is defined in terms of chastity, and her parents represent conventional morality in the story. But unlike Pamela and Clarissa, who do make *choices*, Charlotte seems to possess no independent substance at all. She is the ultimately passive heroine, wafted about by the forces which surround her. At first presented as the ideal child and the darling of her parents' heart, she then comes under the total influence of her French teacher LaRue, who persuades her to elope with Montraville, a British soldier about to begin an American assignment. Once in America, she makes no friends despite the fact that Montraville has failed to keep his promise of marriage, and Charlotte can see that his affection is waning. (He is courting a pleasant young woman of means; Charlotte's parents were respectable but poor.) A potential benefactress acquaints herself with Charlotte, but pride prevents Charlotte from expressing the extent of her need. Finally, alone, penniless, and desolate, Charlotte dies giving birth to a daughter. Metaphorically, Charlotte's death said that there was simply no place in society for an unwed mother.

Mrs. Rowson is emphatic in her statements that even the worst marriage is preferable to a fate such as Charlotte's. Although her initial statement in the "Preface" states that "for the perusal of the young and thoughtless of the fair sex, this Tale of Truth is designed," Rowson's moralizing on marriage indicates that her Tale is intended for disillusioned wives as well. The story portrays no character in the role of a spurned but forbearant wife, but Mrs. Rowson describes the remnant blessings of such a state in one of the book's longest narrative interruptions. "Who can form an adequate idea of the sorrow that preyed upon the mind of Charlotte?" Rowson asks her readers, and then answers her own question:

> The wife whose breast glows with affection to her husband, and who in return meets only indifference, can but faintly conceive her anguish. Dreadfully painful is the situation of such of a woman, but she has many comforts of which our poor Charlotte was deprived. The dutious, faithful wife, though treated with indifference, has one solid pleasure within her own bosom, she can reflect that she has not deserved neglect—that she has ever fulfilled the duties of her station with the strictest exactness; she may hope, by constant assiduity and unremitted attention to recall her wanderer, and be doubly happy in his returning affection; she knows he cannot leave her to unite himself to another: he cannot cast her out to poverty and contempt; she looks around her and sees the smile of friendly welcome, or the tears of affectionate consolation on the face of every person whom she favours with her esteem, and from all these circumstances she gathers comfort . . .[8]

Variations on the seduction theme, all featuring heroines whose fates seem to hang by their chastity belts, proliferated in the decades following the Revolutionary War. Notable among these were the first novel written by a native American, William Hill Brown's *The Power of Sympathy* (1789), and Hannah Webster's *The Coquette* (1797), among others, as well as numerous Gothic thrillers which featured a passive and virtuous heroine continually on the brink of ravishment by the villain.

By about the 1830s, however, the seduction theme had lost its central position in popular literature, having been replaced by themes closer to Rowson's advice to disillusioned wives. Helen Papashvily, whose book *All the Happy Endings* records her studies of the nineteenth-century domestic novel in America, claims that there were good reasons for the decline of the seduction story.[9] According to Papashvily, such novels simply failed to reflect any reality that the nineteenth-century

American woman could identify with. The combination of prosperity, lingering frontier conditions (in which women and children remained productive), and an overpopulation of males helped to make marriage relatively easy for women in this country during the nineteenth century. As Papashvily put it, to give away freely what one could put up for competitive bids seemed more like stupidity than passion or folly. After the sensational aspect of the seduction theme wore thin then, it no longer remained a topic of popular literary sympathy.

But making the actual feminine lifestyle into interesting reading was not an easy task, even for women writers. Frances Trollope, mother of British author Anthony Trollope, was disturbed by the female lifestyles she observed during her travels in America between 1827 and 1830. She described the life of many city women as alternating between boardinghouse and the Dorcas sewing circle. According to Trollope, these women shared little time with their husbands and spent most of each day doing fancy stitchwork or exchanging religious gossip with each other.[10] Twenty years later, James Fenimore Cooper painted a slightly different but no more exciting picture when he reflected about the American wife that "Her husband and children compose her little world, and beyond them and their sympathies, it is rare indeed that her truant affections ever wish to stray."[11]

Ironically, for men, the period from 1830 to 1850 was a time of optimism and increased faith in the achievements of individuals. The "Age of Jackson" brought universal white male suffrage and free education, in addition to a wave of general prosperity. Though women could take advantage of the new educational opportunities (and many middle-class women did), they could not go on to apply their new abilities in the political realm or in the world of work.

In her excellent article "The Lady and the Mill Girl: Changes in the Status of Women in the Age of Jackson," Gerda Lerner emphasizes that after 1830, class differences must be recognized when discussing American women.[12] She argues that stepped-up industrialization benefited lower-class women early on since it gave them economic opportunities in the mills and factories. Since teaching was the only organized profession which admitted women during these years, however, and only at wages less than half those of men, middle-class women continued to look on the role of housewife as the best and only realistic option. Once married, of course, working outside the home was unthinkable. To the contrary, a primary measure of a businessman's success was the degree of luxury and idleness in which he could maintain his wife. In reality, however, the "work" involved in constant child-bearing and routine domestic management, especially given the very unhealthy clothing styles and the lack of any real physical exercise, wore many women into an early grave.

Helen Papashvily has argued that the nineteenth-century domestic novel alleviated the isolation and frustration of a majority of these literate middle-class women in the same way that activism in the budding woman's movement alleviated these symptoms of powerlessness for a more select group of politically aware women. Though Papashvily's conclusion that the domestic novels "encouraged a pattern of behavior so quietly ruthless, so subtly vicious that by comparison the ladies at Seneca appear angels of innocence" seems a bit overdrawn, the evidence indicates that these novels did articulate the problems faced by middle-class housewives, thereby providing a sense of communal sympathy and implicitly suggesting some alternative means of mitigating or solving these problems.

Although there were many capable chroniclers of domestic melodrama prior to 1850, including Catherine Maria Sedgwick, Lydia Sigourney, Caroline Howard Gilman, Hannah F. S. Lee, and T. S. Arthur, the form really came to fruition in 1850 with the publication of Susan Warner's *The Wide, Wide World*. Some measure of the influence of the book is indicated by the fact that it quickly became the overall best seller in America, at last surmounting the record set by Rowson's *Charlotte Temple*, published over a half century before.

Like *Pamela*, *The Wide, Wide World* was received as a moral treatise. Alexander Pope, though disdainful of Richardson's literary abilities, had said of the former work that it "would do more good than many volumes of sermons."[13] By comparison, the Newark *Daily Advertiser* claimed that *The Wide, Wide World* could do "more good than any other work, other than the Bible."[14] This is no coincidence, for since novel reading was still in widespread dispute, authors who wished to enjoy any measure of success interjected much spirituality into their narratives.

In fact, it was the perfect blend of what one critic has called "Home and Jesus" that ensured the unique success of Warner's first novel. Most of the earlier nineteenth-century domestic novels had contained *too* much sermonizing, *too* many conversions and happy deathbeds, *too* many self-sacrificing heroines and not enough glorification of the home routine as women knew it. *The Wide, Wide World* mixed religion and domestic detail in just the right proportions. The plot is simple. Orphaned Ellen Montgomery goes to live with her aunt and grandmother in the country. Having been a sheltered city girl, she must learn all the domestic skills from scratch. This she does with many mistakes and much aplomb, in the process winning the affection of her various tutors. Eventually, she marries a handsome well-born clergyman (wives of the clergy had special status in the nineteenth century; they were believed to be the purest of the pure) and inherits a fortune.

Sassy and self-righteous, Ellen does her share of hymn singing, sermonizing, and converting of sinners, but she has a variety of other, more interesting experiences as well. The novel contained minute descriptions of homey landscapes, travel abroad, preparations for social events and the events themselves, fashions for all occasions, and household furnishings. In addition, Warner, who claimed she loved to read about good eating, wrote about it skillfully as well. Ellen learned all about pickling, preserving, baking, buttermaking, and everyday cooking of all types. And despite the humble country income of her relatives, she managed to wrangle lessons in all the accomplishments considered proper for a prosperous middle-class young lady. She went to school, took music lessons, and even became proficient in French.

Susan Warner was well qualified to write about the finer side of American domestic living since, until her father's business failures forced her to turn to writing for a living, she had lived the life of a leisured young lady. In fact, circumstances rather than conscious design forged the careers of most of the domestic novelists. Like Warner, almost all the popular writers were educated members of the middle class who put their literary training and past experiences to good commercial use when they were forced to earn their own living.

Needless to say, Ellen had many imitators. One of the earliest, the heroine of *Queenchy*, came from the pen of Susan Warner herself. Orphan Fleda was even more industrious than her predecessor, and she was competent as well. She studied up on the most current agricultural methods, which she not only applied dawn to dusk to her uncle's run-down farm (thereby making it into the pride of the county) but also taught to the other farmers in the region as well. She also performed the duties of the farm wife, teaching, nursing, raising vegetables and flowers, baking, canning, preserving, putting up maple syrup, and even cobbling shoes. Interspersed among all this activity, she nonetheless found ample time to observe all the religious amenities and eventually, having proved her mettle, she married a young Englishman.

Other popular orphans included Maria Cummins' Gerty, heroine of *The Lamplighter* (1854), Marion Harland's Ida of *Alone* (also 1854), and Augusta Jane Evans' Edna Earl, heroine of her classic *St. Elmo* (1866). Inevitably, each was rewarded for her self-sacrificing and religious zealotry with a husband. Edna Earl even required that her handsome but unprincipled guardian make an emotional conversion to Christianity as a condition of their marriage.

The best remembered of the orphan-makes-good school of domestic novels, however, were the Elsie books, written by Martha Finley between 1867 and 1909. Actually, Elsie Dinsmore was a psychological orphan only since her father was alive. At the outset of the series, though, he rejected all care of Elsie who he blamed for her mother's death. By the end of the first book, however, precocious Elsie has made her father a convert to both Christianity and domesticity, and he remained an important character throughout the rest of the series. Elsie eventually married an old friend of her father's, who died seven children later, leaving Elsie (much like Pamela now) as the dispenser of advice, as well as medicine and Bibles to the poor folks living in the region of her plantation home.

A major variation on the domestic theme involved the victimized wife, and the most famous practitioner of this genre was a woman whose own life closely paralleled that of her heroines. Baptized Emma Dorothy Eliza Nevitte, Mrs. E. D. E. N. Southworth by her own account had a tragic childhood and difficult, if not tragic, adulthood. She was the plain older sister to a "parlor favorite" younger sister, who ironically later became the successful novelist's dependent. Having attended school until the age of sixteen (a lengthy education for the time), Southworth taught school for four years, married at twenty, and was husbandless at the age of twenty-five with two children to support. After a brief stint at teaching, she turned to writing, producing over seventy popular novels between 1849 and 1887. Although the details of her brief marriage and separation were never published, Southworth's preoccupation with deserted wives suggests that she was writing and rewriting a story that she knew personally only too well.

Southworth's books certainly reflect what must have been the fantasies of deserted or neglected wives. In her first novel, *Retribution* (1849), the deserting husband was punished only with remorse at the premature death of the wife he realized too late that he loved. The trouble with this formula, however, as Mrs. Southworth apparently realised quickly, was that the perseverant and saintly wife got no tangible reward. In her second novel, *The Deserted Wife,* she set the pattern that she would repeat in subsequent novels. Unwilling to become the vassel of husband Raymound, Hagar openly asserts her right to individuality and thereby incurs Raymound's ire and the disapproval of her friends. Only when Hagar becomes sickly and nervous, however, does her husband desert her. Without wasting much time on self-pity, Hagar gets a job as a concert singer in order to support her three children and, in the process, wins fame and fortune. On a concert tour in Europe, she runs into Raymound, by this time bankrupt. He is captivated by her beauty (and no doubt her fortune) and pleads for a reconciliation. In the spirit of self-righteous condescension, Hagar takes him back.

Although Southworth's plots are mawkish, they stemmed from the author's principled awareness of the inequities in the power balance between nineteenth-century husbands and wives.[15] In *The Deserted Wife* she reflects:

> It was strange, queer—a few words had been pattered over by a fat old gentleman in a gown; and lo! all their relations were changed. It was curious; her very name and title were gone, and the girl, two minutes since a wild, free maiden, was now little better than a bondwoman; and the gentle youth, who two minutes since might have sued humbly to raise the tips of her little dark fingers to his lips, was now invested with a life long authority over her. Yes, it was curious! and the spirited girl was in doubt whether to laugh or cry; and the expression of mingled emotions on her face blended into one of intense interest and inquiry as she met his gaze and smile, which she could not help fancying patronizing and condescending, as well as protective and loving! But this new relation, this new position, this new owning and being owned—it was very unique! very piquant![16]

The desertion theme was not the only popular element in Southworth's novels, however. Papashvily points out that, as opposed to many of her sister authors of this period, Southworth consistently received good notices from reputable reviewers; she was believed to possess real talent. She certainly had a knack for weaving a complicated story. Her books were especially well loaded with long-lost (but crucially rediscovered) friends, illegitimate children, half brothers and sisters, double cousins, and the like. And she also used spirituality in unique, sensational, and even macabre ways. Good and bad characters were gifted with "animal magnetism," "mesmerism," or "physiognomy," various names for the means of exerting supernormal power over the will of others. In *The Deserted Wife*, for instance, the evil minister, Mr. Withers, mesmerizes pure young Sophy into marrying him.

Especially for the time period, however, Southworth's novels were conspicuously free of overt religious moralizing. Instead, Southworth advocated a more practical approach to the problem of evil, an approach involving hard work, perseverance, and a sort of faith in faith—a belief that there *will* be a brighter day. Unfortunately, that brighter day, metaphorically anyway, never really comes until the errant spouse is back in the domestic fold. Southworth did not see beyond marriage as the proper and normal state for women. Through the lifestyles of her industrious heroines, though, she implicitly urged women to be prepared for productive alternatives if the traditional one failed.

Another important strain of the domestic novel has been called the "social novel." Insensitive, domineering, or even deserting husbands were not the only evils afflicting women's lives, and many novels crusaded against problems that were believed to have a more social origin. A particularly potent offender was alcohol. In the middle classes, drinking was usually a masculine prerogative only, but women viewed themselves as the victims when a husband became too attached to the bottle. Although many novels dealt with the problems caused by the alcoholic husband, probably the best known and most influential was T. S. Arthur's *Ten Nights in a Barroom* (1854), which is really the story of the drunkard's female relatives/victims.

Saloons, of course, were largely associated with city life, as were a number of other evils in the domestic social novels, including loose women, gambling halls, charge accounts, and boardinghouses. While in many ways the ancestors of the modern apartment complexes, the boardinghouses differed in that residents had little or no part in food preparation, ate in a common dining hall, shared a common "sitting room," and were forced to retire to their bedrooms when they desired privacy. It was expected that single people would seek such accommodations, but the novels swarmed with disapproval of young married couples whose first "home" was a boardinghouse. The consensus was that such a lifestyle got any couple off to a bad start since the wife was not enabled to exercise her proper role in cooking and maintaining the house.

Although national political issues were almost never the concern of the domestic novelists, there was one notable exception in the issue of slavery. Most novelists were apologists for the institution, choosing when they mentioned it at all to focus on the little kindnesses that a good Christian mistress could do for her servants. According to this philosophy, which extended to poor whites as well, the lowly existed to allow opportunities for their betters to learn and demonstrate charity. During the 1850s, however, as the tension between the North and South mounted, a few novelists turned their pens to describing the miseries of slavery.

The most powerful antislavery novel and also perhaps the best of all the sentimental domestic novels was, of course, Harriet Beecher Stowe's *Uncle Tom's Cabin* (1852). A daughter in the renowned Beecher family, Harriet was both the daughter and sister to famous preachers, and she married a respected minister as well. Heavily encumbered by her duties as housewife and mother, she nonetheless wrote several pieces of short fiction before *Uncle Tom's Cabin*, mostly in order to pay for unexpected household needs. Not surprisingly, Stowe was frankly committed to the didactic mission of fiction, and even these earlier pieces always had moral messages.

Well aware of the intricate mesh of difficulties that freeing the slaves would bring to the United States, Mrs. Stowe's visions of plantations of freemen in Canada and of utopian colonies in Liberia were no more or less naïve than the "solutions" offered by other abolitionists. Solutions to the problem aside, however, slavery, *in principle*, was intolerable to Stowe; she saw it as a corruption of master as well as slave which ultimately deprived both of their humanity. In order to illustrate this for her readers, she focused in *Uncle Tom's Cabin* on that most sacred of institutions, the family.

Without doubt, Stowe aimed *Uncle Tom's Cabin* at the women on both sides of the Mason-Dixon Line, and particularly the mothers. Her strategy, startling at the time, was simply to portray black people with the same needs, feelings, and religious convictions as white people. In this regard, it is no coincidence that the novel's two most lingeringly memorable scenes form a parallel structure. One portrays the tragic death of a white child—little Eva St. Claire—and the other portrays a mother's heroic flight over the ice, in order to save her infant from the living death of slavery. Stowe knew that women would identify with and weep over the forced separation of families, the death of loved ones, a mother's driven instinct to protect her child, the sale of pure young girls, the sexual violation of women, and the use of women as "breeders," whether the victims of these travesties of the family were white or black. Even the novel's detractors (and there were many; fourteen proslavery novels almost immediately challenged *Uncle Tom's Cabin*) admitted that "a nation's sympathy has been awakened."[17]

Just as *Uncle Tom's Cabin* brought visibility and sympathy to the victims of slavery, the nineteenth-century domestic novels, taken as a whole, gave middle-class housewives a sense of shared destiny and common, if difficult, alternatives to that destiny. For one thing, these novels argued that life was more interesting than it might seem. The carefully detailed and often sensual descriptions of such tasks as cooking and gardening argued inherently for the pleasure involved in these domestic chores. Furthermore, the novels suggested that self-improvement or ministering to the needs of others were always options for the woman whose present life bored her. For the desperate or very courageous, there was even paid employment.

Still, the dominant metaphors in the novels suggested powerlessness and isolation. Although kinship ties abound—sometimes discovered only at the novel's end—they are often abstract relationships of blood only, since feelings of love and loyalty must often be won. Husbands and guardians are the arbiters of authority, but they rarely exercise their power lovingly and most often they outright abuse it.

It is within the context of powerlessness and isolation that the image of the religious heroine takes on special significance and becomes almost a defining characteristic of the "nineteenth century" domestic novel, as opposed to later strains. It is in fact through religion that the "moral fantasy" of this type of melodrama is realized. Recall that, as John Cawelti defines it, the basic fantasy (Cawelti calls it a "moral fantasy") of the melodrama is the belief that the controlling forces of the universe are benevolent, no matter if evidence may appear to exist to the contrary. In the case of the nineteenth-century domestic novels, the negative evidence consists of orphans, dying children, derelicts, abandoned and neglected wives, seducers, misplaced relatives, cruel relatives, and a host of other apparent evils. But through religion, and specifically the promise of an afterlife, all is reconciled for the heroine of the domestic novel. Even Southworth's heroines possess a guiding faith, which if not labeled religion has all the earmarks nonetheless. And, of course, their faith is always justified in the end.

In addition, however, the domestic novelists seemed to urge females to use religion as a weapon in their battle against oppression from males. Papashvily argues plausibly that women in the novels used religion as a source of power, in effect substituting their interpretations of God's will for the will of unkind and unprincipled earthly authority figures.

As Papashvily put it, appealing to religion had the effect of transforming insubordinate wives and daughters into martyrs. Within this context, too, the exhibitionistic self-sacrificing practiced by so many heroines can be seen as their means of asserting the right to choose their own fate—even though such "choices" of necessity ran counter to their real needs and desires. Ultimately, of course, the self-sacrificing heroine is vindicated and rewarded, generally with a husband.

The particularly nineteenth-century strain of the domestic novel, with its focus on "Home and Jesus," began to fade rapidly in the 1880s, to be replaced by a new variation which historian Frederick Lewis Allen has called "home and sugar."[18] Popular culture historian Russel Nye sees Grace Livingston Hill, who wrote the first of her eighty domestic romances in 1882, as a transition figure leading to a more cheerful type of domestic fiction.[19]

Other practitioners of the cheerful school of domestic fiction focused on the adventures of children and adolescents, producing such classics as Kate Douglas Wiggin's *Rebecca of Sunnybrook Farm* (1903), Lucy Montgomery's *Anne of Green Gables* (1908), and Eleanor Porter's *Pollyanna, The Glad Girl* (1913). The queen of this genre, however, was Gene Stratton-Porter. Porter added the beauty and soul-saving qualities of nature to the home-and-sugar recipe and came up with twenty novels, several of which were million sellers. Some of her familiar titles include *Freckles* (1904), *The Girl of the Limberlost* (1909), *Laddie* (1913), and *Michael O'Halloran* (1915).

Laura Jean Libbey's optimistic stories of Pamela-style working girls were also popular during the closing decades of the nineteenth century. Libbey condescendingly aimed her stories to the newly literate immigrant members of the working class, and her astounding financial success revealed that Richardson's tale of "virtue rewarded" had lost none of its appeal. Heroines of books like *Only a Mechanic's Daughter*, *A Romance of the Jolliest Girl in the Book Bindery*, and *Willful Gaynell, The Little Beauty of the Passaic Cotton*

Mills resisted the wiles of seducers and eventually were rewarded with a husband. In essence, the novels of Libbey and her imitators gave urban working girls basic lessons in how to achieve respectability by the dominant middle-class standards —as always, the keys were sexual purity and marriage.*

Even the more optimistic versions of the domestic formulas, declining since the 1880s, faded into obscurity by the 1910s. Russel Nye thinks that the domestic vogue was essentially supplanted by public interest in historical romances and the so-called local color stories. Of these, the historical romance had special interest for women.

The type really derives from the novels of Sir Walter Scott whose first historical narrative, *Waverley*, was published in 1814. Although Scott's romances were very popular at the time, they are long and tedious, with too much emphasis on history and not enough emphasis on the romance for the modern reader. The form became more personable after the success in 1880 of Lew Wallace's *Ben Hur: A Tale of the Christ. Ben Hur* had just the right blend of history, romance, religion, adventure, and melodrama to sell over four million copies. Reprints have also enjoyed periodic resurges in popularity, particularly in the reformist 1890s and the religious 1950s. Other classic titles from the turn-of-the-century period include Charles Major's *When Knighthood Was in Flower*, Maurice Thompson's *Alice of Old Vincennes*, and Mary Johnston's *To Have and To Hold*.

In recent decades, too, particularly in the 1930s and the 1950s, a large number of the best-selling hardcover novels have been historical romances. Classics from more recent years include Margaret Mitchell's *Gone With the Wind* (1936), Lloyd Douglas' *The Robe* (1942), Thomas Cos-

---

*By comparison, it is interesting to think of two turn-of-the-century "elite" novels in which the working girl heroine gave in to seduction —Stephen Crane's *Maggie: A Girl of the Streets*, and Theodore Dreiser's *Sister Carrie*. Maggie became a prostitute and eventually committed suicide; Carrie became a famous actress, but she never found happiness.

tain's *The Silver Chalice* (1952), and James Michener's *Hawaii* (1959). Again, these novels have a flavorful blend of romance, history, and adventure. In addition, though, there are a number of historical romance *series* which contain novel after novel written to the standard formula also found in the modern "Gothic" and Harlequin romances, which will be discussed later. Some of the most simplistic are really costume pieces set in the past as an excuse for the heroine's very untwentieth-century naïveté about sex. These books, which contain no historical "event" at all, are designed especially for young adolescents.

As the case of the domestic novel illustrates, however, best-selling fiction in general, with the exception of the pulp magazine variety, tended to become less and less formulaic after World War One. Instead, the moral fantasy of the formulas was discarded in favor of more complex characterizations and more ambiguous resolutions to dilemmas. For the first time, writers destined for "elite" critical recognition appeared on top-ten best-seller lists. Examples include F. Scott Fitzgerald, Edith Wharton, Ernest Hemingway, and John Steinbeck for the immediate postwar period.

Courtship and family life continued to be focal to popular novels during the late 1910s and the 1920s, but less often was the traditional melodrama or romance formula portrayed. Edith M. Hull's *The Sheik* (1921), for instance, was a conventional romance since the heroine, a frigid socialite, and her kidnaper, a virile Arab chieftain, eventually fall in love and marry, thereby conquering seemingly unsurmountable obstacles posed by the differences in their social status and sexual attitudes. Gertrude Atherton's *Black Oxen* (1923), however, turned the formula on its head when Countess Marie Zattiany, rejuvenated to youth by a gland transplant, walks away from the man she has fallen in love with to marry an Austrian political leader and help in the postwar reconstruction work.

Likewise, in the domestic melodrama *The Brimming Cup*, by Dorothy Canfield Fisher, the moral fantasy of an ultimately benevolent universe is upheld since despite the sophisticated arguments of modern-day seducer Mr. Marsh, Marie Crittendon elects to remain in the country with her husband and children. Earlier versions of this tale would perhaps have mandated conversion and/or death for Marsh, but in the 1920s it is enough that he return to the city alone. In Anne Douglas Sedgwick's *The Little French Girl*, on the other hand, one of the principal "good" characters in the novel is a high-class professional paramour, conveniently living in France. Though misunderstanding and conflict ensue with her chaste young daughter (who is the heroine of the book), the mother never "reforms" and the question of sexual ethics is not resolved.

After the 1920s, best-selling novels focusing on family relationships departed even further from the standard melodrama formula. The new ingredients were sex, scandal, and an attempt at realistic portrayal which was foreign to previous domestic novels. Erskine Caldwell's *God's Little Acre* (1933) and Grace Metalious' *Peyton Place* (1956), sexual shockers about rural and small town life, reversed most of the stereotypes of the domestic novel, setting new all-time sales records in the process. In these novels, family life is brutal and incestuous, "nature" brings starvation and physical lust (but no soul-saving), and people who escape to the city are envied.

The more traditional versions of the domestic melodrama and the sentimental romance formulas didn't disappear, of course. Far from it. These standard pleasers were transferred *in toto* to a newer and even more popular medium—the movies. The chapter on movies picks up their story there. Meanwhile, as new formulas became popular with fiction readers, there came to be a distinction between "quality," hardbound best sellers, of the type that appeared on top-ten listings, and more specialized "lowbrow" formula fiction usually published in paperbacks. Some critics even went so far as to pose a three-deck system of ranking fiction. British critic Queenie D. Leavis, in her 1930s analysis of *Fiction and the Reading Public*, popularized the terms "highbrow," "middlebrow," and "lowbrow" as a means of differentiating between say an Ernest Hemingway novel; a novel by an average novelist whose work might be selected by a book club or appear on a top-ten sales chart; and a Western, a detective story, or a light romance.[20]

Leavis was alarmed enough about "lowbrow" fiction to write a book to condemn it. Her concern was that formula-style reading was becoming so popular that the "highbrow" and even the well-meaning "middlebrow" authors would soon be totally unappreciated and without audience (and their critics with them). Although in retrospect Leavis' fears seem overdrawn and paranoid, she was correct in her prediction that formula-style fiction would only increase in popularity, particularly after the explosion of paperback series in the late 30s.

One formula which enjoyed increased popularity in the 1930s as a result of the paperback boom was the classical detective story. Although different in most respects from the romance and melodrama formulas typically preferred by females, the nonviolent detective novels have enjoyed considerable popularity with women. Edgar Allan Poe invented the form in the 1840s, but it was not until Conan Doyle published the first of his Sherlock Holmes tales, *A Study in Scarlet*, in 1887, that its popularity was assured. For the next fifty years, the public's taste for mystery and detection was appeased by stories about a succession of low-key private eyes, including, in addition to Holmes, Philo Vance, Hercule Poirot, Ellery Queen, Charlie Chan, Perry Mason, and many others much like them.

Since the detective is the focal character in these stories, it seems likely that the characteristics of the detectives themselves have contributed to the appeal of this formula for women. In the first place, the male detective is always decisive and commanding but without interjecting physical machismo. The detective is also moral and dependable; he is committed to justice and humanity rather than "the law," per se, so he can be counted on to do the "right thing." For example, Hercule Poirot once failed to turn in a murderer because she was an old lady with a terminal illness. In addition, though, the detective is asexual. He can be counted on to help those in need—often women—without exacting a sexual price. No doubt some women would see these as ideal masculine traits. And several of the detectives also have unique mannerisms that endear them to women: Philo Vance is, unself-consciously, a social snob; Hercule Poirot is a fidgety little man who is also a gourmet; Watson is a gossip.

John Cawelti has suggested another reason why the detective story might have appeal with upper-middle-class women, who he claims are avid readers. Cawelti notes that these women, like men of this class, are given heavy guilt conditioning to achieve when they are children. Notwithstanding, they are blocked from the male world of achievement as adults and are expected to find satisfaction as housewives. Cawelti says that there is therefore a constant inner war between the achievement drives (which produce guilt feelings) and the drives to remain within society's expectations. "Such a tension could lead to an interest in stories in which an authoritative figure proves that someone else is guilty," Cawelti states.[21]

No doubt the broadest appeal of the classical detective story for persons of both sexes, however, derives from the problem-solving theme. In this regard, some critics have compared mystery stories to crossword puzzles—reading one is a means of giving the brain a minor workout without worries about failure or responsibility.

Once the detective formula had proven itself so immensely popular with adult readers, it was inevitable that a watered-down version would be created for the juvenile market. On the one hand, boy detectives like the Hardy Boys followed neatly in the pattern of previous juvenile adventurers including the Rover Boys, Motor Boys, Racer Boys, and the juvenile inventor Tom Swift—all created by the prolific Stratemeyer syndicate. But when Edward Stratemeyer introduced teen-age detective Nancy Drew, he revolutionized literature for adolescent girls.

Previous books written for girls were largely descendants of the Elsie Dinsmore series or of Louisa May Alcott's *Little Women* (also part of a series). These titles were moral tales, filled with sentiment and domestic trivia. In sharp contrast, the *Nancy Drew* series (written since 1930 by Stratemeyer's daughter Harriet S. Adams as "Carolyn Keene") tapped vital fantasies of adolescent girls for the freedom, adventure, and mobility they associated with the lives of men and with the world beyond the home.

Nancy herself is poised, intelligent, attractive, and more than moderately well-to-do. Her widowed father, Carson Drew, is a famous lawyer who treats his only daughter more like a business associate than like a teen-ager. In fact, he often refers to her as his assistant and sometimes solicits her help. Nancy has a "professional" reputation all her own, though, having solved a large number of important mysteries. Policemen, even in cities distant from her own posh suburb, know of her work and assist her at the merest request. Perhaps most intriguing for the female reader, however, is Nancy's mobility. At eighteen, she owns her own blue roadster, which she drives (and parks) with precision, and whenever she needs to travel to more distant spots, she has but to say the word, and her father provides all necessary expenses.

Although Nancy clearly prefers the adventurous world normally reserved for men, she is distinctly feminine as well and frequently uses her charm to win the confidence of people she wishes to investigate. Nancy has a large and varied wardrobe (every adolescent girl's dream), which includes sports clothes and fancy evening attire in addition to the suits she prefers for most of her detective work. Every book contains at least one scene in which Nancy relaxes with hot tea and "delicately frosted cakes"—always as someone else's guest, however. Nancy even has a boyfriend, Ned Nickerson, though not even in the swinging sixties was Ned allowed a single embrace.

Nancy may represent an impossible ideal, but the drawbacks to being too feminine or too unfeminine are portrayed subtly but vividly by her two sidekicks—silly, plump, boy-crazy Bess Marvin and short-haired, insensitive George Fayne. Bess is too lost in nostalgia (or in thoughts of chocolate sundaes) to recognize a clue when it is staring her in the face; George, at the other extreme, doesn't have *enough* imagination to see beyond appearances. In addition, Nancy's poise and charm are highlighted as relief from Bess's frivolity on the one hand and George's gruffness on the other.

Judging by the phenomenal sales of the Nancy Drew books (over 60 million by 1975) and by the long life of the series, the Drew character may well represent an archetype of the modern "liberated" woman. After all, she is independent, mobile, productive, respected as a skilled professional, and her life has excitement and adventure. All this with domestic comfort, female companionship, and the loyalty of two men thrown in as well. But as Bobbie Ann Mason, author of *The Girl Sleuth* has observed, even though Nancy *acts* about thirty, she remains eternally eighteen (and wealthy and lucky, I would add).[22] As a result, she never has to confront such problems as "marriage versus career," aging, job discrimination, or affirmative action suits. Nonetheless, her image is inspiring.

At about age fifteen, however, most girls start to read romances, a formula many will remain addicted to throughout their adult lives. Though the movies and later television were quick to capitalize on the love theme, romantic fiction lost none of its popularity after these media became prominent because the intimacy of the reading process allowed the reader to assume a close identification with the heroine in a love story, thus living the fantasy of ecstatic and triumphant love along with her. The authors of the modern Gothic mystery romances have maximized on the intimacy between reader and heroine, moreover, by telling the story, almost diarylike, in the heroine's own words. (Again, though, Samuel Richardson was ahead of them, since he achieved this type of intimacy by composing his novels in the form of letters.)

When a potential reader walks into her local paperback bookstore or drugstore to select a book, she may well have over fifty titles at any given time to choose from—just in the romance section. To the uninitiated, all the covers look pretty much alike, but there are subtle distinctions which the seasoned reader recognizes and interprets as others might unconsciously translate abbreviations like "Mr." or "Ms." Some covers carry the picture of the heroine against a plain background (sometimes just her face); she is young, radiant, perhaps slightly wistful. The potential buyer knows these are light romances. If the magic word "Harlequin" appears on the cover, then the reader knows she is buying one in a long series (now over 2,000) of immensely popular British-originated romances.* Working-girl heroines, interesting locales, a love plot uncomplicated by mystery, history, or superfluous characters—these are the attractions.

The buyer passes on. Other covers picture a young woman wearing the long, elaborate skirts of the past—often with a décolletage bodice. Surrounding the cover lady are other symbols of the leisured life of long ago—perhaps a sailboat, a horse and carriage (with footman or driver), or a candlelit ballroom filled with gaily dancing couples. These are the descendants of the historical romances, usually less historical and more romancy than their predecessors. If the reader wants to, she can consult the paragraph on the back of the jacket to locate just the period of history she is most interested in—all are times nostalgically associated with conflict and romance, such as the Civil War, the American Revolution, or the reign of Napoleon.

Finally, there are the Gothic mystery romances—their covers picture a terrified young woman fleeing for her life.

*Harlequin Enterprises, the Toronto-based arm which sells to the United States and Canada, sold 80 million books in 1975.

Her dress may be contemporary or historical, but she is always running alone at night and outdoors, presumably escap-
ing the evil in an ominous old mansion or house positioned
in the distant background. Frequently, a single light shines
from one of the windows in the faraway house.

Despite the differences suggested by the covers, the three
major romance variations are basically alike in most respects,
including plot, the relationships between the characters, the
possible settings, and so forth.

The basic plot line of all the romances goes as follows: An
inexperienced young woman meets an enigmatic and commanding older man and they get off to a bad start. Anywhere
from three encounters to several months of constant companionship later, the heroine realizes she loves the hero but this
only increases her distress, either because she 1) knows for a
certainty he doesn't love her (the Harlequin romances), 2)
suspects him of some evil deed (the Gothic mystery romances), or 3) thinks he has been captured by the enemy or
that he is on the "wrong side" in some historical conflict
(the historical romances). Often the heroine leaves or starts
to leave the hero shortly after this point (in terror for her life
in the Gothics). Then, after a few chapters in which the heroine misinterprets everything going on around her, the hero
reveals that he has loved the heroine from the beginning, explains away all her confusions, and the curtain falls as he begins to discuss marriage.

The hero is always the heroine's superior in every visible
way, and his only immediately discernible fault is a conde-
scending air.

> Dane Ryland, apparently, was something of an enigma.
> Well-bred and occasionally good-humored, clever and
> possibly overwhelmingly proud of the fact that he had
> put himself at the head of the Hotel Mirador. (Harle-
> quin, *Hotel Mirador*)

> Lou felt her heart lurch slightly at the sight of the hand-
> some profile, the unyielding chin, the strong brown

hands, and the quiet strength of the broad frame slouched easily in a swivel chair. He looked, she thought, as if nothing would ever daunt or defeat him. He'd never understand what it was to feel helpless, insecure, lonely, and untrusted. (Harlequin, *The Outback Man*)

As with his father, my first impression of Raoul de Valmy was that he was remarkably good-looking; but where age and illness had given the older man's looks the fine-drawn, fallen-angel quality he had mocked to me on our first meeting, there was nothing in the least fine-drawn about Raoul. He merely looked tough, arrogant, and, at that moment, furious. (Gothic mystery romance, *Nine Coaches Waiting*)

The hero is usually about ten years older than the heroine —generally in his early thirties—and of higher social or economic status. If the heroine is a nurse, then typically the hero is a doctor (though sometimes the heroine may be a doctor, in which case she is usually a pediatrician whereas the hero has a more technical specialty like surgery); if she is a penniless governess, then the hero is the rich young man of the household. Even if she is rich, he is richer. The historical romances are more flexible with this part of the formula, since either hero or heroine may *appear* to be of lower class than the other at the outset, but typically their status is equalized by the end of the book.

The hero is also much more aggressive and self-confident than the heroine. Though most contacts between the hero and heroine occur by chance, the hero initiates any planned meetings; he also initiates their first embrace (often the only one in the book) and any discussion of their mutual attraction for each other. He appears to hold the upper hand in any disagreement, and he frequently is curt or sharp in his speech with the heroine.

By contrast, the heroine is young, unsophisticated, almost never wealthy, open enough with her feelings to occasionally make a fool of herself but passive and insecure when it comes to social graciousness or showing her affection for the hero. In short, the heroine has nothing whatever to recommend herself to a heartbreaker like the hero. (Quite frequently, the hero *has* a past reputation as a heartbreaker.) The following descriptions of heroines are typical.

> Eden's smile grew rueful as she popped a chocolate into her mouth. What a nuisance to be only nineteen and the owner of looks that seemed to give people the impression that she had not yet fathomed the mystery of the birds and the bees. . . . (Harlequin, *Love's Prisoner*)

> At twenty she was a big girl, well-built and handsome, though she lacked the picture-book prettiness of the currently admired Gibson girl. Her thick hair was blue-black and glossy with health and her dark eyes had a way of looking at the scene about her with eager curiosity. There was always a touch of the dramatic in Sara. The lift of her chin, the set of full lips that were not always soft, betrayed a determination that had not yet learned to be wise. (Gothic mystery romance, *The Trembling Hills*)

The heroine's more-than-redeeming quality, however, is that she is good. She stands up for what she believes in even if it earns her the displeasure of others; she is self-sacrificing; she loves children and knows just how to care for even the most troublesome child; and she is loyal—we know this by the way she stands by the hero even after misunderstandings lead her to believe him guilty of indifference or worse.

The reader identifies strongly with the heroine's goodness, moreover, because she is always privy to the heroine's thoughts and knows for sure that her intentions are always to do the "right thing," usually to help someone else. Being privy to the heroine's thoughts also allows the reader to learn about the heroine's insecurities regarding her relationships with other people, particularly the hero. Since this insecurity is so sympathetically portrayed and since it is justified by the superficial differences between the heroine and other characters, being insecure comes off as a painful but "humanly" natural trait in these novels, and one which is associated with goodness.

It is crucial to her status as heroine, moreover, that she be good and that the reader know it for a certainty, because there is often another female character in the novel who, judging by superficial characteristics, seems much more interesting than the heroine. The "other woman," who is usually some type of rival for the hero's love, is always young, beautiful, sophisticated, and often rich as well. She has a great deal of charm and personality, but she has perverted these traits by using them to obtain selfish and usually mercenary ends.[23]

It should be emphasized that modern romances, like much nineteenth-century fiction, take female rivalry for granted. By contrast, however, the heroine almost never has a female friend who is a peer. Sometimes the heroines will befriend an older lady or a small girl, but almost never do they have trusted companions of their own age. One possible explanation for this is that the friend would almost necessarily be more interesting than the heroine and so the reader wouldn't know who to sympathize with.

It is worth noting in this context that the hero also has no true peers in these novels, but this is because he stands so far above other male characters in appearance, drive, and frequently wealth and social status. When the hero has an apparent rival for the heroine's love, he is always *less* sophisticated and not quite so good-looking as the hero—ironically, a more natural peer for the heroine. In short, the hero wins out over rivals by superiority; the heroine, it would seem, by inferiority.

The modern romances also contain some similarities in the settings. All the novels take place in exotic, out-of-the-way places—stereotypically settings for romance. Only exotic cities like New Orleans or San Francisco among U.S. locations qualify. Usually, the novels are set in a foreign country, either on a lonely moor or estate or else in an atmospheric city or village. The British-published Harlequins, however, can also take place on a whaling boat, in the jungles of South Africa, or in the wilderness settings of any of Britain's colonies. Since all of history is shrouded in mystery and inherently imbued with a romantic quality, the settings in the historical romances have earned their exotic flavor as a result of the events which took place there. Furthermore, the characters are inevitably very wealthy, and houses and clothing are luxurious. Escape to the past via the historical romance is always an escape to a prosperous past.

In addition to the slight variations in setting, there are also other differences between each type of romance, differences so minor, however, that they might not seem worth mentioning fifty years hence. For one thing, the heroes of the Harlequins are upper-echelon professional men (like doctors and business tycoons), whereas the heroes in the Gothic mystery romances and the historical romances tend to be aristocrats. In part, this is because the Harlequin series began as "nurse and doctor" tales. Since the working hero has been continued, though new professions have been added, however, it seems likely that readers of the Harlequins are primarily working-class wives. On the other hand, readers of the "Gothics" and the historical romances, who are presumably already married to professional men, dream of life among the idle rich.

One might well suppose that the "Gothic" and "mystery" elements of the Gothic mystery romance would be their most unique and distinguishing characteristics, but this is not the case at all. As critic Joanna Russ has pointed out, the "mystery" reduces to a "secret" and most of the "Gothic" terror is in the heroine's own paranoid mind.[24]

Some authors and critics of the Gothic mystery romance have claimed ancestry for it in the eighteenth-century Gothic novels written by Anne Radcliffe and in the classical detective story. The Gothic claim is hardest to justify since even events as potentially horrible as murder are not placed in a horrible context: a rifle shot narrowly misses the heroine; a small boy fails to fall over a weak bannister; an evil woman shoots herself, but the shot is heard from afar and the body is never described.

By contrast, the original Gothics were structured around chilling episodes like the disappearance of persons, or the appearance of ghosts, crumbling cliffs, and moving castle walls. Though the heroine's life and virginity were continually imperiled by the villain, the "romance" with the hero was primarily a plot contrivance, rather than a source of emotional tension in the novels.

On the other hand, like detective stories, every Gothic mystery romance has a villain or villainess—someone who has already committed a crime, usually against a member of his own family. But the heroine does nothing at all to determine who the evil party is. She doesn't want to pry into other people's business, and besides, she forces herself to trust the hero. Since the heroine is too passive to actively investigate the mystery, she is left to spend her time *wondering* about people and attempting to read their facial expressions. This is a state much more suggestive of the lifestyles of most women, though, according to critic Russ. "When the most important person in your life is your man, when you can't trust him (and can't trust anyone else), it becomes exceedingly important to "read" other people's faces and feelings," Russ states.

It is a fact, though, that the Gothic mystery romances do contain an element of adventure not present in other romance formulas. As several critics have noted, "romance" is about as close to adventure as most heroines in popular culture ever get. Though exceptions exist to prove the rule, almost all the cowboys, detectives, and other adventure heroes are male. The phenomenal sales of the "Gothics," however, indicates that women like their romances spiced with adventure. In part, this is because danger has an erotic quality about it when taken in small doses. It calls to mind the Freudian image of a scared little girl running to find safety in Daddy's arms, or one step down the line, of the sweety little bride calling her big strong husband into the kitchen to kill a tiny spider. Ultimately in the Gothic mystery romances, of course, the naïve young heroine finds comfort from the danger-that-never-seemed-too-real in the arms of the strong and sexual hero.

In the final analysis, however, all authors of the modern romance formula are working to achieve the same goal—a romantic experience for the reader. The emotional build-up between the hero and heroine is therefore very important, and all of the authors create this build-up by making the hero the object of the heroine's strongest emotions. Their first encounter is always highly charged, though one or both is usually angry at the other for some reason: the hero thinks the heroine has taken a job as his aunt's companion in order to leech upon the family fortune; by accident, the hero nearly runs down the heroine on a dark winding road; or the heroine simply finds the hero too arrogant to bear. More unpleasant encounters may follow, but sooner or later the hero and heroine find themselves in a situation in which they are having a good time "in spite of themselves." Then follows an opportunity for touching, like a dance. And at long last—often on the last page of the book—there is THE KISS. This first kiss is the erotic explosion for which the entire rest of the book was foreplay.

Since a mild eroticism is key to the appeal of women's romantic fiction, it is fascinating to compare these books to the overtly sexual, "hard-boiled detective" formula which became immensely popular with men after World War Two. It may come as a surprise to some that the romance and hard-boiled formulas portray similar structural relationships between male and female characters. But, since the point of view is masculine in the hard-boiled novels, girl doesn't get boy. Boy gets girls. And not on the mouth with a kiss, but, eventually, in the guts with a bullet.

Although female readers early-on found expression of their mythic dreams in Rowson's *Charlotte Temple* and Warner's *Wide, Wide World*, books whose overall sales were not topped until the mid-twentieth century, it remained for the hard-boiled detective novels of Mickey Spillane to similarly strike the heartbeats of the masses of American males. Each with sales in the four and five millions, seven of Spillane's books have outsold all other mystery and detective fiction in America. In addition, on the overall best-seller list between the years 1895 and 1965, including sales of both hardbound and paperback books, the same seven titles appear among the top-thirty best sellers.

The success of the Spillane novels has a special significance, furthermore, since they represent the penultimate expression of the first fictional formula for men (excluding pornography) to deal explicitly with sexual relationshps between men and women.

Probably the first novels to hold widespread appeal for men were James Fenimore Cooper's "Western" classics, *The Leatherstocking Tales*. Together, they relate the life of eighteenth-century woodsman Natty Bumpo, whose most beloved companion was a noble Indian savage, Chingachgook. Thereafter, the motif of the male companions, battling together the forces of the wilderness or of evil, became a standard in adventure fiction. Functionally, it took the place of male and female romance. Women are sometimes "the prize" in the adventure stories, of course, but when they are, it means that the hero's adventuring days are about to conclude. In many Westerns, for instance, the hero's acceptance of civilization is symbolized by his marriage to the schoolmarm or rancher's daughter (*after* the adventure is over).

Not until the hard-boiled detective novel was there a mass-selling fictional formula which combined violence and sex in just the right manner. *I, The Jury*, Mickey Spillane's first novel, sold over five million copies alone. Although some claimed that Spillane was just a pornographer in disguise, there was enough "redeeming social value" in his detective tales to keep Spillane on fairly reputable best-seller lists for several years.

Six of Spillane's first seven books have as their protagonist private eye Mike Hammer. Like the heroes in the women's romances, Mike is arrogant, commanding, self-confident, and virile—a natural lady's man. And, also like the romance heroes, Mike prefers women who are domestic, passive, and virginal—at least he says he does. But his sexual conduct indicates quite another preference.

Velda, Mike's fiancée, secretary, and occasionally second gun, is set forth as the Ideal Woman in the Spillane novels. She is a perfect blend of "mother" and "sexual toy." Velda comforts Mike after his close calls, cries whenever his good name or his life are in danger, and she asks no questions about his frequent sexual escapades. Velda, of course, is a virgin.

But Velda is a very odd virgin. Spillane's lingering descriptions reveal her as a sexually ripe young woman, big-busted, long-legged, and "with hair like midnight." Velda also provides Mike with continual reaffirmation of his masculinity. Even while he is laid up on a hospital bed, recovering from multiple bruises, burns, and lesions, Mike is irresistible to Velda.

> Her hands were soft on my face and her mouth a hot, hungry thing that tried to drink me down. Even through the covers I could feel the firm pressure of her breasts, live things that caressed me of their own accord. She took her mouth away reluctantly so I could kiss her neck and run my lips across her shoulders. (*Kiss Me Deadly*)

It is clear that Velda is a virgin only because Mike wants her that way. He wants his "wife" to be a virgin when they get married. As Mike tells Velda in one of the novels, "I'm just afraid of myself, kid. You and a bedroom could be too much. I'm saving you for something special." (*One Lonely Night*)

But while Mike is saving Velda for "something special" (though scenes like the one quoted above don't sound as if much is saved), he feels perfectly free to engage in sexual relationships with all the other women who make themselves available to him. Spillane hereby clearly endorses the double standard of sexual conduct. The implication is that men should choose their sexual conquests from among the "lower classes," or the "already tainted," since the women Mike has affairs with always have questionable pasts and frequently are suspects in the crime he is investigating.

The women have something else in common. They exude sexuality—of the Marilyn Monroe, Jane Russell, Brigitte Bardot variety. Mike repeatedly expresses his scorn for skinny women—the type that model clothes. He goes for the 1950s movie types, though naturally he doesn't put it that way. Despite their experience, furthermore, all of these women are sexually starved. They throw themselves at Mike because he is violent. The other men they've known were weaklings or near-impotents and now they are looking for a *real* Man. They want a brutal sexual experience, and Mike gives it to them.

The overall emotional build-up of the Spillane novels, then, is created by a carefully constructed rhythm of sex and violence. In general, Mike's sexual episodes are immediately followed by an act of violent assault, usually murder. In addition, these episodes take place in dark, out-of-the-way places: stereotyped settings for rape. In *I, The Jury*, murder suspect Mary Bellemy lures Mike into the woods, takes off all her clothes, and seduces him. Mike returns to the tennis match they had left just in time to discover a fresh murder victim—a female. In *Kiss Me, Deadly*, Mike picks up a hitchhiker who almost immediately makes a pass at him. Mike resists and, soon after, his car is run off the road by a car filled with Mafia agents who strip and torture the hitchhiker and then kill her. In *One Lonely Night*, Mike meets a frightened woman being chased down a deserted bridge at night. He kills her pursuer and turns his attention to the woman, with his gun still in his hand. She takes one look at the "kill-lust" in Mike's face and jumps over the bridge to her death.

Violence and violent sex work together to produce the

strong emotional experience created by reading a hard-boiled detective novel, so it is no coincidence that the villains of Spillane's most successful novels inevitably prove to be women. Since Mike executes the villains at the end of each novel (to make sure that "justice" is done), the rhythm in Spillane's novels reaches its final climax in what John Cawelti calls "violence as orgasm."

The extreme popularity of the early fifties version of the Spillane formula, with its contradictory images of women as housewifely, passive, and virginal (Velda) versus aggressively sexual and living outside the social norms (the amoral or criminal types that Mike makes violent love to) indicates that the G.I. Joe reader may have left his Tiger Lily overseas and returned home to marry the girl next door, but that the wartime sexual code was not so easily forgotten.

But while G.I. Joe was busy with his Mickey Spillane book, his wife or sweetheart was reading about romance, Gothic-novel style, moodily anticipating the single kiss and the magic word "marriage" on the last page of the book. Clearly, the signals between the sexes were on their way to getting crossed.

For a time, the movies saved the day. With television taking over the family audience, the movies were freer to present sexier, more male-oriented images of women during the 1950s. This they did, but with a concession to the female audience as well. It was understood from the beginning that the characters played by the movie sexpots like Marilyn Monroe, Jayne Mansfield, and Kim Novak *really* wanted a husband and house in the suburbs just like every other woman—and wouldn't settle until they got it. So men and women could compromise on the movie version—he would provide the ring and the house in the suburbs and she would put on her push-up bra and try to think sexier.

But in private moments—alone in the world created by her own mind and by the book in her hands—the woman of the fifties (and the sixties and the seventies) returned to the safety of the familiar fantasy. Climbing into the heroine's chaste and barely pretty body, she turned back the clock to her future housewife days, becoming again a passive and sought after young woman—who would be claimed, dominated, even loved just for the price of existing.

2.

Images of Women on Television

Feminists often complain that television portrays only the most traditional and outdated images of women, many of which are overtly sexist. It is an easy charge to support. For example, a study of evening dramatic-type programs made during the 1974–75 television season revealed that men outnumber women slightly in comedy, by about two to one in dramas, and by an overwhelming eight to one in drama/adventure series.

What this means is that female characters are concentrated in programs like the evening comedies, the morning game shows, and the afternoon soap operas where the structure of the program type inherently stereotypes them into "situated" roles symbolic of the housewife lifestyle. By contrast, men are typically portrayed as cool, competent professionals. On the soap operas, they may have feet of clay (which is why they are "situated" like the women), but on the evening drama and drama/adventure programs, where females rarely and families never intrude, the heroes have exciting, often highly mobile jobs, which allow them to serve others and have close relationships with male peers as well.

The present chapter will examine in some detail each of the major daytime and evening TV formulas to better explain how television fosters this dichotomy between the situated woman and the male superhero. But first, a brief history of the medium is in order.

Television became America's number-one entertainment media almost overnight. In 1948, there were 172,000 television sets in operation; in 1950, there were more than 5 million; in 1960, nearly 50 million. In the middle seventies, it is conservatively estimated that 95 per cent of all American homes (poor as well as affluent) have at least one television set. A recent survey indicated, moreover, that the *average* American spends twelve hundred hours per year watching television, as compared to less than four hundred hours per year reading all printed media combined. For example, the A. C. Nielson rating company reported in 1974 that almost 30 million people watched "All in the Family" every Saturday night. Without doubt, TV is the number one spectator sport of the American public.[1]

Television derived its content from both radio and the movies, and in the process, it sucked much of the lifeblood from both media. When radio came into its own in the 1920s, competition was feared by the movie industry at first, but it soon became apparent that the new medium was best at presenting a type of program quite different from the standard movie fare. All during the big band era, for instance, evening performances were aired live and one could listen or dance in one's own living room; sports and news events were also broadcast live and often from the scene. Radio provided a "you were there" quality for its listeners which was very different from the movie experience and did not really compete with it. Without the visual component radio drama was radically different from movie drama. Carefully orchestrated sound effects supplied a scenario all their own.

Since the radio was located in the home and available for constant use, the patterns of daily program distribution evolved naturally and carried over to television intact. Women were home during the day, so daytime radio was aimed at them. Game shows and talk shows were aired in the morning, and the most popular afternoon programs were the soap operas. In *The Unembarrassed Muse*, Russel Nye reports that in 1938 the average housewife listened to 6.6 radio soap operas each afternoon; some heard as many as 22.[2] Serializing drama was nothing new—remember that Richardson's *Clarissa* had been issued in seven "volumes," magazines often serialized fiction, and films of adventure and escape were frequently serialized for the matinee movie audience. In developing the soap opera, then, radio simply adapted to its own use one of literature's staple forms—the sentimental domestic melodrama—and dished it out in meager daily doses. By contrast, nighttime programs consisted of a mixture of variety shows, one-line comedians, situation comedies, and adventure series drawn from popular fiction and comics. These programs were designed for Dad and the kids as well as for Mom.

When television's popularity became a sure thing in the early fifties, programs and stars transferred in toto from radio to TV, including comedians like Bob Hope, Jack Benny, Milton Berle, and the team of George Burns and Gracie Allen; musicians like Perry Como, Bing Crosby, Kate Smith, and Dinah Shore; situation comedies like "Ozzie and Harriet" and "My Favorite Husband" ("I Love Lucy"); and drama/adventure hits like "Perry Mason," "The Lineup," and "Mr. District Attorney." Kiddie favorites like "Superman," "The Lone Ranger," "The Cisco Kid," and "Jungle Jim" were hits as late afternoon (afterschool) and Saturday morning programs. Stripped of most of its entertainment fare, radio became largely a news service and disc jockey medium in the late 1950s. Like the movie industry, radio largely targeted its appeal to the teen audience after television controlled the family market.

The relationship between TV and movies was somewhat more complex, however. By the middle seventies, movie stars and television stars had become virtually interchangeable. In

the early fifties, however, television was having no dealings
with movies and movie actors except to steal their audiences.
As the chapter on movie images explains, during the same
time period that sales of television sets were soaring, movie
attendance was precipitously dropping. The large matinee audiences, primarily women, dried up almost totally, and the
audience for evening showings became increasingly dominated by teen-agers, young adults, and the dating crowd. For
the housewife and the family with young children, television
offered the best of radio and movies combined. And officials
of the commercial networks were careful to see that programs
were suitable in every way for women and children.

Having learned its lesson from the movies, the television
industry was a cautious self-censor from the beginning. To
avoid taking chances with profits, television stuck to a very
few tried-and-true program formulas and confined characters
within those formulas to behavior and attitudes guaranteed
to be approved by a majority of the American people. As an
ironic aside, media conservatism almost kept Norman Lear
from acquiring a network for his first hit production, "All in
the Family," in 1970. There was a longstanding taboo
against prime-time characters cussing, drinking beer, or expressing un-American attitudes like racial and ethnic prejudice, but Archie Bunker did all three. The first night that
"Family" was aired, Lear stationed an overload staff of telephone operators on the CBS lines to take complaints. To everyone's surprise, none came.[8]

Archie Bunker may be a beer-drinking bigot, but in many
other ways he is the typical situation-comedy-style husband
and father. This is the case because media officials are reluctant to tamper too much with a good thing. The remainder
of this chapter, then, will be devoted to a discussion of the
images of women versus men portrayed by TV's major,
money-making formulas. During the daytime, these include
game shows, talk shows, and soap operas; during the evening
—situation comedy, drama, and drama/adventure series.

Commercial television begins each weekday with the early

morning news and discussion shows.* Since "The Today Show" began in the early 1950s, however, the hosts of these daytime eye-openers have almost all been male. These programs are clearly designed as send-offs for the working person, and since only a few token females have ever been seated behind the wide desks with the male moderators in their business suits, the stereotype that only men are serious professionals is subtly reinforced. The few women like Dorothy Kilgallen, Betsy Palmer, Barbara Walters, and Betty Furness, who have appeared at various times on the morning talk shows, however, have projected a special image of intelligence, charm, and dignity which has rendered them peers of their male colleagues and popular with viewers. It is just that there have been far too few of them.

It should be noted that in late 1976, Barbara Walters began a five-year, five-million-dollar contract with ABC to join newsman Harry Reasoner in presenting the ABC evening news. As such, Walters became the first evening anchorwoman in major network TV. Female reporters have appeared on national evening news since the early 1960s, however, and their numbers have been increasing in recent years. Even so, television networks are far behind in meeting minimum affirmative-action quotas. In her book *Women in Television News*, Judith S. Gelman cites a 1973 study which found that of 41,000 full-time employees in broadcasting, only 24 per cent are female. And of these, 89 per cent are in "dead-end clerical jobs."

Understandably, most of the regular female faces appear during the daytime hours when female viewers provide the bulk of the audience, and over the years, there have been a great many morning conversational series featuring a female host and aimed especially for women. Most of these have

*There are also a number of children's programs aired during the early morning hours. Athough these programs would doubtless make an interesting study from the standpoint of female images, I have not included them because of lack of time and resources to give them proper consideration.

originated at the local or regional level, but some, including such favorites as Arlene Francis' "Home Show," Julia Child's "The French Chef" (educational television—ETV), Dinah Shore's "Dinah's Place," and recently Walters' "Not For Women Only," to name a few, have been syndicated nationally. Each series is focused somewhat differently, but all are directed primarily to the housewife. Program content indicates, furthermore, that the nationally syndicated programs are typically planned with the upper-middle-class, educated housewife in mind.

Nuts-and-bolts cooking, sewing, and housekeeping are not discussed on these programs. Instead, guests include celebrities, who often talk about their private lives, and experts on topics like storing furs, sauce cooking, and repairing picture windows. "Not For Women Only" is a slight advancement on this theme since "issues" like mental illness, rape, ecology, and gambling are discussed in addition to more traditionally female topics like fashion and dieting.

By about 9:30 A.M., however, the daytime game shows have started to dominate TV fare. This seemingly innocuous style of program holds an obvious advantage for the busy housewife, since it doesn't demand her full attention and since the programs can be "listened to" as effectively as watched. In addition, programs which ask questions of some type give her something on which to work her brain while making the beds, doing the dishes, and diapering the baby.

Over the years, there have been several different types of game shows, appearing at various times of the day. Many of the most popular early programs, such as "What's My Line?" and "I've Got a Secret," focused on a panel of celebrities. Variations on this format still existed in the middle 1970s in shows like "Celebrity Sweepstakes" and "Hollywood Squares." During the middle fifties, the big-money shows like "$64,000 Question" (on radio, it had been the "$64 Question") caught the imagination of viewers. After the TV quiz scandals of 1958 and 1959, however, the emphasis switched to audience participation, and shows like "Beat the Clock," "The Price Is Right," and "Let's Make a Deal" were the hits.

The majority of the quiz programs have been aired during morning hours, however, and on most of the morning shows two or more contestants from the studio audience compete against each other for cash, automobiles, vacations, and various domestic items like washing machines, TVs, and electric can openers. In fact, since these programs are aimed for an audience of housewives, everything from the image of the emcee and the voice of the announcer, to the image of contestants and the type of prizes won reinforce the stereotype of woman-as-housewife/consumer and man as professional/ provider.

On the game shows, the emcee is a male entertainer who is acting the part of a professional know-it-all. Producers of game shows make it clear that the emcee is not supposed to be a "star," per se, since the game is intended to be the focus of interest. That makes the image of the emcee all the more insidious, however. He is calm, cool, professional, and always dressed in a business suit. Not infrequently, when a contestant makes a wrong guess, the emcee fills in additional information about the answer, as a college lecturer might do to add perspective to a student's knowledge on a certain subject. The audience is subliminally urged to accept the emcee as a genuine expert, then, rather than as an actor who has memorized these lines as he might any other.

Likewise, game show announcers are always males with the look and sound of professional businessmen. The announcer's voice is cool, deep, authoritative. When he describes that new car or that forty-eight-piece set of sterling silver dinnerware, he sounds as if he knows what he's talking about. The desire for the prize escalates among contestants and viewers alike. Significantly, almost all of the viewers and a majority of the contestants whose consumer urges are being titillated are women.

As John Kenneth Galbraith has convincingly argued, a

major function of housewives in a full-employment, consumer-based economy is to "administrate" the purchasing of a wide assortment of personal and household goods, a time-consuming task.[4] Vance Packard and others have gone on to claim, moreover, that to keep the economic wheels rolling, many more goods and services must be purchased than people really need.[5] Among other things, what this means is that an atmosphere must be maintained in which buying in itself is viewed as a good or approved thing to do, so that people, and particularly the unemployed housewife segment, will want to spend as much time and money as possible in buying the trappings of the good life.

In the broadest sense, then, the morning game shows are symbolic shopping sprees in which a deluxe assortment of household goods and dream vacations (to take one away from the dreary household reality) can be purchased by the housewife for a flick of the television dial. In addition, these programs might even inspire her to go out to the real shopping center later on and seek out some of the goods so expertly advertised.

The popular "Queen for a Day" program, which ran for nearly a decade beginning in the middle fifties, tried to award prizes to the "contestant" with the greatest need. The catch was that the would-be queens had to tell their hard-luck stories to a studio audience which then voted on the most oppressed housewife by applauding for her at the end of the show. Applause was registered by an applause meter, which had a high reading of ten, though even the sobbiest contestant rarely ranked above an eight. Producers of the program were frank to admit their opinion that housewives watched the program to convince themselves that however hard or boring their lot might seem, it was roses compared to what some women suffered.

Just as "Queen for a Day" was leaving the air in the middle sixties, a new type of sexist afternoon game show began. Substituting younger, more beautiful-type people, programs like "The Dating Game," "The Newlywed Game," "Dream

Girl," and "Family Game" used laughter and inane repartee as the device to reveal the superficiality, if not the outright suffering, present in relationships between couples and families.

On "The Newlywed Game," for example, a panel of four couples who had been married less than a year competed for a jackpot-type prize awarded at the end of each show. Husbands and wives took turns predicting how their spouses would answer questions like "What is the funniest thing your husband (wife) does the last thing each night?" or, "When rolling over to awaken you in the morning, which compass direction does your husband (wife) turn?" (When asked the latter question, one dizzy-looking blond female responded by lisping, "Is East a compass direction?") Couples were encouraged to banter over every petty answer, and the confrontations between spouses were the highlight of the program.

Although most of the game shows are aired during the morning hours, those that invade the afternoon and early evening are much more emotional. In the case of the afternoon programs, this is perhaps the case because producers want them to compete effectively with the highly emotional soap operas. Again, a majority of the contestants on such programs as "The New Price Is Right" and "Let's Make a Deal" are women. These women, however, can barely contain their squeals and wriggles and overall exuberance when the emcee chooses *them* to play the game. As each new prize comes rolling in, moreover, they jump up and down, clap their hands and kiss and embrace the emcee (who remains cool, smiling, and only mildly contemptuous) in a mad show of gratitude. Female contestants and home viewers may see this undignified display as "all in fun." But since the emcee is ever a stoic and since male contestants express their happiness with a grin and a handshake, the stereotype of women as more emotional and irrational than men is strongly reinforced by such programs.

Beginning about noon, soap operas take over the daytime

TV fare. Since the genre became fully entrenched in the late 1950s, housewives have been able to watch half-hour episodes almost without interruption from about eleven in the morning until about four each afternoon. Though titles have varied over the years as less popular soaps were phased out and new ones were added to replace them, there have always been close to twenty separate programs for viewers to choose from at any given time. In the middle seventies, some of the most popular shows, including "Days of Our Lives" and "As the World Turns," have gone to full-hour episodes without any decrease in popularity.

Though soap opera came to television via radio, its true roots are firmly in the nineteenth-century sentimental domestic novel. Characters in soap operas interact in a series of overlapping domestic melodramas, as marital problems lead to affairs followed by divorce and remarriage, where the cycle inevitably resumes, varied only by lawsuits, tragic illness, and sudden death. At any given time there are usually three or four featured subplots, but only one reaches crisis proportions at a time. The basic theme of all plots is *suffering*. More superficially, however, some of the most frequent themes involve:

the evil woman
the great sacrifice
the winning back of an estranged lover/spouse
marrying her for her money, respectability, etc.
the unwed mother
deceptions about the paternity of children
career v. housewife
the alcoholic woman (and occasionally man)

For example, the 1975 plot of award-winning soap opera "The Young and the Restless" went as follows:

Background: Newspaper owner Stuart Brooks and wife Jennifer have four daughters: introvert Les; promiscuous Lauri—who is really Jen's child by Dr. Bruce Henderson, Stuart's best friend, unbeknown to Stuart and Bruce;

loving, self-sacrificing Chris, who married Snapper Foster from the poor Foster family against her family's wishes (Snapper has since risen beyond his background by becoming a doctor); and Peggy who is attending college. They all live in Genoa City, somewhere in the northeast U.S.A.

1975 plot: Shy Les, an accomplished pianist, fell in love with Brad Elliott, who came to Genoa City without explaining his past. (He had been a neurosurgeon in Chicago, but he quit his profession after he accidentally killed his illegitimate son on the operating table.) Popular, outgoing Lauri felt she had always lived in Les's shadow, since the family had been supportive of the older sister, feeling Lauri could take care of herself. Lauri was also in love with Brad, who she seduced and tried to keep from Les. Thinking Brad would marry Lauri, Les had a nervous breakdown during a piano concert and was hospitalized. Brad gave her the courage to recover and eventually they were married. Lauri retaliated by writing a book about her sister's breakdown.

After a brief interlude with her publishing agent, Lauri next became sexually involved with wealthy Phillip Chancellor, who was married to alcoholic Kay but secretly in love with young hairdresser Jill Foster, sister of Snapper Foster. When Phillip finally got a divorce and told Kay he would marry Jill, Kay tried to kill them both in an auto accident. Only Phillip died, but not before marrying Jill in the hospital. Kay got the marriage between Phillip and Jill annulled, but Jill was already pregnant with Phillip's child. The problem became complicated when Jill's father, Bill Foster, reappeared after deserting the family nine years before. Jill's mother had just decided to declare him legally dead and marry someone else.

Meanwhile, Jennifer Brooks suddenly became "discontented," claiming things had never been right in her marriage with Stuart. Bruce Henderson, Jennifer's lover of long ago (and Lauri's real father) said he would divorce his wife and he and Jen could have a wonderful life together. Before Jen could ask Stuart for a divorce, he

collapsed from a heart attack. After Stuart recovered
however, Dr. Bruce discovered a lump in Jennifer's breast
and she had a radical mastectomy. Then daughter Lauri
fell in love with Mark Henderson, Bruce's son and they
planned to be married. Jennifer finally stopped the wedding by telling Mark that Lauri is his half-sister. And
on it goes.

Characters in the soap operas are mostly middle-class
white, suburban, professional, or other white-collar workers
Some of the newer serials have included families from lower
or working-class backgrounds, but the story then involves the
rise of one or more family member into respectable middle
classhood. There are no television soap operas exclusively
about lower- or working-class family life. There are also no
all-black soap operas. There have been a smattering of black
characters on various serials, but no family grouping has yet
been introduced in toto.

The lack of complete black families on soap operas is
clearly prejudicial, since all soap opera characters gain their
aura of respectability via family ties. New characters with
projected longevity for a series are added in family groupings
By contrast, the more transient characters (who are usually
white, of course) are introduced singly, often with implica-
tions of a "dark secret" in their pasts.

Most soap operas are structured around relationships involving two or three extended family units. As such, community and peer approval, or disapproval, comes directly from
family members who often represent the values of their respective generations. Though fathers tend to be philosophical
(apathetic?) about children's troubles and mistakes (there
are exceptions), mothers are always ready to interfere in the
lives of even their grown children.

As opposed to the almost equal distribution of male and female *characters* on the daytime serials, the *audience* is almost
all female, most of them housewives. Writers and producers
of the soaps claim surveys indicate that about 15 per cent of
the audience is male, but even if true, this proportion seems

elatively insignificant. Clearly, the serials are geared for the housewife viewer. In fact, in 1970 Russel Nye quoted the supervisor of NBC daytime programs as claiming that the aim of the serial is to give the viewer assurance "that her middle-class values are fine, that giving up what she thought of as a career in favor of marriage is fine, that life's little problems are the ones that really count, that apple pie is not really fluoridated."[6]

The fact that most of the viewers are housewives, however, doesn't mean that women on the serials are portrayed primarily as housewives or that the housewives are always the sympathetic characters. What it does mean, though, is that the importance of jobs, whether held by women or men, is subordinated to the importance of personal relationships and family life. In this way, the world of the housewife is closely approximated, and the situation is created whereby men and women are full-fledged peers of one another.

During the fifties and much of the sixties, most women were portrayed as housewives by the soap operas. However, during the past decade, more and more career women have been portrayed. Since the overall structure of soap opera demands that men and women be equals, careers engaged in by women are often on a full parity with those of the men in the program. There have been several female doctors, lawyers, and businesswomen of various sorts, in addition to the inevitable nurses, who are concentrated on programs taking place in hospitals.

The attitude toward working women on the serials is generally supportive, so long as these women don't work so hard that they neglect family responsibilities. Even good, well-meaning women can fall into the trap of devoting too much time to their jobs, in other words, and it is a mistake for which they always pay dearly. Witness the case of Kathy Phillips in "Search for Tomorrow." Kathy is a lawyer who has proven herself a good woman by accepting the responsibility of husband Scott's stepchild by a former marriage. Now Kathy has the opportunity to do a major out-of-town merger

case for her firm. She and Scott agree she should go, but th
case strings out longer than expected. Scott misses Kathy, s
he uses a minor problem with the stepson as an excuse to as
her to come home. Kathy remains with her case, however—
choosing to honor her job commitments against Scott'
wishes. As punishment for this act of insubordination, Scot
allows himself to be seduced by college girl Jennifer and a
break-up of his marriage to Kathy ensues. Since Kathy is basi
cally a good person, she finally gets Scott back, but the in
terim suffering for all concerned has been immense.

In real life, most working persons no doubt carry some jol
preoccupations home with them at night. On the serials
however, the best men, like the best women, are sensitive t
the every glance and voice inflection of their spouses. Such
undivided attention may well mirror a vital fantasy of man
housewives for the total attention of their husbands.

Despite the focus on family life, however, very few smal
children regularly appear on soap operas. Still, the *desire* fo
children and/or the threat of pregnancy provides a majo
theme for much of the drama. Even women doctors in these
soaps seem to be living in a pre-Pill era with inadequate con
traceptive knowledge. The lack of birth control precautions
on the part of soap opera characters is more than a means of
thickening the plot, however. It is also a reinforcement of old
Victorian stereotypes about the asexuality of "good women."
Women are not prepared with contraceptives because the
do not plan to engage in sexual relationships. When a good
woman is involved, sex always means true if unpremeditated
love on the soap operas. Only weak or evil characters desire
to have sexual relations without love or with more than one
person at a time. Likewise, people who are "really in love"
prove it by having a child together.

Since men and women are equal on the soap operas
"good" characters and "bad" characters exhibit similar value
regardless of sex. "Good," however, is associated with trait
traditionally stereotyped as female, such as love, compassion
family loyalty, and the willingness to sacrifice and suffer

"evil," on the other hand, is associated with traits long stereotyped as masculine—including cutthroat professional ethics, excessive involvement in work, neglect of family, infidelity, and so on.

For the majority of the characters on the soap operas, right and wrong are not determined by any code or by a set of principles, but rather by subjective assessments of the needs of self and others. The good people consider the needs of others, especially loved ones, first, even if they must commit the "great sacrifice" to do so. Bad people, by contrast, act to meet their own selfish needs and desires, letting the chips fall where they may.

The serials present strong dichotomies between good and evil. Rarely are there legitimate conflicts in which two people honestly differ as to what is right and what is wrong. One party inevitably has an ulterior motive or is using or victimizing other people involved.

Frequently, good and bad characters are played directly off against one another. In one set of episodes on "As the World Turns," for example, "good" Kim Dixon was compared and contrasted with "bad" Susan Stewart since both of them were in love with Susan's ex-husband, Dr. Dan Stewart. Beautiful, sophisticated Kim was trapped into a loveless marriage with Dr. John Dixon, who was blackmailing her to remain with him for the sake of his medical career. He knew that Kim had spent one night with her brother-in-law during his separation from her sister and that a pregnancy resulted from that affair. Kim had married John to have a father for the child, which died. Afterward, John threatened to tell Kim's sister about the affair if she left him. Miserable, Kim sought guidance from a minister who gave her the spiritual courage to withstand her suffering. Later, Kim fell in love with Dan, whom she met several times accidentally while taking long walks in the park. Since she knew she could not leave John, however, she refused to think about Dan, and once when he tried to proclaim his love for her, she told him he didn't want to hear it.

Meanwhile, Susan Stewart was deliberately trying to get her ex-husband back. Whereas Kim thought of the needs of others first, Susan thought only of her own selfish interests. Kim remained faithful to John, though she did not love him; Susan, on the other hand, used longtime boyfriend Mark in an attempt to make Dan jealous and thereby win him back. Kim developed a loving relationship with Dan's daughter; Susan, a doctor not interested in the responsibilities of children, merely used her daughter as bait to lure Dr. Dan. Whereas Kim turned to a minister in her confusion, Susan turned to the bottle and became an alcoholic.

Viewers were thus encouraged to identify with Kim, the victim, and to deplore Susan who victimized others. In subsequent episodes, however, Susan also became a victim and thus a character to be "sympathized" with when she became an alcoholic and lost her daughter in a custody suit.

More than anything else, then, the soap operas present the image of woman as victim and encourage viewers to identify strongly with that image. Except for a few older characters who have already passed their baptisms by fire, good characters seem doomed to recurrent victimization. Although men as well as women can be victims, this is the case because such men exhibit "female" traits like the willingness to suffer and sacrifice. Most generally, however, it is the women who suffer most, revealing their agony in wringing of hands, heavily upheld heads, and dewdrop eyes, just barely fighting away the tearful outburst that will come sooner or later anyway.

Fortunately, the suffering ends at nightfall. Like daytime TV, programs aired during prime time fall broadly into categories, including situation/domestic comedy, drama, and drama/adventure series. However, only one category of evening programming portrays an even balance of male and female characters—the situation comedy.

When the schedule for the 1976 television season was announced, *TV Guide* reported that CBS network officials were privately referring to Monday night as "ladies night." The prime-time lineup included four situation comedies:

"Rhoda," "Maude," "Phyllis," and "All in the Family." To be sure, "ladies" starred in three of the four shows, but the meaning of the phrase "ladies night" included the audience as well. Network officials were simply confirming what has been common-sense knowledge all along—that women are the primary viewers of the evening comedies.

It stands to reason. The situation comedies are the only dramatic-type evening programs that portray women as the full peers of men, and occasionally as their superiors. Early fifties comedies like "Life of Riley," "Ozzie and Harriet," "The Honeymooners," and "Make Room for Daddy" set a pattern of the foolish husband and sensible wife that has often been repeated.

By contrast, in drama and drama/adventure programs, men are the heroes, and women are victims or window dressing. The differences in male and female roles on comedy versus the drama programs exist largely because of stereotypes regarding the "proper sphere" of men and women. Situation comedies, where female characters are concentrated, deal exclusively with close interpersonal relationships, usually in a family context; drama and drama/adventure programs, on the other hand, are about the world of work.

Situation comedies are, in many respects, just soap operas with the frowns turned upward into smiles, and the tears dried up with gusts of laughter. Marshall McLuhan put it succinctly when he said that "behind all comedy is a grievance." All dramatic-type comedy inherently poses an adversary situation, and the most basic and most frequently used team of adversaries, in fiction, movies, and television, is the married couple.

On the soap operas, the "natural" adversary relationship between men and women leads to a chain of jealousies, extramarital affairs, divorces, child-custody fights, and a host of related traumas. Because of the large number of characters and the deep commingling between community members on the soap operas, characters can be allowed to change spouses, jobs, friends, and personalities with a fair degree of regularity.

Situation comedies, on the other hand, utilize a small cast of regulars, two or three settings, and depend on occasional guest characters to add novelty to the plots.

Both men and women, then, are "situated" on the situated comedies. Conflicts may come and go, but it is clearly understood by the audience that, at least for the duration of the TV season, the cast of characters will remain the same from week to week—that is, that the interpersonal relationships established between characters will remain intact. This adds a certain optimism and lightheartedness to even the most dire of conflicts and aids the course of comedy on the programs.

The TV sitcom has always been a "family affair." During the 1950s, typical comedies like "I Love Lucy," "Ozzie and Harriet," "The Donna Reed Show," "Make Room for Daddy," "Father Knows Best," "The Real McCoys," and "Leave It to Beaver" portrayed complete nuclear families consisting of mother, father, and one or more children. By the middle 1960s, however, television began reflecting the escalating divorce rate (it had been skyrocketing since 1950) by portraying a host of single parents, still with their school-age children. To round out the nuclear family illusion, however, a spouse substitute was always provided for the lone parent.

Interestingly, spouse surrogates for the female lead on such programs as "Here's Lucy," "Petticoat Junction," "The Partridge Family," and "The Ghost and Mrs. Muir" were always of the opposite sex. By contrast, spouse substitutes for bachelor fathers on programs like "My Three Sons" and "Family Affair" were sometimes male. Since TV portrays the most conservative values, the implication is that marriage is considered more normal and obligatory for women than it is for men. Women are portrayed in confining relationships with men even when they are single and allegedly career oriented.

In fact, the small, family-sized cast, close, indoor settings, and the recurrent presence of spouses or male-spouse substitutes combine to create a lingering image of women as house-

wives on the situation comedies. This image is further reinforced by the fact that work itself is de-emphasized on the
sitcoms.

In many situation comedies, characters are stipulated as
having jobs, although they never appear at work on the program. It is a long-standing gag among television buffs that
Ozzie Nelson, of the long running and immensely popular
"Adventures of Ozzie and Harriet," never worked or mentioned a job of any sort. In the prosperous fifties when employment was taken for granted, it was just assumed that
good-natured Oz had some legal means of providing for his
wife and two sons. In the middle seventies, however, an
allegedly employed house-husband such as Walter Finley
("Maude") will make infrequent comments about his job to
remind the audience that he has one. Occasionally, the job
may even be incorporated into the plot, as it was once when
Walter became a religious zealot in order to sell a large order
of construction supplies to the church. Only by tearing up
the church's check could Maude get Walter to make a "do-
nation" of the supplies.

As is true on the soap operas, it is common in the middle
seventies for women in the domestic comedies to be employed, but money-making is never an apparent goal. In fact,
they are only shown at their jobs when interpersonal dilemmas are at issue. Rhoda Morgenstern ("Rhoda"), for instance, is a window dresser, but the principles of window
dressing have never been discussed on the program, and we
have never seen an example of her work. Instead, "work related" episodes center around conflicts with Rhoda's assistant, Myrna, a well-meaning young woman with very poor
judgment where male clients are concerned. Likewise, Emily
Hartley ("The Bob Newhart Show") is a schoolteacher, but
the plot only takes her to school when it can also provide an
excuse for star Bob Newhart to be there too. Maude Finley
allegedly sells real estate, but she has never closed a deal on
the program.

For seven successful years, the "Mary Tyler Moore Show"

provided an interesting variation on the typical domestic arrangement in the situation comedies. On this show, Mary Richards' work colleagues were actually a surrogate family. Most episodes took place at work, but they always involved interpersonal conflicts and misunderstandings. The cast of the show portrayed members of a nightly news team, and their respective job positions roughly suggested their positions in the surrogate family. Lou Grant, the program director, was the stern, masculine, and all-business father figure; Mary, as producer of the news show, was the mother figure, of course; Murray, her assistant producer, was like a mature teen-age son; and Ted Baxter, the egocentric, laughing-boy newscaster, who had to be told every word he was to say and given plenty of time to rehearse even the shortest of lines, was the precocious child. Other situation comedies had used the work situation to provide surrogate family groupings, of course, including such favorites as "Our Miss Brooks," "Susie," "Get Smart," and "The Doris Day Show," as well as the military comedies "McHale's Navy," "Hogan's Heroes," "Gomer Pyle, USMC," and "M*A*S*H."

Most typically, however, the heroines of the sitcoms have been actual housewives whose daily dealings with husbands, children, other relatives, and friends lead to mild conflicts and misinterpretations which are easily resolved after every ounce of comedy has been milked from them.

For example, one of the best comedies of the middle 1960s was Emmy award winner "The Dick Van Dyke Show," starring Van Dyke and Mary Tyler Moore as a happily married couple with one son. This program also contained a surrogate family grouping since Rob Petrie's (Van Dyke) work associates were regulars on the show. Rob and his colleagues, Buddy and Sally, were portrayed as the writers of a TV comedy program. (In a neat reversal of roles, the real writer of "The Dick Van Dyke Show," Carl Reiner, appeared infrequently as the star of the show allegedly written by Rob, Buddy, and Sally.) Again, relations between the writers were warm, and differences arose from misinterpretations. The only adversary relationship that was built into the program's basic situation and was thus recurrent on every show was the relationship between the writers of the comedy program and Mel, the show's producer. Mel was a sourpuss who disliked everybody on general grounds.

"The Dick Van Dyke Show" was exceptionally well conceived, though unfortunately many of the gags built into the situation had mild sexist overtones. For example, Mel got his job in part because he married the star's sister. (He was also bald and overly sensitive about it.) Sally was middle-aged, single, and always on the lookout for a good catch. Buddy and his wife, "Bubbles," had their ups and downs. But each episode featured a unique dilemma, generally spawned by a misunderstanding between two characters.

In one episode, Rob's parents come for a visit. Rob and wife, Laura, are delighted, since they have a good relationship with the folks. Before dinner, however, Mrs. Petrie gives Laura a family heirloom as a treasured gift. After the fanfare, Laura opens a small box and finds a grotesque brooch, in the shape of a map of the United States, with a tiny jewel to indicate the birthplace of every member of the Petrie clan. The scene is hilarious, with much of the comedy carried by Mary Tyler Moore's ingenious use of voice inflection to indicate shock, then disbelief, and finally a subtle humor at receiving such a monstrous gift. Never overtly losing her composure, however, Laura pins on the brooch and expresses sincere gratitude for being made the custodian of the prize family keepsake.

After dinner, Laura and Rob have a good laugh over the brooch, agreeing that as soon as his parents leave, it will get the deep drawer treatment. Meanwhile, however, the folks are taking Laura and Rob out for dinner the next evening, and Laura guesses she will have to wear it one more time. Disaster strikes when the brooch gets knocked off into the dishwater and mangled by the garbage disposal. Too aghast to tell even Rob, Laura takes the brooch to a jeweler the next day to see if damages can be repaired. The jeweler restores it to a semblance of its former appearance but, in the process, rearranges some of the stones.

When Mrs. Petrie first notices that one of the stones is missing from its accustomed place, she is horrified; the last time a stone dropped out, that family member died within weeks. She soon notices that the whole brooch is different, however, and the hoax is up. As a final coup d'état, Mrs. Petrie reveals that she has hated the brooch all along, which is why she was so eager to pass it along to Laura. In this episode, then, Laura's potential conflict with her mother-in-law resolved itself into the most superficial of misunderstandings. Everyone was on the same side all along, if only they'd known it.

Occasionally, situation comedies have been structured around the frustration involved in being a housewife. Metaphorically, these shows have all suggested that a woman's special talents must be sacrificed to the married state as a condition of getting and keeping a man.

The archetypal frustrated wife was Lucille Ball's Lucy Ricardo of the extremely popular and long-running "I Love Lucy" show. Portrayed as the wife of Cuban band leader Ricky Ricardo (played by Desi Arnaz, Ball's husband at the time), Lucy's problem was that she desperately wanted to get into show biz herself. Ricky Ricardo categorically disapproved of his wife working, however, though the plot conveniently made Lucy inept at performing anyway. She could neither dance, carry a tune, nor act; she was even too fat (not a standard size twelve) for a chorus line. In real life, of course, Lucille Ball was a successful veteran of numerous movies, including musicals, and she possessed all of these skills to a refined degree. For purposes of comedy on the program, though, Lucy continually tried to steal her way into Ricky's act, only to make a fool of herself in the process. All her *mis*performances were hilariously funny, of course, but nobody, least of all hubby, Ricky, stops to think that Lucy Ricardo might have talent as a comedienne. Ironically, Lucy Ricardo's failures were the great success of Lucille Ball, and to this extent, the central metaphor of Lucy's ineptness is ironic.

Denied any challenging activity outside the home, Lucy effectively remained a child, forever engaging in crazy pranks and schemes. When not conning her way into a performance, one of Lucy's favorite pastimes was to chase down stars in unlikely places in order to obtain their autographs. She was assisted in these escapades by her childlike landlady/best friend, Ethel Mertz, and sometimes by Ethel's husband, Fred. After hearing Lucy propose some preposterous scheme, Ethel typically clapped her hands together, took a big gasp, and replied with her classic line, "I don't know, Lucy, sounds awful risky."

Even Ricky occasionally dropped his plastic band-boy smile to yell uncontrollably at his wife in Spanish when one of her schemes was exposed. Lucy was the biggest baby of all, however, and when Ricky descended to her level of childish irrationality, she simply gaped open her mouth and started to bawl. This effectively forced Ricky to resume the father role, assuring his little Lucy that her silly pranks would go unpunished if she promised not to do anything so foolish again.

The immense popularity of the "I Love Lucy" program is an interesting phenomenon in itself. Surely the primary reason is the considerable talents of the stars, especially Ball herself. In addition, though, the theme of a housewife spicing up her ho-hum life in bizarre, exciting ways and, in the process, becoming even briefly involved with famous movie stars must have tapped a vital fantasy of many women whose lives were less eventful.

Later comedies gave the wives more illusive, magical powers which these women happily agreed to shelve in order to seem like ordinary housewives and thereby keep their ordinary husbands happy. "I Dream of Jeannie," for instance, has sexy Jeannie as the wife of an ordinary-looking Air Force pilot. She refers to him in private as "Master" and responds automatically to his every command. By contrast, he feels free to confine her to her bottle if she shows the slightest intention to act on her own initiative. Since she is intended to represent the perfect embodiment of male fantasy, however, Jeannie doesn't mind. She adores her master, and her only real concern is that he might be lured away by another, perhaps more "normal," woman. To ward off this possibility, she devotes a major portion of her magic energy to surreptitiously supervising his contacts with other females.

In the popular comedy "Bewitched," beautiful and good witch Samantha, who fell in love with ordinary mortal Darrin Stevens, has agreed as a condition of their marriage to practice no more witchcraft, even of the good kind. Week after week, however, trouble is created when one of Samantha's zany witch or warlock relatives casts a spell that inadvertently threatens Darrin's business relationships. Then, of course, Samantha must use witchcraft to cover up the previous trickery or to dispel the previous spell. Over and over, the point is made that the best thing "Sam" can do for her husband's career is to be as sweet, ordinary, and housewifely as possible. The very *last* thing that Darrin wants is for people to know that his wife has special capabilities. So Samantha does her best to seem "normal."

In a short-lived 1970s version of this theme, a program called "The Girl with Something Extra" had the young wife of a lawyer gifted with powers of extrasensory perception. With such a talent, you might presume that she would be busy predicting the next political assassination or natural disaster. But no—the good wife used her powers to smooth over domestic trials with in-laws and friends, and occasionally to help her husband with his law practice.

A discussion of situation comedy would be incomplete without taking some special notice of recent trends in female images. The dominant image of women in the sitcoms has always been the housewife, and it continues to be so in the 1970s. Primarily as a result of the success of Norman Lear's "All in the Family," however, some new variations in the housewife image have recently been presented to viewers.

Although "All in the Family" has had a major effect on all

situation comedy in the 1970s, its success may largely be attributed to the strong acting abilities of the cast and to the strange chemistry of the different coexisting types. The program revived the theme of the working-class family, fairly well extinct since the late 1950s when popular programs like "The Life of Riley" and "The Honeymooners" (a regular segment of "The Jackie Gleason Show") went off the air. "All in the Family," however (which is based on a similar Canadian series), varied the older formula by adding a "hippie" son-in-law who married the "shop-rat's" daughter and then moved in with the in-laws while completing his graduate school education. (During the 1976 season, the Stivics moved next door.) Carroll O'Connor is superb as bigoted shop-rat Archie Bunker, and Rob Reiner, as Michael Stivic, makes a credible "liberal" sparring partner. Physically, both men are portrayed as overweight, unkempt, and lethargic. This is important since it means that the cards are not artificially stacked in favor of one or the other based on appearance.

Though surveys have shown that viewers tended to agree exclusively with *either* Archie *or* Mike, no matter what the conflict, Jean Stapleton and Sally Struthers, who star as Edith Bunker and Gloria Stivic, portray the values of working-class women with a charm and optimism that makes these values universally sympathetic.

Edith Bunker's devotion to family life forms the core of her personal philosophy. This is what enables her to survive Archie's criticism of her cooking, her singing, her religion, and her friends with only a mild smile for a rebuttal. In one episode, Edith discovers that a friend is contemplating divorce because her husband is tired of her and has begun having affairs. The friend tells Edith that she and Archie are practically the only people she knows who are happily married. "What's your secret?" she asks. "Oh, I ain't got no secret," Edith replies with a slightly embarrassed smile. "Archie and me still has fights, but we don't let 'em go on too long. Somebody always says 'I'm sorry,' and Archie always says, 'That's OK, Edith.'"

Like her mother, Gloria is also a peacemaker. Her character has slowly changed and developed over the five years that
the series has been on the air, however. At the beginning,
goldilocks Gloria, whose ringlets surrounded a not-quite-
grown-looking face was perpetually in a turmoil over Archie
and Mike's bickering. But over time, she has gained an independence and sense of personal responsibility that refuses to
be intimidated by either husband or father.

More than the individual characters, however, it is the
basic structure of "All in the Family" that has been so
influential. Although previous situation comedies used adversary dilemmas of a subtle and mild nature, often focusing on
misunderstandings and misinterpretations, "Family" has focused on conflict and disagreement, per se, usually of an issue-oriented nature. Initially, the conflict in viewpoints between Archie and Mike sparked most of the comedy on the
program. In these conflicts, Edith and Gloria acted as media-
tors and peacekeepers. Very soon, however, the show
branched out to do episodes on a number of social and political issues—sometimes with quasi-serious overtones—specializ-
ing in the sensitive issues of racial and religious prejudice. To
better tap the adversary viewpoints involved in racial conflict,
an equally bigoted black neighbor was created for Archie in
the person of George Jefferson. Eventually, the Jeffersons
spun off into a program of their own.

The portrayal by "Family" of adversary issue-oriented
conflict, peacekeeping wives, and black neighbors, who finally
"moved" into a sitcom all their own, represented innovations
which have had a large impact on female television images.
Programs like "Maude," "Phyllis," and the shorter-lived
"Fay," in addition to the Mrs. Grant character on the "Mary
Tyler Moore Show" were built around adversary conflict over
women's issues. It should be emphasized, though, that the
Women's Liberation Movement gained a peak of nationwide
publicity in 1970 and 1971, thereby rendering women's issues
topical enough to be of interest to the mass of conservative
prime-time viewers.[7] Running parallel to the new inde-

pendent and free-thinking images of women, however, is the motif of the peacekeeping wife popularized by Edith and Gloria. This image was carried forward on such popular programs as "Rhoda" and "Good Times," after the initial ardor of the woman's movement had subsided in the middle seventies.

The Florida Evans character on "Good Times" also represents part of another 1970s trend—the trend toward all-black sitcoms. "Beulah," a stereotypical portrayal which found a receptive audience in the 1950s, focused on the antics of a black maid. Then, in 1968, a comedy program about a young black nurse, "Julia," achieved some notice because of the talents of its star, Diahann Carroll. Judging from the success of the Mary Richards character ("Mary Tyler Moore Show") three years later, however, the Julia character, being not only black but a working woman as well, was ahead of her time. By contrast, the all-black programs of the 1970s have featured family dilemmas of the type which have always been the staple of situation comedy. As a result, they have found a multiracial audience among long-time devotees of the genre. Though racial issues and innuendos have been used to spark comedy on programs like "The Jeffersons," "Sanford and Son," and "Good Times," bitterness is never allowed to overshadow the love between family members, which is the real theme of these programs.

A final trend of the seventies, the spin-off phenomenon, which has produced programs like "The Jeffersons," "Good Times" (derived from "Maude," where Florida Evans was the housekeeper), "Rhoda" (former best friend of Mary Richards on "The Mary Tyler Moore Show") and "Phyllis" (also from MTM show), seems to indicate that the bonds between soap opera and situation comedy are becoming even stronger. The most confining aspect of the sitcom has been the necessity of keeping the cast size small. But through the use of spin-offs, new characters can be added ad infinitum, and old familiar characters can be allowed to change, develop, and potentially, to grow into more challenging and contemporaneous roles. So far, spin-off roles have been at least as traditional as those portrayed on the parent program, but the potential for a wide range of variations certainly exists.

One TV critic theorizes that the sitcom formula itself has spun off into other TV genres. Horace Newcomb's *TV: The Most Popular Art* has as its central thesis that the situation comedy is television's basic model, after which other formulas have become increasingly patterned.[8] Newcomb believes that *all* television formulas—including the sitcoms, Westerns, mysteries, doctor and lawyer shows, and adventure programs—are more like each other than like the literary formulas they are descended from. To illustrate this thesis, he cites the appearance of family surrogates in programs of all types.

Newcomb realizes that the family or in group has become television's staple unit in part because of the small size of the television screen. Only a few faces or forms can be distinguished clearly at a time. In addition, however, Newcomb thinks that intimacy, *per se*, has become a value within television formulas. "Television is at its best," he says, "when it offers us faces, reactions, explorations of emotions registered by human beings." In other words, TV is best at portraying close, interpersonal relationships, like those that exist in a family.

If it is true that television's basic unit is the family, it is disturbing that on a great majority of drama and drama/adventure programs, it is a family without women. There are a few exceptions to this womanless world of drama and drama/adventure, however, and one of them is on its way to launching a whole new genre for evening television—"family drama."

Family drama began during the 1972–73 television season with a single program, "The Waltons." Based on the childhood experiences of the program's creator, Earl Hamner, Jr., the series is about a large Blue Ridge Mountain family living out the Depression on love and the father's backyard sawmill. So idyllic is the presentation of family life that many viewers, accustomed to family bickering on the evening sitcoms, considered the series controversial at first. Mike Stivic of "All in the Family" summed it up for these viewers when he accused mother-in-law Edith of forming false notions of what a family should be from watching "The Waltons." "No family is really like that," exclaimed Mike. Four years later, however, the program has already become a television classic which has inspired several short-lived imitators and one successful one, "Little House on the Prairie."

The Walton clan consists of mother and father, Olivia and John Walton, in their early forties, and their seven children. John's parents, who are referred to affectionately as Grandpa and Grandma by community members, also live with the family. As early reviews of "The Waltons" observed, the moral tone of family life is set by John and Olivia. John is a rough-hewn lumberman, whose simple philosophy of life is written all over his smiling, weathered face. He believes in the "decent" things—hard work; providing for loved ones; extending compassion and a helping hand to those in need. Olivia also believes in the simple, traditional values—taking care of her family; helping others; serving as an example of soft-spoken and patient love for her children.

According to the message of the program, however, love and helpfulness comes only within the family as in group. Life within a happy family is the highest type of fulfillment possible according to the program. No career, no dream is worth the effort if family life must be jeopardized in the process. As a result, a number of professional persons, including an actor, an airplane pilot, a writer, and a historian, have been stereotyped as conflict-ridden and partially unfulfilled. Olivia herself gave up a career as a singer in order to pursue full-time what she believed to be the higher calling of housewife.

Though the parents set the moral and emotional tone for the household, the oldest son, John-Boy, has been the central character of the program. Patterned after Hamner, the series creator, the "adult" John-Boy is now a successful writer living in California. He is relating events that happened to his family when he was a teen-ager, still aspiring to be a professional writer. At the end of the 1977 season, John-Boy finally left his Blue Ridge home for New York City, there to start his career as a novelist.

It is hard to predict where the focus of *The Waltons* will lie in the future, but thus far, the series has really been a saga of a boy growing into manhood. Women are important to the program, but only in the most traditional of roles. Three of the children are girls, but they are generally shown in situations which teach them about nurturing behavior. For example, sister Erin, fourteen at the time, learned not to be overprotective when she had to send a beloved captured fawn back into its natural environment. By contrast, John-Boy and Jason, the oldest sons, have been pictured branching out into the world of work and handling demanding conflicts with peers and occasionally with parents. It is inherent to the context of "The Waltons" that boys grow up to be strong and resourceful wage earners. Girls grow up to be housewives. On one episode, oldest daughter Mary Ellen claimed that she wanted to become a doctor. This seemed hard to believe, however. More likely, we think, she will follow her mother's example and lay aside plans she was capable of realizing in order to be the moral nexus of her own Walton-type family. After Mary Ellen married a doctor in the 1976 season, the latter alternative seemed a certainty.

Once "The Waltons" had established the fact that family drama of a more serious nature could be as popular with evening viewers as the family comedies, imitations were inevitable. The best of the imitations to date has been "Little House on the Prairie," based on the *Little House* books by Laura Ingalls Wilder. This TV series features a nuclear family comprised of mother and father in their thirties, two school-age daughters, and one female toddler. The overall youth of this family stands in sharp contrast to previous frontier families such as those portrayed on the Western classics of "Bonanza," "The Virginian," or "Big Valley." In these series, parents were middle-aged or older, and children were adults or in their late teens. In common with earlier versions of farm living, however, the Ingalls family lives in a recently settled, western community in which law and justice are still heavily in the hands of local community leaders. Despite their youth, Charles and Caroline Ingalls provide moral leadership for their town.

"Little House" is not a Western in the usual sense, however, because the action is nonviolent. Even in situations where violence looms heavily as a threat, peaceful solutions, but without the rhetoric of surrender, are worked out. No doubt the civilizing presence of a woman and female children is largely responsible for creating the context in which resort to violence would never seem justified.

But Caroline Ingalls and her daughters are not portrayed as prissy weaklings who need the protection of men. Criticism of the series which claims that the roles are too stereotyped and not reflective enough of pioneer conditions is unjust. Numerous episodes have shown the women fending capably for themselves and levelheadedly responding to such emergencies as a snowstorm or a fire in the barn. The daughters, too, are as resourceful and independently responsible as the parents. Male children could be cast in their roles without changing any of the stories.

As far as images of women are concerned, then, family drama of the "Little House" variety is somewhat superior to family drama Waltons style. Like Olivia Walton, Caroline Ingalls is also occasionally guilty of "sMother love," but there is never any doubt that, if need be, Caroline could manage alone. In one "Waltons" episode in which John briefly took a job in a nearby community, however, Olivia lasted only four days before calling at his boardinghouse to express loneliness and depression. Also, at ages eight and ten, the Ingalls girls seemed more mature than did the Walton daughters as teen-agers.

By contrast with the family dramas, on most evening

dramas women are not deemed important enough to hold any major role. Instead, these programs feature a professional male as the principal character/superhero. Drama programs of the past have focused on the professions of law and education as well as medicine, but during the seventies most of the superprofessionals have been doctors. These doctors radiate a perfect blend of sympathy and rational responsibility toward their patients, who are often female and frequently friends of the doctors as well.

Commonly, medical (and formerly legal or educational) larly on the long-running and popular series "Marcus Welby, or Joe Gannon to the patient's personal problems. Particularly on the long-running and popular series "Marcus Welby M.D.," the patients' illnesses often seem to follow as direct retribution for some "sinful" act. In one 1974 episode, for example, a prostitute refuses to be operated on for breast cancer because she knows it will ruin her business; naturally she dies. In a 1970 episode, a popular high school girl engages in premarital sex and gets pregnant. Afraid to tell her social-climbing mother, she goes to a back-alley abortionist. Her ultimate punishment is a complete hysterectomy.

With rare exceptions, on the medical programs parents are presented as irrational and incompetent. Children are continually portrayed as the victims of their parents'—and particularly their mothers'—overprotectiveness, inability to face facts, and general emotional weaknesses. For instance, in one episode of "Marcus Welby" an overprotective mother of a young deaf girl refuses to give permission for her daughter to have a delicate operation to restore her hearing. The mother is desperately afraid that the child will either die during the operation or that some facial distortion will result. Later, the daughter gets lost in the city, and after the mother has spent a long night in panic, the girl is finally found by a night watchman. Kind, paternalistic Marcus Welby is at last able to persuade this weak and possessive woman to do what is best for her child.

Although one superprofessional is the star character on

each drama program, he has always been portrayed in a fa-
ther-son type relationship with another male in his profession.
It is clear that the bonds between the two men are deeply
personal. Marcus Welby is father figure to his young assistant
Steven Kiley, for instance. On the other hand, Joe Gannon,
the main star of "Medical Center," has a father figure in the
hospital's chief of staff, Dr. Lockner. The older doctors ex-
pound the more traditional wisdom, and the younger men are
more contemporary and "causey." This pattern of portraying
two doctors in a mentor/learner relationship dates back to
the earliest TV doctor programs, moreover—think of Kildare
and Gillespie or Casey and Zorba. Programs about lawyers
and educators have also followed this pattern.

Occasionally, women appear in minor regular roles, in part
to round out the illusion of a family. These women are only
window dressing, however, since they never participate in the
action of plots. During the 1975 season, Consuelo, the nurse-
receptionist on "Marcus Welby" was featured in one episode
—but as a patient!

An exception to the usual all-male pattern of professional
drama was the program "Room 222," which was aired between 1969 and 1971. This series grew out of the "relevance
movement" of the late sixties, which also produced such issue-oriented programs as "Mod Squad," "The Young Lawyers," and "Storefront Lawyers." "Then Came Bronson," the
program about a motorcycle drifter, was a variation on the
relevance theme.

"Room 222" dealt with dilemmas facing students and
teachers in a large high school. The main characters included
a white principal in his fifties, a black male history teacher in
his thirties, a black female counselor in her thirties, and a
white female teacher fresh from college. Though an improve-
ment over programs with no female professionals, this series
nonetheless portrayed the men as more capable and dignified
than the women.

Alice, the beginning teacher, is full of foibles as she tries to
learn her new role. She acts more like a high school cheer-

leader than like a teacher, and it is clear that her acceptance by students is largely on a peer basis. As the counselor, Liz is portrayed in a female support role which she nonetheless has difficulty performing. She is prone to fits of emotionalism and must consult Pete, the history teacher, or Mr. Kaufman, the principal, when serious counseling problems arise. In contrast to the women, Dixon and Kaufman are portrayed as always calm, rational, and competent—with just the right words to placate angry students and teachers alike.

Although family dramas like "The Waltons" and programs like "Room 222" have raised the proportion of women in the drama category to about one female for every two males, in the drama/adventure category men have always outnumbered women by at least a ratio of eight to one. Only during the 1970s have female regulars begun to appear in any quantity on adventure programs. In general, however, women have been confined to the roles of victims and transient love interests on the popular adventure shows; only sporadically have women risen to the status of regular characters.

During the 1950s and most of the 1960s, the Western dominated TV adventure-type programs. Women, however, were by and large second-class citizens on these programs, if they appeared at all. Several of the most popular Westerns, including "Wagon Train," "Have Gun, Will Travel," "Wanted Dead or Alive," and "Bonanza," had no regular female characters at all. As a result, women were mere episodes in the lives of the Western superheroes.

Critics of American popular culture, including especially John G. Cawelti, have argued convincingly that the Western is the basic formula after which other American adventure formulas have been patterned.[9] Since the Western is basic to American literature and media, it is significant that it is a genre which inherently excludes women. In the traditional Western, the pioneer or cowboy superhero is strong, virtuous, and almost infallible. He acts as a civilizing force, bringing law and order to ruthless outpost communities, but as soon as the town is safe enough for the womenfolk, the cowboy hero rides out to new adventure. The Western hero respects women, but he prefers the company of men. Women mean stability and stagnation, and by nature the Westerner feels called to roam.

Likewise, in the television Westerns, women frequently represented stability—the interlude between exciting adventures. On westerns like "Have Gun, Will Travel," "Maverick," and "Wild Wild West," a brief scene between the superhero and an unnamed female often framed the action of the story. These women were always saloon girls, however, or at minimum they had the look of ill-repute. It was clear that the hero's attachment was transitory and that the call to the brave world of men would occasion only a fleeting regret.

Sometimes a woman figured prominently in the hero's adventure, but if the two became romantically involved, separation or death for the female character was mandatory by the end of the episode. If the temporary heroine had a sexually tainted past, she was either killed at story's end or else she was banished "back East" where no one would be the wiser. If the heroine was a "good girl" who won the superhero's love, her death was a foregone conclusion. I remember once as a kid getting terribly excited when I read in *TV Guide* that Little Joe Cartwright was to be married in that evening's episode of "Bonanza." As I read on, however, I discovered it was the first of a two-part episode. My heart sank. I knew that the wife would die in the second part, as, of course, she did. (Interestingly, Little Joe *has* gotten married in a way, since Michael Landon plays an adult version of his "Bonanza" character in his new role as Charles Ingalls on "Little House on the Prairie.")

Although several of the TV Western heroes were loners, many of the most popular series featured a family or family-like grouping. On some of these programs, including such favorites as "The Virginian" and the highly sophisticated "Gunsmoke," there was a female regular who appeared briefly in some or most of the episodes. On "Gunsmoke," Kitty, proprietor of Dodge City's saloon and Marshal Matt

Dillon's presumed girlfriend, was portrayed skillfully by Amanda Blake for over twenty years. Her appearances were frequent in the 1950s, but unfortunately they steadily dwindled during the sixties and seventies. A token Western of the late sixties contained a female principal character. "Big Valley" featured the considerable talent of veteran movie performer Barbara Stanwyck in the role of Victoria Barkley, the widowed matriarch of a giant western landholding. The show was noticeably patterned after the popular "Bonanza" series, and Victoria was a strong female version of the Ben Cartwright character. As a very subtle example of sexual stereotyping, however, Victoria's children included three unmarried adult sons and a pretty teen-age daughter. Had the daughter been the age of any of the sons but still unmarried, she would have been considered an old maid. As for the sons, however, their "freedom" allowed them greater mobility and adventure.

Though it has only limited significance for the image of women on television, one of the most notable changes to occur in TV's short history has been the disappearance of the once immensely popular TV Western. Critics have been quick to notice that the theme of law-and-order maintenance was passed down from the Westerns to the crime drama programs which now dominate in the drama/adventure category. That this should have happened in the late sixties seems reasonable, given the national situation in the United States at the time. As the tempestous sixties closed, the American people wanted reassurance that law and order was possible and that society was not breaking down. Civil rights demonstrations and demonstrations against the Vietnam war were common occurrences on college campuses and in large cities across the country. The large following of law-and-order extremist George Wallace, as a third party presidential candidate in 1968, is one indication of the seriousness of the average citizen's concern over street violence. The crime drama dealt "better," that is, more concretely, with the law-and-order issues posed in the 1960s. The Westerns simply could not reassure the public that the "system" wasn't breaking down.

In the middle 1970s almost all drama/adventure programs are subclassified in *TV Guide* as "crime drama." The pattern of the straight-laced, just-the-facts-ma'am cop first suggested in 1952 by the "Dragnet" series, moreover, has gradually won out over more free-lance crime fighters. The current version of the supercop is of a highly professional, even analytical crime fighter, someone who radiates a college education and good breeding. This is true for uniformed policemen on such programs as "Adam-12" and "The Rookies," and their nonuniformed affiliates on shows like "Hawaii Five-O" and "Streets of San Francisco" as well.

Typically, the policemen on the crime dramas are portrayed as members of teams in which the personal ties seem almost as binding as the professional ones. Over the decade of the crime drama's great popularity, however, only a few women have appeared as members of these family-like teams.

Surely the relative absence of women in action roles in Westerns and crime dramas stands as proof of a strong sexual stereotyping in this country which relegates women to nurturing and supportive roles and men to roles defined by conquest and adventure. In the broadest of metaphoric terms, these stereotypes suggest the difference between home and work, but even in the post-liberationist era of the 1970s, those women who work still choose or are assigned the subordinate, supportive positions.

Beyond the well-entrenched, practical consequences of sexual stereotyping in the world of work, however, there are a number of *symbols* which our culture deeply associates with femininity and masculinity, respectively. The most ultramale of all symbols, of course, is the gun. This in itself may be the reason why women have figured so negligibly in TV Westerns and crime dramas. As far as many people are concerned, for a woman merely to hold a gun is a travesty of her femininity.

The thesis that women and guns don't mix in our cultural

mythology (and thus on our most popular media) is given support by the fact that, up until very recently, the few women who have made their way into the ranks of the drama/adventure superheroes have done so sans gun. The best of these superheroines used the special skills of the martial arts to ward off assailants and to immobilize and capture criminals; a more anemic group relied on their "feminine wiles," that is to say their powers of persuasion and deception.

The best of the crime drama heroines, and perhaps the best role thus far created for any woman on television, was Emma Peel of the British series "The Avengers." Played by Shakespearean actress Diana Rigg, Emma Peel was an "internationally educated daughter of a wealthy shipowner and youthful widow of a famous test pilot." She and John Steed (symbolic name) were free-lance undercover agents who got most of their assignments from a man in a wheelchair whose code name was "Mother." (One time a woman gave them their orders and *her* code name was "Father.") Plots were bizarre—a flavorful combination of crime detection, spy story, and magic, frequently acted out in elaborate costumes. In one episode, for example, Emma and Steed intercepted the plot of a diabolical scientist to make people into robots. (He had already made a robot of himself.) In another, the duo uncovered a plot to poison England's soil.

The truly intriguing aspect of "The Avengers" series, however, was the unique portrayal of the heroine. Not only was Peel gorgeous, sophisticated, and sexually mature (the fact that she was a widow took care of that), but she was also capable, independent, even haughty—and a judo expert. Although she sometimes used her judo skills against capable female antagonists, it was not uncommon for her to take on as many as six men at a time. Though Emma Peel could dress with dignity as the occasion demanded, for rounding up spies and criminals, she preferred all-leather pants suits.

"The Avengers" began a long and popular run in England in 1961, although it was not purchased for distribution in the

United States until 1966. Before Diana Rigg took the part of Emma in 1964, it had been played by Honor Blackman who quit to become Pussy Galore in the James Bond movie *Goldfinger*. Despite the popularity of "The Avengers" in this country, however, no American Emmas were forthcoming. Instead, the general mold of American crime drama heroines was carved out by the heroine of another series which made its debut in 1966—Barbara Bain's "Dana" of "Mission Impossible."

Except for an almost stoic sobriety, Dana was a more normal—that is to say unexceptional—heroine than the often fiery Emma. Also rarely allowed the use of a gun or other weapon, she relied instead on her cool wits to perform her part of the "mission" and to save her from any dangers encountered along the way. The series was structured perfectly to make such a female role credible. Dana was the lone female member of a special team called the "IMF" which undertook top secret missions on behalf of national security. The team leader was warned at the outset of every mission that if members of the team were detected or apprehended in the course of their operations, "the Secretary will disavow all knowledge of your activities." In sharp contrast to the brash, shoot-em-up blundering of most crime fighting, then, subtlety and careful maneuvering were of the essence.

Dana was also portrayed as the full peer of her IMF team members. She had an important function to perform in connection with each mission, and a crucial behind-the-scenes job as well, since she was portrayed as the make-up artist who crafted all of IMF's brilliant disguises. When Barbara Bain quit the series, she was replaced by younger actresses, thereby instituting the typical middle-aged man/young-woman structure commonly found in spy and detective novels. Bain, however, was allowed to have the over-thirty look, carried off successfully by the same type of chiseled attractiveness and sophistication that graces male characters in such roles.

Between 1966 and 1974, women in adventure series grew increasingly anemic. The science fiction series "Star Trek" made its debut in 1966, with three regular female roles. Despite an obvious attempt to people the starship *Enterprise* with a multiracial, heterosexual crew however, the male "WASP" image dominated. For one thing, the three feature characters, Captain Kirk, Mr. Spock, and Dr. McCoy were male, and Kirk and McCoy projected a white-Anglo-Saxon-Protestant image.

In addition, the three female crew members were placed in stereotypical support roles, one as a nurse, one as the captain's personal yeoman (whose sexiness he found distracting), and the third as the communications officer. During the 1966 season, black communications officer Ohura was often shown entertaining crew members during relaxation breaks with impromptu musical numbers. During these episodes, she stood out as friendly, talented, and as an agent of good will among crew members. During the show's second and third seasons, however, the general atmosphere surrounding adventures grew more tense and these pleasant interludes were omitted. When this happened, Ohura became just another secondary crew member, evoking subliminal images of women perpetually on the telephone. Her role was further diminished, moreover, because Captain Kirk consistently took over the communications function whenever important messages were being received or transmitted. By contrast, he never assumed the controls of the male navigators.

In the late 1960s, teen-cop Julie of "Mod Squad" became the first female side-kick in a crime drama series. Most passive of all the adventure heroines, Julie used neither gun nor judo to ward off an antagonist. Commonly she served as a decoy, positioned in the enemy's midst until such time as superteen cops Pete and Linc could rescue her. Slim, blond, and freckled, Julie's success frequently depended on her prettiness and her look of naïveté. As an example of the way in which popular programs are imitated, the "Mod Squad" format was transferred almost in toto to the 1970s hit "The Rookies." Captain Greer of "Mod Squad," the father figure, become Sergeant Ryker of "The Rookies"; Julie became nurse/public servant Jill Dago; white teen-cop Pete and black teen-cop Linc became uniformed rookie cops Mike (Jill's husband) and Terry respectively; rookie Chris was thrown in for good measure. The role of the female side-kick on "The Rookies" was even less important than it had been on "Mod Squad," however, since only unwittingly did Jill Dago become involved with the criminals and misfits who cause trouble for her husband and the other rookies.

As Sally McMillan, wife of police chief "Mac" McMillan (Rock Hudson) on "McMillan and Wife," Susan St. James briefly revived the trend toward using the wives and female relatives as assistants/confidantes for a more debonaire set of crime fighters. The best show to use this theme, however, was the 1950s detective series "The Thin Man," starring Peter Lawford and Phyllis Kirk in the Nick and Nora roles which William Powell and Myrna Loy had popularized for movie audiences of the thirties. Although both series used witty dialogue between the married couple to add a comic touch to the program, Sally McMillan was a comic character, per se, who, in the manner of the old "Get Smart" comedy, made jokes even when a gun was being pointed at her.

Likewise, black policewoman Christie Love ("Get Christie Love") was a comic heroine of an adventure series which in other respects seemed to take itself seriously. Since all of Christie's work associates were white as were most of the criminals she rounded up, she was often the lone black figure on the program. It was often hinted that Love lured her way into the confidence of white criminals by an amorous attachment, but differences between a competent undercover professional and the sleazy roles she might affect to apprehend criminals were never drawn by the Christie Love character. To work associates and criminals alike, she appeared the cheerful jokester. To be sure, she was always dressed and groomed at the peak of middle-class fashion, but the image of the "smiling darky" came through anyway. As a result, the Christie Love character was a regressive image of black females on television.

In the middle seventies, producers of crime drama programs are at last allowing heroines to carry and use guns, however. The most satisfying characterization of the new female supercop is portrayed by Angie Dickinson in her role as Pepper Anderson in "Police Woman." Like Christie Love, Detective Anderson must occasionally assume roles overtly suggestive of prostitution. When she does, however, the fact that she is assuming a role is never in doubt. In strategy sessions with her partner and other colleagues, Anderson is as cool and competent as anyone. She is also a crack shot who sometimes outshoots her partner in practice sessions on the police pistol range. This doesn't threaten him, however, since Pepper has saved his life on several occasions. Furthermore, Pepper is conventionally feminine, but with a hint of a rough background in her face which makes her devotion to police-work seem all the more credible.

During the 1976–77 television season, several new drama/adventure heroines entered the field as television executives tried to maintain interest in the crime shows while responding to mounting citizens' protests against TV violence. Sex, they reasoned, might make a good substitute for shoot-outs on these programs. So far, the strategy seems to be working.

Two shows have been particularly successful—"The Bionic Woman," starring ingenue-faced Lindsay Wagner (a spin-off of the popular "Six Million Dollar Man"), and "Charlie's Angels." The latter program has made an overnight sex symbol out of one of the three angels, former Alberto Balsam girl Farrah Fawcett-Majors. Though plots inevitably require the heroines to appear partially unclothed at some point in these programs, sex is not the only theme of the shows. Bionic "Jamie Sommers" is clever, athletic, competent, and equipped with three bionic limbs and a bionic ear. As such, she is the physical superior of any male antagonist. Charlie's three angels are also bright and assertive and they carry guns which they aren't in the least afraid to use. Winning the confidence of attractive male suspects is often called for in both series, but the heroines never lose sight of their duty to enforce the law. And in the case of "Charlie's Angels," the camaraderie, loyalty, and affection among the females themselves is stressed in every episode.

Females other than principal characters appear more frequently than regulars on the adventure programs, but they are cast as victims or criminals. Unlike the Western heroes, crime drama professionals rarely dally sexually with females as this would be a violation of their professional code. But studies have shown that most of the victims on violent programs are females or members of minority groups. One might argue that if women weren't portrayed as victims or criminals, there would be very few female roles at all on the crime dramas. This is true, but it might be a better state of affairs, since the experience of being a victim is never conveyed. Instead, the emphasis is always on the male crime fighters, whom the audience is expected to identify with. Insofar as women and disadvantaged minorities are the victims, the structural message of the programs becomes, "White male might is right—let the weak beware."

By contrast, of course, the afternoon soap operas focus almost exclusively on the process of being victimized—on what it feels like to be a victim. Surely, one of television's most sexist "crimes" is to encourage women to identify with the victimized while at the same time encouraging men to identify with the victors. This is deep, structural inequality.

3.

Images of Women
in Movies

It is no secret that movies of the late 1960s and 1970s have pictured men as the ideal soul mates for each other. It is the male characters in such pictures as *Butch Cassidy and the Sundance Kid*, *The Sting*, *Easy Rider*, *Midnight Cowboy*, *The Godfather*, *Pat Garrett and Billy the Kid*, *Dirty Harry*, *The French Connection*, *The Towering Inferno*, and *Jaws* (to name only a few of the most popular ones) who possess mutual understanding, affection, and the complementary personality traits that provide the real "love interest" for the plots. To paraphrase from Leslie Fiedler, they are *cultural homosexuals*, since they imply by their actions that the only lasting, spiritual, and productive relationships exist between men.[1]

Men in these films not only have each other, but they also have a mission of some sort—a job to do. The male superheroes in such 1970s thrillers as *The Towering Inferno* and *Jaws*, for instance, must rescue an entire community of people from eminent extinction. A host of supercops work in teams to eliminate crime. Marlon Brando and sons have "the family" to take care of in *The Godfather*. Pictures like *Easy Rider* and *Midnight Cowboy* show the heroes helping each other find meaning in life—they are in search of their souls.

By contrast, women in films of the past decade have been portrayed without mission or job of any type and often without peers of either sex. With the exception of the steadily dwindling escapist musicals, the few starring vehicles allotted to women have largely portrayed them as sexual or social misfits. The rare "happy ending" for such movies usually means that the heroine has come to some brink of awareness about her own needs. Think of Shirley MacLaine in *The Apartment*, Lee Remick in *Days of Wine and Roses*, Joanne Woodward in *Rachel, Rachel*, Julie Christie in *Darling*, Elizabeth Taylor in *Who's Afraid of Virginia Woolf?*, Ann Bancroft in *The Graduate*, Jane Fonda in *Klute*, Mia Farrow in virtually all her movies, Cloris Leachman in *The Last Picture Show*, Glenda Jackson in *Sunday Bloody Sunday*, or Goldie Hawn in *Shampoo*.

It was not always so. For several decades, movies portrayed strong and often productive women as the peers and partners of men and occasionally each other. Women used to be the big stars, and even through the fifties they frequently outbilled their male costars. To a young generation raised on women-as-extras, this is hard to believe. The best proof comes from watching the old movies themselves. In addition to the late, late shows, there are the late afternoon matinees—right after the soap operas every afternoon. Here one can see young, beautiful Bette Davis as the iron-willed southern belle in *Jezebel*; one can watch men sacrificing everything for the love of first the young, then the middle-aged, Joan Crawford; one can watch lawyer Kate Hepburn winning a case on feminist principles against husband Spencer Tracy in *Adam's Rib*, or see Kate as the missionary who, with riverboat captain Humphrey Bogart, engages in a daring mission to sink a German gunboat in *The African Queen*.

Two excellent book-length studies have also appeared in the past three years to help revive images of strong female movie roles during this lowest period for women in movie history. In *From Reverence to Rape* (1973), Molly Haskell states that, with too few exceptions, the image of women in

the movies has been created by the men who made the films
—primarily the writers and directors.[2] Increasingly as the
fifties and then the sixties wore on, Haskell thinks that
actresses found themselves in the hands of homosexuals,
downright misogynists (women haters), and men with peri-
scopic views of women as sexual toys or, worse, as incidentals.

In comparison to the acid brilliance of *Reverence* (and the
book is very funny too, in a cynical sort of way), Marjorie
Rosen's *Popcorn Venus* (1975) is indeed like a bowl of but-
tery popcorn treats.[3] Tidbits from stars' lives, plot summaries,
information on divorce rates, employment trends, fashions,
and popular music—all are there. Insofar as possible, Rosen
explains female movie images by referencing dominant cultural conditions of the time. When cultural trends fail to explain certain images, however, she relates them anyway, saying only that "Hollywood expediently ignored reality."

Of course the history of female images in film is as old as
the media itself. In 1876, Thomas Alva Edison invented the
phonograph, and by 1889, Edison and his assistant, William
Kennedy Dickson, had developed the visual equivalent—the
Kinetoscope. It was a large black box with a peephole lens
and a hand crank. One looked through the lens and, for
about thirty seconds, watched a moving filmstrip lighted
from behind by an electric lamp. The showings were sometimes co-ordinated with a phonograph to provide sound, but
sound and sight were only crudely matched.

By the late nineteenth century, most cities had year-round
amusement parks where one could take the family for a pleas-
urable outing without spending too much money. Edison's
patented Kinetoscopes were installed in the penny arcades of
these amusement parks all over the country, and for a penny
a look, one could see a variety of moving scenes including nature settings, slapstick comedy acts, dancers, acrobats, and so
on.

That sex would be a major attraction of the big screen was

foreshadowed during the era of the peep shows. Films such as *Taking a Bath,* or *How Bridget Served the Salad Undressed* were big sellers, whereas features like *Surf at Dover* or *Otters at Play* brought in comparatively meager returns.

It became apparent that if the movie images were projected onto a large screen many people could watch at once. Edison resisted the idea, however, because his penny machines were bringing in a good deal of money and he feared a loss of profits. Nonetheless, in April of 1896, the first public performance on a large screen was given in New York. The first movie was comprised of a series of vaudeville acts and the audience was astounded, considering the new medium marvelous, even magical. Viewers found themselves deeply involved and strangely exhilarated by the experience of watching the action approach and then recede away from them on the screen.

The first makeshift movie theaters that began to spring up were amusement-parlor owned. Eventually, they proved so successful that arcades were converted into auditoriums which showed films full time. Initially, the audience for the vaudeville-like films was primarily male. As more features with plots were produced, proprietors attempted to broaden their audiences by encouraging women and children to attend. Sometimes movies would be advertised as "especially for ladies and children."

By 1907, the gross income from film production exceeded that of legitimate theater and vaudeville combined. Admission was usually five cents. The popularity of the new medium continued to increase, moreover, and by the end of World War One, moviemaking was the fifth largest industry in the United States. Movie theaters sprang up everywhere. From their amusement-park beginnings, they expanded into vacant stores in the poorer sections of big cities, where, throughout the teens, working-class audiences comprised the majority of the fans. By 1920, most small towns had movie theaters too, and increasing numbers of middle-class people in cities and towns were also becoming regular attenders.

Several factors combined to create overly stereotypic film images of women during the 1910s. Probably most important were the artistic constraints imposed by *silent* filmmaking, the self-conscious profit orientation of the movie industry, and the moral climate in the United States at the time. Without benefit of sound, and thus of dialogue, early movies had to rely entirely on the physical activities of the characters to convey personality. Since a plot always requires a contest or conflict of some sort, moviemakers tended to play strongly opposed types against each other. In general, the battle reduced to good versus evil, with good represented by a young, pure female and evil represented by a wicked woman, or "vamp," or else by a would-be seducer. In the early Westerns, this formula for creating plot became the popular good-guys-in-white versus the bad-guys-in-black theme.

In the many movies which used a female to symbolize goodness, the heroine was always very young (often prepubescent), sweet, unmarried, and, *of course*, a virgin. She reserved sunny smiles and affectionate hugs for her family and appeared properly bashful in the presence of men and strangers. Such heroines were expected to love children and puppies and to shed tears of sympathy for the lonely and needy. The names of some of the stars who continually played such roles, including Blanche Sweet, Arline Pretty, and Louise Lovely, were symbolic of their stage characteristics.

The vamp, on the other hand, was just as sexual and sophisticated as the heroine was asexual and naïve. She was portrayed as almost magically irresistible to all men; any man would leave his wife for her. She was clearly evil, moreover, since she ruined men simply for the fun of it. A variation on the vamp was the sophisticated-woman-from-the-city. In this case, the woman not only represented personal evil, but her characterization also implied that city values in general were corrupt.

In addition to heroines and vamps, the silent screen had an ample supply of long-suffering mothers—women who worked their hands to the bone for unappreciative husbands and children. Such characters were expected to be respected, however, since they symbolized self-sacrifice, righteousness, and the authority of wisdom.

Male characters were heavily stereotyped in the early silents too, of course. Often the hero lived in or came from a small town, and he had the look of rugged virginity all over him. He was a walking embodiment of all the boy scout virtues—kind, courteous, generous, and on and on. By contrast, villains usually had the taint of the city on them. Though the villain always had sexual designs on the heroine, he was usually involved in robbery, murder, or kidnaping as well.

Since the movie industry was self-consciously profit oriented, there was little incentive to risk changing these standard images and stories which had proved to be such moneymakers. The movie industry was already expanding at a breakneck speed. Why take chances when success beyond belief was already in the hand and there might be thorns in the bushes?

And in retrospect, it seems obvious that these movie formulas, with their simple solutions to questions of good and evil, filled a strong need for working-class Americans in the early years of the twentieth century. Several historians have convincingly argued that the country as a whole really lost its collective innocence during the decade which couched World War One.[4] Up until the years just before World War One, America considered itself an agrarian nation with a set of values different from, and superior to, the values of older, more congested and more sophisticated Europe. Despite the fact that the United States was rapidly urbanizing (it would be more than 50 per cent urban by 1920), Americans clung to an image of themselves as rural innocents—living in the open air, independent, self-sufficient, chaste, and with enough of the world's blessings to go around for all.

Movies gave members of the swelling working class, perhaps one generation removed from urban migration or emigration from a European farm or village, a nostalgic look backward to a time and a condition that they knew in their hearts was gone forever. In its place they found themselves living in crowded tenements; uncertain of their next paycheck; often unable to speak the standard language of the land; the victims of unscrupulous landlords, businessmen, and insurance salesmen; and the pawns of corrupt politicians. But beyond the struggle for personal survival, there was the carnage of the Great War, and afterward, red scares, violent labor disputes, women's rights, and jazz. No wonder images of simplicity and innocence were so eagerly sought.

One heroine provided these images best—Mary Pickford. Tiny, small-featured, and haloed with blond, dangling ringlets, Mary portrayed rural innocents in a series of movies patterned after children's fables. In such roles as Little Red Riding Hood, Rebecca of Sunnybrook Farm, the orphan in *Daddy Long Legs*, Pollyanna, and Little Annie Rooney, Mary championed the cause of the orphans against the rich kids.

Pickford, however, was not a child. She began her movie career in 1909 at the age of sixteen (when she was already older than most of her parts) and continued to play children until the age of thirty-two. Her primary fans were adults, however, and men viewed her as a desirable sexual partner despite the extreme youth of her roles. In part this was because Pickford's offscreen life as the wife (until 1935) of heman actor Douglas Fairbanks was public property, and many men no doubt fantasized about the actress herself as opposed to her roles. In addition, though, this interest in the childheroine is no doubt one more indication that females were (and, by and large, still are) expected to be sexually passive.

Pickford was the first screen superstar, and her popularity has been credited with starting the star system itself. Initially, studios did not give out stars' names. In Mary's case, the public made up one of its own—"the girl with the curl." Companies quickly learned from this that the public became

attached to specific actors and actresses and that a certain audience was guaranteed for any picture they appeared in.

Most screen heroines during the teens were of the Mary
Pickford variety—sweet, young virgins. Next to Mary, the
best and probably most popular of these was Lillian Gish.
Gish was Mary's underside—the other half of the story of
what happens to orphans. With a look of premature tragedy
on their sweet, young faces, Gish's heroines went from innocence, through defilement or threat of defilement, to death or
hairbreadth rescue. As such, movies like *Way Down East*
(1920), *Broken Blossoms* (1919), and *Orphans of the Storm*
(1921) are firmly in the tradition of the eighteenth- and
nineteenth-century sentimental novel.

Way Down East has most of the elements of stock sentimental seduction stories like *Charlotte Temple*. Gish's Anna
is married in a mock ceremony. As punishment for her fool-
ishness, the lover deserts her. An infant born of the union
dies, and in final retribution, the father of a man who would
redeem her by legitimate marriage banishes her outside,
presumably to her death, in the midst of a blizzard. In *Broken Blossoms*, an Oriental falls in love with fifteen-year-old
Gish, whose father is a child-beater. Though almost drooling
over her sleeping body, the Oriental at one point resists the
temptation to molest her sexually, and a subtitle makes the
point that "She is pure still." Later, the father beats Gish to
death; the Oriental carries her body home; and then he stabs
himself.

The man responsible for launching the careers of both
Mary Pickford and Lillian Gish was D. W. Griffith, who was
owner of Biograph, the first successful movie company. All of
Griffith's heroines were young, small, tight-featured females
with the figure of a young boy. In part there were technological reasons for selecting very young actresses during the
early silent period, since lighting was still crude and
blemishes difficult to disguise. In addition, though, Griffith's
personal preference for the company of very young females
was well known in his own time. (At the age of sixty-one,

finally released from his unhappy first marriage, he married a young woman of twenty-five whom he had known since she was thirteen.)

Griffith's detractors have argued that since the early movie-maker had little interest in adult women, the female roles he constructed were inherently demeaning. A southern gentleman from Kentucky, Griffith put women on the proverbial pedestal, both on and off the stage. It is possible that Griffith feared female sexuality as much as he claimed to believe in chastity, but, regardless, he remained consistent in his portrayals of innocent women, even into the roaring twenties.

Critic Marjorie Rosen thinks that the notorious "vamp," Theda Bara, was a transitional figure between Griffith's pure maidens and the more sexual heroines of the 1920s. Bara starred in almost forty movies in her short but immensely popular career which lasted from 1915 to 1918. Rosen thinks that Bara avoided threatening prewar audiences by overdoing the sexual image and in effect portraying a characterization of it. Women knew that she was *too* aggressive for male taste. After all, didn't she ruin or kill every man by the end of each film? And if that was not enough, she was fat in an era which no longer cherished plumpness. In short, she was just *too much*.

Whereas Griffith had satisfied the silent screen's need for strong dichotomies by posing battles between good and evil, virgin and defiled, Cecil B. De Mille obtained the same result in the 1920s by using hubands and wives as adversaries.

Like most domestic fiction, De Mille's movies were advice columns for keeping marriages together. Unlike fiction, though, there was little true suffering; problems were rectified through material rather than spiritual means; and happy reunions were prescribed for the end of each movie. The titles to De Mille's movies were little messages in themselves: *Don't Change Your Husband, Why Change Your Wife?, The Gold Bed, For Better or Worse, Forbidden Fruit, You Can't Have Everything*, and so on.

By focusing on a marriage, De Mille was able to legitimize

sex on the screen. To better do this, however, he introduced
the traditional *settings* of sex and undressing—namely, bedrooms and bathrooms—to the movie screen. He highly
glamorized these functional rooms, however, by picturing
large, exotic beds, sunken bathtubs, wall-sized mirrors, and
ornate trimmings of the most lavish sort. Griffith also invented several means of displaying more of the heroine's
lovely body than clothing styles permitted. Preparing for the
bath became a standard. Another means was to show the heroine tossing in troubled sleep, inadvertently exposing a thigh
or part of a breast. A third was to picture the heroine trying
on clothes during what came to be the mandatory shopping
spree. In fact, De Mille was the first director to turn movies
into fashion shows as well, by requiring that actresses wear
different clothes during every scene.

In private life, De Mille was apparently a faithful husband
to his lifelong wife and a good father to their three adopted
and one natural child. De Mille's film philosophy of marriage
was more complicated, however. Dalliance in extramarital
affairs was branded as fun and beneficial even though
"wrong"; monogamy, by contrast, was branded as "good"
though apparently boring. In his movies, bored or neglected
spouses turn for comfort to someone else of the opposite sex.
When the affair is discovered, however, the jilted mate
spruces up and wins the wandering partner back. Women,
like the wife in *Why Change Your Wife?*, do this by buying
new clothes and getting a new hairdo; men, like the husband
in *Don't Change Your Husband*, by developing inner
strength or by becoming more attentive.

Since divorce was not an option in these pictures, they
were reassuring to a public concerned by publicity of the rising divorce rate. Historian William L. O'Neill has argued,
however, that in America divorce has largely served as a
means of preserving the nuclear family system.[5] This is so because divorced individuals tend to "seek a second chance"
and to remarry quickly instead of adopting alternate sexual
and child-rearing arrangements. In the De Mille movies,

promise of "reform" and future monogamy is always the basis of reconciliation. Metaphorically, then, the plots also subtly suggest that a *second* marriage has a chance for success (translate monogamy) if the parties vow to turn over new leaves.

The archetypal heroine of De Mille's early domestic movies was Gloria Swanson. In her various roles she played a young and affluent former flapper who had married well and was now having trouble with her prize. Crystal-eyed and with a face that looked good from any angle, Swanson became a symbol of the growth and prosperity of the movie industry during the 1920s. Her glamorous roles carried into her personal life as well. For her third husband she married a European nobleman, thereby becoming one of the first movie stars to officially establish the link between aristocrats abroad and America's own aristocrats of the silver screen. Although Swanson has continued to perform into the seventies, her superstar status declined during the 1930s. To Depression audiences, Swanson represented all the false hopes of the previous decade.

Running parallel to De Mille's domestic melodramas were movies that directly exploited the twenties concern regarding changing morals among the young. These movies were full of tight-dancing couples, girls and boys driving unchaperoned in automobiles, and alcohol-laced punch bowls. The book *Flaming Youth*, after which the 1923 movie was patterned, has flapper Pat Fentriss making love to her older beau. This was too much for the movie version, which, at the conclusion of the story, has starlet Colleen Moore jump off a boat into the ocean to avoid seduction.

The definitive flapper, however, was Joan Crawford. The Crawford image of invulnerability, which hardened into statue by middle age, was apparently perfect to convey youthful rebellion in early movies like *Our Dancing Daughters* (1928). Marjorie Rosen notes that in two studies done in the early thirties on the effect of movies on young people, Crawford was repeatedly cited as a behavioral model by teen-age girls. Despite the fact that Crawford's characters either reformed or suffered tragic ends, teen-agers chose to remember only the fun on the way. "These modern pictures give me a feeling to imitate their ways. I believe that nothing will happen to the carefree girl like Joan Crawford," said one sixteen-year-old after watching *Our Dancing Daughters*.[6]

If Joan Crawford was the ideal flapper, Clara Bow was the ideal *Pamela*-style working girl. In the middle and late twenties, Bow made a series of movies in which she played a lowly working girl really working at getting a husband. Sometimes she is attracted to a married man in these pictures, but before the movies end, a suitable partner always appears for her. In *It* (1927), based on Elinor Glyn's book, lingerie salesgirl Clara goes after the new boss and gets him. After this movie Bow was known as the gal who had "IT"—a spritely brand of sex appeal that guaranteed both good times and, eventually, the loyalty of a good man.

Most of the working-girl films showed their heroines at blue-collar or service occupations. They were factory workers, chambermaids, housemaids, cooks, dishwashers or, one step up the ladder, they might be hatcheck girls, clerks or, at best, stenographers. This was a fair reflection of reality since by 1930, still less than 18 per cent of female workers were employed in white-collar or professional jobs. Nonetheless, during the 1920s, women did make inroads into the professions in greater numbers than in any previous decade. Marriage was still viewed as the best "job" for all women, however. In part, then, portraying women in low-status occupations from which marriage provided a truly rewarding escape reinforced the standard marriage norms.

In contrast to the feminine appeal of the domestic and romantic plots, comedy during the silent era aimed to satisfy a masculine audience. As Molly Haskell has convincingly argued, physical comedy, performed by such silent film stars as Laurel and Hardy, W. C. Fields, Chaplin, and the Marx Brothers, was unappealing to women not only because it suggested macho power plays, but also because women and "the home," per se, were the comedians' natural adversaries. After all, some woman worked all afternoon to bake those fluffy pies that got so unceremoniously thrown into the foil's face (splattering freshly cleaned walls and carpets all the while).

The few silent films that remain, however, show that a number of female stars, including Mary Pickford, Colleen Moore, Gloria Swanson, Bea Lillie, Marie Dressler, Mabel Normand, Bebe Daniels, Clara Bow, and Marion Davies, were talented mimics. These stars occasionally played an allegedly plain but good-sport, personality-girl heroine who was contrasted with a glamour goddess, often an actress. In these films, the personality girl won the hero by mimicking the glamour girl, thereby revealing her pretentiousness.

By the late twenties, all the popular silent formulas were well developed, and a multitude of variations on the tried-and-true themes insured heavy profits. In his extensive history of American popular culture, Russel Nye claims that 1926 was "probably the movies' best year." There were over 20,000 theaters across the country, and nearly 800 films were produced for an audience of 7 million daily and 9 million on Sunday. Approximately 500 of the movie theaters built during the twenties cost $1 million or more; they were dream palaces for folks to dream in. New York City's lavishly architectured Roxy Theater, built in 1927 and demolished in 1960, was the epitome of luxury. It had more than 6,000 seats; a lobby for 2,000; three organ consoles and a 110-piece orchestra; 125 ushers; a ballet corps; hospital, and a catering service.[7]

The addition of sound in the closing years of the decade increased profits even more, though production costs were increased too. The technology for sound movies was available throughout the twenties, but not until Warner Brothers, in dire financial trouble, produced *The Jazz Singer* with Al Jolson in 1927, did the revolution actually get under way. *The Jazz Singer* was really a silent film with musical segments spliced in, but so speedy was the transition from silents to sound that by 1931 there were only two silent films on the commercial market.

Sound created vast new possibilities which moviemakers were quick to exploit. Before the stock-market crash in late 1929, a number of flashy musicals were made which featured full orchestras, choruses of bathing beauties, tap dancers, and crowds of laughing people. In the early years of the Depression, when glamourous extravaganzas started to lose money, the producers of the new gangster movies discovered outdoor noises and brought them to the screen. Audiences thrilled to the sound of squealing tires, grinding brakes, smashing bottles, and to the chatter of machine guns. Horror movies used screams and sound effects to create suspense and terror.

Many popular stars made a direct transition from silent to sound movies, including Swanson, Crawford, and, until her voluntary retirement to go into producing in 1933, Mary Pickford. Clara Bow lost out, however. The nasal quality of her Brooklyn accent was incompatible with the "IT" image. Actors with high-pitched voices and stars with offbeat accents, lisps, or other speech impediments fell by the wayside as well.

Sound greatly vitalized the screen image of many performers, however; and it literally created others. The craggy voice qualities of James Cagney, Humphrey Bogart, and Edward G. Robinson (who later refined his voice for more refined parts) were ideally suited to the gangster, he-man roles they played in the early thirties. The humanizing effect of sound was also crucial to the success of the early thirties screen goddesses. Only the mysterious European accents of Greta Garbo and Marlene Dietrich made their overt sexuality intriguing rather than threatening. In the comedy genre, Jean Harlow's high-pitched nasal voice was the comic anecdote for her sensual and classy good looks.

The screen images of Garbo, and of Dietrich in her early movies, really defy description. Fortunately, their films are now being circulated, both on television and in full-screen editions, largely shown to college audiences. In attempting to describe Garbo and Dietrich, critics have used words like "masculine" and "androgynous" in part because both actresses conveyed a highly charged, self-confident, and strangely self-sufficient sexuality. In addition, in their various roles, both portrayed individualized, but intensely moral, personal codes of conduct. In United States culture, it is quite simply the belief that only men can possess these qualities.

By contrast, in eighteenth- and nineteenth-century France, a certain class of women, called the *demimonde*, enjoyed affluence and a degree of prominence. Prostitutes by American standards, these sometimes powerful women provided sexual and often intellectual stimulation for the wealthy bourgeois and noblemen who were willing to support them. Some of the beautiful and talented ones became actresses. Others lived on the fringe of respectability—wealthy, sought after, the objects of wives' jealousies, but with the future ever an uncertainty.

Emotional independence was crucial to a demimondaine's survival, and it was this European, cosmopolitan image of emotional distance coupled with sexual involvement that Garbo and Dietrich, actresses at first dependent on male patronage themselves, conveyed so well.

Ironically, Dietrich's demimonde image was molded by an American from Brooklyn, Joseph von Sternberg. (The "von" was an artificial acquisition; Dietrich called the director "Sternie.") In the late twenties Sternberg met Dietrich in Berlin, where she was an overweight, small-time actress. He reportedly ordered her to lose weight and began the indoctrination process whereby she was to learn the sizzling poses and gestures that made her famous.

Dietrich made only seven films with Sternberg in the early thirties—including *The Blue Angel* (made in Germany), *Morocco, Dishonored, Shanghai Express, Blonde Venus, The Scarlet Empress,* and *The Devil is a Woman*—but they created her legend. The demimonde image is clearest in *Blonde Venus*. For American audiences, Sternberg has Dietrich married to Herbert Marshall, but she sleeps with gambler Cary Grant to get money for an operation to save Marshall's life. Recovering from the operation, Marshall learns about the affair and is horrified. When he threatens to take their son away from her, Marlene flees with the child. Thereafter, the battle becomes survival at the expense of sexual exploitation. But Marlene does survive, through lowlife prostitution and then a career as a cabaret performer which takes her to Paris and eventually brings her wealth and fame.

Garbo played demimondaines in two of her pictures, *Anna Christie* and *Camille*. But in all of her pictures she is defined by a consumptive love relationship. In the beginning of her movies, she is portrayed as apparently whole and self-satisfied, if exotic. She has no true peers, but she has worked out a lifestyle that guarantees emotional survival—whether as the wife of an older man, a ballerina, a spy, or a queen. Then enters the great passion, and Garbo sacrifices everything for it. Generally the ending is ironically tragic; her lover is killed accidentally, or else he leaves her. Garbo's ending is death or great pain. Metaphorically, then, the all-devouring love is incompatible with survival.

Garbo was not a heroine of the seduced-and-abandoned variety, however. Neither was she a vamp. Haskell has called her "autoerotic." Embracing her lovers, she looked like a child dancing around a Christmas tree piled high with presents. Through it all, she seemed wrapped up in a private ecstasy. No other actress has portrayed sexuality so joyously. Although the endings of her movies show Garbo's plans shattered, she is rarely the victim of one man's cruelty or of larger social ills. She is a martyr to nothing but her own previous joy, which she chose to experience, knowing well the possible consequences. Dietrich's version of the demimondaine character is more calculating and more enduring, but Garbo's has a taste of heaven on earth.

If Garbo and Dietrich epitomized transcendent sexuality on the screen, Jean Harlow epitomized the common. As an amoral, bad-girl heroine, she was the moral equivalent to the gangster heroes she played with in her early pictures. Harlow's good looks seemed almost accidental in the context of her raw, nasal speech and the obvious lack of social graciousness which she portrayed. Whether as Wallace Beery's naïve, smart-cracking, *nouveau-riche* wife in *Dinner at Eight* or as Clark Gable's sexy, smart-cracking secretary in *Wife Versus Secretary*, Harlow always radiated an effusive sexuality, uninhibited by restricting social norms, who compared to other women looked cheap, but who made these other women look stuffy in the process.

Mae West, the fourth screen goddess of the early thirties, was also a star created out of the new sound medium. In the case of West, who wrote her own films, it wasn't so much how she talked but what she said that brought down the house, not only on her but eventually on all the screen's sex goddesses. Many critics have pointed out that West's portrayal of a nineteenth-century grand dame was less sexy than disturbing to most men and women. It was also very funny, however. Because of her large size, the "dress-up" quality of her clothes and her preference for stud-type males, several critics have called her a thinly disguised caricature of a homosexual drag queen. Her sauntering walk, low husky voice, and the stare that looked a man up and down reinforced this image. It seems likely in retrospect that the gay illusions, coupled with West's obvious power over her men, were the really threatening aspects of her movies. Her dialogue, however, gave censors their excuse to bring the sex issue to public attention and to finally exorcise altogether, in the name of religion and childhood, overt sexuality from the screen.

West was the master of the one-line *double-entendre*. Greeting a beau at the door, she remarks, "Is that a gun in your pocket, or are you just gladda see me?" Or, gawking over West's array of diamonds, a lady friend says "Goodness!" "Goodness had nothing to do with it," retorts Mae. But it was reportedly the song "A Guy What Takes His Time" from the movie *Diamond Jim* that really spurred into action the would-be censors, including Mary Pickford (by now part owner of United Artists), publishing magnate

William Randolph Hearst, the Catholic National League of
Decency, and the Daughters of the American Revolution.

Before the 1933 Production Code was drawn up, censorship had been an interindustry affair. In the early twenties, a
series of alcohol and drug-related accidents involving industry
limelighters created considerable scandal. As a result, the
Will Hays office was set up in 1922 largely as a public relations and internal monitoring department. Censorship of the
silent movies themselves was never seriously considered, however.

But, like children, it seems that sex was only acceptable as
long as it was seen and not heard. The addition of sound to
movies was, in and of itself, threatening to many critics of
popular culture, since they believed it enhanced the medium's capacity to influence its audience. Studies done during
the early sound period reflect this concern. Even before the
initial results were in, however, would-be censors had made
up their minds that the medium's two most popular genres—
the sexy comedies and the gangster films—must go. The violent gangster films began to edge their way back in the mid-
thirties, but censors kept a vigilance over screen sex for three
and a half decades.

As originally drawn up, the Production Code was designed
to enforce, on the screen at least, the most conservative of
American norms and values. Marriage was to be portrayed as
sacred, but passion was discouraged, even between married
people. Twin beds were mandatory. There was to be no expo-
sure of the sex organs of men, women, children, or animals,
whether real or stuffed. "Perversion" (which was defined to
include miscegenation) was forbidden. Violence, unlike sex,
was not strictly forbidden, but the Code required that it be
portrayed as spiritually *and financially* futile.

Molly Haskell seems justified in dividing movies into "Pre-
Code" and "Post-Code" categories. In the immediate wake of
the Production Code came a number of superwholesome pictures featuring family life and children, including such classics as *Little Women* as well as the Shirley Temple, Andy

Hardy, and Judy Garland movies. Besides Westerns, which never provided starring vehicles for women, the most popular genres in the post-Production Code decade, however, were musicals, romances, and the screwball comedies.

Fred Astaire and Ginger Rogers made their first musical as a duo, *Flying Down to Rio*, in 1933. Although, in actual courtship, dancing is often a prelude to sexual intimacy, on screen it served as a great substitute for it. Dancing was a real source of release and a major source of entertainment throughout the Depression. Far from competing with the big bands, moreover, movie musicals used them. Astaire and Rogers introduced or popularized new dances like the continental and carioca which quickly spread to dance halls everywhere.

Before she teamed up with Astaire, Rogers was just another blond actress of the gold-digger variety. In combination with Astaire, however, she gained a chic and wholesomeness that has made her one of the screen's enduring images of the lady. Musicals are inherently optimistic, and even during the Depression they could use exotic settings without being offensive to poor audiences. The message of these movies was that the couple that danced together eventually romanced together.

Since sex, even between married people, was excluded under the Code, movies went to extreme measures to drag out the more innocent stages of the romancing. Movies, like fiction, prolonged the courtship by interposing carefully contrived obstacles between the lovers. As Molly Haskell has pointed out, however, the best movies in this genre always featured couples that were well matched in terms of that indefinable "chemistry" that makes a love relationship credible. In these cases, the postponement functioned to provide an opportunity for both parties to cast aside roles and to get to know themselves and each other more deeply.

A number of actresses starred in the screwball comedies, including Irene Dunne, Carole Lombard, Claudette Colbert, Ginger Rogers, and Jean Arthur. In any of their typical pairings (which included Cary Grant, Clark Gable, Jimmy Stewart, Gary Cooper, Charles Boyer, John Barrymore, and others) they portrayed the weaker, dizzier, less stable of the twosome. And they were always the pursued. For example, Colbert's role as a runaway heiress in *It Happened One Night* won her an Academy Award in 1935. In this film, reporter Clark Gable (significantly for Depression audiences, the worker of the two) helps Colbert understand responsibility and find purpose in life.

The best of the screwball comedies, though none but the last was a financial success as a first release, was the trilogy which Katharine Hepburn made with Cary Grant in the late thirties. In the first two, *Bringing Up Baby* (1938) and *Holiday* (1938), Hepburn plays characters who are just as wealthy and wacky as any of their predecessors, but who are unredeemed by their beaus in the end. Instead, Hepburn converts Grant to her irresponsible code, albeit his characters were both likely candidates from the start.

The third number in the Hepburn/Grant trilogy was successful in part because the haughty Hepburn character is made to eat humble pie at the end. *The Philadelphia Story* (1940) began as a hit Broadway play with Joseph Cotton and Van Heflin as the male leads. For the movie version, however, Hepburn substituted James Stewart and Grant to add even greater star luster. In its broadest outlines this movie is like the previous two. As before, Grant plays an eccentric and Hepburn plays a society girl. This time, he is an aristocratic cynic who sees Hepburn for the zany snob she really is, but is intrigued by her and loves her anyway. In other words, he has the upper hand. Audiences loved it, and Hepburn biographer Gary Carey suggests that there was more than a little personal vendetta against strong and outspoken Kate in the audience willingness to enjoy her in this role.[8]

Like many of the screwball comedies, melodramas of the thirties also used the high society theme. Stars such as Kay Francis and Norma Shearer played neglected wives who typically sought sexual adventure or appreciation from another man, only to be punished by death or "rewarded" by reunion with their spouses by the end of the movie. The Shirley Temple musicals were also high-society melodrama, since it was never doubted that the little urchin would go from rags to riches before movie's end, usually taking along a friend or relative with her. Should she be rich at the movie's beginning, she would find happiness without sacrificing her wealth.

If the movies of the twenties exaggerated reality by emphasizing wealthy couples and the party-time life, movies during the Depression created its inverse fantasy. Those who were not independently wealthy had jobs. Even women. A substantial number of thirties films featured working women. Like the twenties heroines they generally had a low-level job like department store clerk, but occasionally actresses such as Claudette Colbert, Bette Davis, or Joan Crawford played professionals. Among movie professionals, reporters were particularly popular. In *Mr. Deeds Goes to Town*, Jean Arthur played a spunky one who wasn't beyond deception in order to get her big scoop. Naturally, she falls in love with her subject (Gary Cooper) in the process, so her best scoop will be her last.

Among purely escapist movies in the thirties, horror films were particularly popular. In movies such as *The Mummy's Ghost*, actors like Lon Chaney played monsters whose depravity was the product of technological overkill. Females were the victims in these movies, but even though the assault usually had sexual overtones—being at night, in bed, and often drawing blood—it was understood that the poor monster couldn't help himself. In fact, before the "accident" that had transformed him, he had usually been the outstanding-citizen type.

The female variation of the monster, however, was not portrayed so sympathetically. Marjorie Rosen has called the series of psychotics played particularly well by Bette Davis as "emotional and moral Frankensteins." In these films, physical deformity was more insidious, consisting of distorted facial expressions, bizarre gestures and the famous Davis evil eye. The Davis monster was not pitiable, however, and in movies like *Dangerous, Satan Was a Lady,* and *The Letter,* there was no indication of the causes for her distress and malignancy. As a result, the message was that *any* woman could become such a monster.

Davis has considerable talent for playing psychotics, and her screen performances have been spellbinding. It is the lack of diversity in her roles that many critics point to as creating her disturbing image. As late as 1962, Davis and coscreen veteran Joan Crawford tried to outhorrify each other in *What Ever Happened to Baby Jane?* It is a shame that such actresses were not allowed to mature in films by portraying the advanced wisdom which age brings, instead of presenting aging women as freaks.

During the early 1940s, movies and movie audiences changed drastically. The nation was at war; the men were over there; and in order to keep home fires burning and to manufacture the necessities of war, 20 million previously unemployed American women entered the labor force.

Included in the men over there were such box-office attractions as Clark Gable, James Stewart, Tyrone Power, William Holden, Robert Montgomery, and John Wayne. In the early forties, audiences, too, were primarily female. The concentration of women in the industry and in the theaters produced a positive result in that some movies showed women working together as true peers, doing men's work and supporting each other through emotional trials. But the Second World War was a devastation to American family life and this was also revealed metaphorically in the movies of the 1940s.

On and off, there had been several isolated movies that portrayed women as peers. Lillian and Dorothy Gish played loving sisters in Griffith's *Birth of a Nation* and again in *Orphans of the Storm.* Dorothy Arzner's *The Wild Party* showed Clara Bow and her girlfriends as affectionate comrades. In the early 1930s gold-digger series, women supported each other in their search for men and success. In an inversion of the women-as-peers theme, the movie based on Clare Booth Luce's play *The Women* portrayed women equally matched in cruelty and sadistic dependence upon one another. In patriotic and often perversely optimistic movies of the forties, however, women were shown working and living together and thinking of the future together. If Johnny died over there, at least his son would have a better world in which to grow up.

The effect of the war on family life was revealed, montage style, by the wildly conflicting images of women in 1940s films. On the one hand, most movies of the decade were purely escapist. By 1943, 40 per cent of the year's films were musicals, and the percentage remained high well into the postwar decade. On the other hand, the forties produced the most satisfying portrayals of men and women as peers. Movies like *His Girl Friday, Woman of the Year, Adam's Rib,* and *To Have and Have Not* captured in their protagonists the perfect blend of opposites. In still another seemingly contradictory vein, a number of movies showed women alternatively as shrews or victims in domestic melodramas where conflict spawned high, and the stakes were life and death.

All of these movies gave testimony to the ambiguous feelings regarding marriage which were induced by the prolonged separation of men and women during the war. War had changed women just as it had changed men. Having once gained self-confidence and the sense of personal worth brought about by working, responsibility, and leading an independent life, many women were unwilling to contemplate giving up their freedom to become housewives. Several studies conducted during the war revealed that only a small percentage of the new female workers wanted to quit their jobs when the war ended.[9]

But at the same time, it was impossible *not* to wish that the war were over. The independent life had its rewards, but it was lonely. Women wanted their men back, but they feared the reunion. Surely, one of them will have changed too much, they thought; the relationship will falter. A few movies addressed the problems of returning servicemen and their wives directly, but most treated the topic only obliquely, through broad metaphors.

The best reunion alternative posed by the wartime movies portrayed men and women on a new peer basis. In Howard Hawks's *His Girl Friday*, Rosalind Russell, ace reporter, is an ideal peer to Cary Grant's business-first editor. Hepburn and Grant were peers of a different sort—two icy sophisticates who gave symmetry, and thus a degree of balance, to each other's eccentricities. Grant and Russell seemed to frame and thus define each other while remaining unique and independent at the same time. Russell's tailored seriousness, her womanliness and handsome beauty added dignity to Grant's impressionistic wit and dialogue. Grant, on the other hand, lent a bit of luster to Russell's almost too-stolid image. At the start of the movie, ex-husband and former boss Grant is trying to get star reporter Russell back on the job. He is more interested in her professional talents than in rekindling their relationship, but this is portrayed sympathetically, since they both are "in love" with their work. Russell has personal as well as professional needs, however, and she is strongly considering settling down to a homebody existence with her new suitor. By movie's end, however, she is reunited with Grant and with the paper, having realized that her life is the work she loves and the people who love it with her.

Another Howard Hawks screen classic of the forties, *To Have and Have Not*, introduced a couple that was to make it together not only in the movies but in private life as well—Humphrey Bogart and Lauren Bacall. Based very loosely on the Hemingway novel, Bogart is again a craggy, good bad-guy hero, operating on the nether side of the law. This time, though, the law is the Vichy government in German-occupied France; World War Two is in its prime; and Bogart's job is to smuggle in supplies and communiqués for the French resistance. Bogart is no hero, however; he thinks of his work as "just business." Bacall is a singer whose classy good looks conceal an iron will and a tough, unhappy background. She seduces Bogart into a "no strings" relationship, but at the movie's climax, Bogart discovers he is indeed tied to Bacall when he has to face the responsibility of deciding whether or not to take her on a particularly dangerous mission. Symbolically, the boat trip seals their union, but Bacall doesn't realize until it is nearly over what a chance Bogey took for her sake and how deeply concerned he has been for her safety. At this point, she is ready to accept their love as genuine.

Director Hawks must be given high praise for the fresh and penetrating images of women presented by Russell and Bacall in these movies. The initial dialogue between Russell and Grant in *His Girl Friday* is still considered some of the best in all of screen comedy. Russell's strength, integrity, womanliness, intelligence, and dedication to her work are all revealed in a fast-paced repartee. Hawks also devoted much time to developing Bacall's facial expressions, voice inflexions, and gestures—all of which he believed were necessary to convey character on the screen. He reportedly made her stand in a vacant lot and scream daily for months in order to lower her voice and give it an offtype husk.

The most offbeat yet most "right" couple of the forties, however, was Katharine Hepburn and Spencer Tracy. The bond of love and friendship which they shared in their private lives has only recently been publicized, but the greatest legacy of their relationship, their films together, has been public property for over three decades. Beginning in 1941, Hepburn and Tracy made a series of sassy comedies in which airy and sophisticated Kate matched wits with salt-of-the-earth Spence. It was noted above that Rosalind Russell was in some ways a more satisfying partner for Grant than was Hepburn. The same comparison can be made between the Grant/Hepburn and Tracy/Hepburn pairing. It is the difference between two big wheels which combine to make a bigger wheel (or heel as the case may be) and two wheels which combine to make a bicycle.

In their first picture together, *Woman of the Year* (1941), Hepburn is a political journalist and Tracy a sports reporter who meet and match in the work setting but find it difficult to make a go of marriage because Kate is unwilling to sacrifice an ounce of her demanding career to the role of wife. The night she is to receive the Woman of the Year Award, Tracy walks out saying, "I've got the perfect lead; the woman of the year isn't a woman at all!" Tracy quickly settles into a bachelor apartment, but Kate develops pangs of regret, so she determines to win Tracy back. Her planned method: serve him a surprise breakfast in bed and promise ever thereafter to be the perfect wife. Kate ruins the breakfast, but Tracy accepts the promise. The implication is that Kate won't be the *perfect* wife, but that she will do the compromising in the future.

Some feminists complain about *Woman of the Year*, saying that the strength of the Hepburn character is mauled by the ending. Others point out, however, that it is the image of Kate as a competent and excited career person that lingers longest. *Woman of the Year* set the basic pattern for the Hepburn/Tracy films, however. Hepburn never gives up a career for Tracy, but she never has life completely on her own terms either.

In *Adam's Rib* (1949), Hepburn comes closest to having her cake and eating it too. Written by husband and wife writing team Garson Kanin and Ruth Gordon (who were close friends of Hepburn and Tracy), this comedy deals directly and complexly with sex role issues which are only now surfacing for serious debate. Hepburn and Tracy play rival lawyers. Tracy loves his wife deeply, but he is proud of her accomplishments in the manner that a husband might be proud of a wife who is a great entertainer at parties. When Hepburn reads in the newspapers about a woman who has shot and badly wounded her husband over his affair with another woman, Hepburn's feminist principles are aroused and she decides to defend the woman. The wife herself (played by Judy Holliday) is guilt-stricken, remorseful, simpy, and eager to plead guilty. Kate, however, convinces her to fight for acquittal, but on grounds the Holliday character can barely understand. Kate rests her case on the principle that there is no fundamental difference between the sexes and on the precedent that in numerous similar cases, men committing crimes of passion had been sometimes acquitted, and sometimes sentenced for justifiable homicide.

As the case progresses, however, Hepburn becomes consumed with righteous indignation for her cause. Unable to disturb Tracy's cool courtroom composure, even in private moments, Kate indeed reverts to parlor tricks to gain her applause. To prove that women are just as strong as men, she has a lady wrestler come into the courtroom and lift Tracy onto her shoulders. When Hepburn wins the case, Tracy demands a divorce. The next day, however, *he* has second thoughts and they rush off to the woods for a second honeymoon.

The few movies which portrayed men and women as true equals were at the top of an amorphous heap of popular thirties and forties movies loosely described as "women's films." At their lowest level, on the other hand, women's films were weepy melodramas like the domestic fiction from which they descended and the TV soap operas to which they would eventually give way.

During the thirties and forties, the movie industry made a large proportion of its profits from the matinee audience. This audience consisted primarily of women who came to see the weepies; it is similar to the same large group that watches television soap operas today. A typical film of this type was *No Sad Songs for Me*, starring Margaret Sullavan. In this film, Sullavan's husband resists the temptation to have an affair with another woman. His reward for his fidelity is that when Sullavan dies, she bequeaths her husband to the other woman, knowing that in the crunch, he had preferred to remain with his wife and family.

Middle-class mores were central to the woman's film just as they are to the modern soap opera. Women's options

consisted of marriage and motherhood only, with occasional
help from such stable social institutions such as hospitals,
courtroom, adoption agencies, and so forth. Careers, when
they existed in films like Joan Crawford's *Mildred Pierce*
(1945) and *Daisy Kenyon* (1947), took back stage to personal, emotional dilemmas. The heroes of the women's films
were the relatively unmasculine listening-ear types. Haskell
makes the point that they demanded nothing of the women
sexually and that this was part of their "safety" and their appeal.

During the forties, women's films in general became more
emotional. Shocking death and lingering illness became staples, and women were alternately portrayed as victims or as
Evil Women. They were victims of would-be murderers in
such movies as *Sorry, Wrong Number* (Barbara Stanwyck,
1948) and *Notorious* (Ingrid Bergman, 1946); of a brain
tumor in *Dark Victory* (Bette Davis, 1939); of psychosis in
The Snake Pit (Olivia de Havilland, 1947) and *Lady in the
Dark* (Ginger Rogers, 1941), or imagined irrational paranoia
in *Suspicion* (Joan Fontaine and Cary Grant, 1941). They
appeared as Evil Women in such movies as *The Maltese Falcon* (Mary Astor, 1941), *Double Indemnity* (Barbara Stanwyck, 1944), and *Possessed* (Joan Crawford, 1947), as well
as the Bette Davis psychotic movies of the type discussed
above. Metaphorically, all of these films were saying that in
ambiguous, poorly understood ways, things weren't working
out between the sexes.

A great many movies made during and directly after the
war were purely escapist, however. Designed with the service-
man or ex-GI in mind, these movies portrayed images of
women which were at great variance with the working-girl
image popular with audiences of real working women. Into
the wartime musical melee danced the sweet little sex kitten
who, underneath the chorus-girl figure, was all mother love.
Betty Grable was the most famous of the new breed of chorus girls. Musical numbers in pictures like *The Dolly Sisters,
Sweet Rosie O'Grady, Coney Island*, and *Song of the Islands*

provided her with the innocent opportunities to reveal her abundant charms. Rita Hayworth, however, in pictures like *You'll Never Get Rich, My Gal Sal,* and *Cover Girl* was not far behind in popularity.

The subtle sexuality exuded by these bosomy stars was sufficiently soft-pedaled to make their movies hits for home audiences, but it was not lost on the servicemen who saw the films abroad. In addition, though, film companies launched campaigns during the war to make starlets like Grable and Hayworth armed services pin-up girls. (The most popular pin-ups were the pictures of Hayworth sitting, with feet tucked under, on an unmade bed and the one of Grable with her rump facing the camera, wearing a skintight swimsuit and smiling over her shoulder.) This was done both in the name of patriotism and in the name of profit. Postmaster General Frank Walker ended all the fun in 1944 when he banned the pin-ups from the mails, but it was too late. "Mammary madness," as it has been called, had already infected the men, and it would soon dominate all movie images of women.

In part, "mammary madness" filled the movie industry's need for fresh images. In the postwar decade, business was deteriorating badly. Nobody, least of all movie officials themselves, could have anticipated the impact that television would have on a medium which had prospered for more than half a century, easily surviving a great depression and a world war as well as competition from radio and the big dance bands.

But the writing was clearly on the walls by the early fifties. In 1947, upward of 85 million Americans attended a movie each week; by 1957, there were less than half that many weekly attenders. (In the middle seventies, it dwindled to less than 20 million.) During the same time period, ownership of TV sets jumped from 172,000 in 1948 to 17 million by 1952. Whereas during the movie's heyday in the late 1920s, audiences demanded and would support upward of seven hundred movies each year, by the middle fifties the industry could afford only about two hundred productions per year.[10]

The movie industry's first response to the television encroachment was exclusionism—barring TV use of filmstrips; forbidding stars to appear on television and so forth. In addition, movies tried to do more of the things television couldn't do at all. The emphasis was on sex and sensationalism, with the latter taking top billing at first. A series of movie spectaculars, largely using biblical themes, began with De Mille's *Samspon and Delilah* in 1949 and continued through *Quo Vadis*, *The Greatest Show on Earth*, *The Robe*, and *The Ten Commandments*. Cinerama, the device whereby a realistic illusion of depth was created by using a huge wide-angle screen and three projectors, was introduced. Cinemascope, another means of creating the same depth illusion using only one projector, soon followed. Though panic would again flare up in the sixties when the spectaculars began losing money, industry personnel thought they had found their mecca when *The Robe* (1953), the first picture to use cinemascope, earned $30 million. (At that time, the record was $33 million for *Gone With the Wind*.)

As was briefly mentioned in the chapter on fiction, the mass media of the 1950s produced highly contradictory images of women. Whether as "future-wife," "mother," or as "sex-kitten," however, the images involved filling the needs of others, specifically men. The conflicting images grew naturally from the wartime separation of the sexes. Men and women both needed and wanted a sexual reunion, but in addition, women must be urged out of the work force and therefore into the home in order for men to have jobs and feel truly masculine (and because any other alternative would create a ripple in the status quo).

In her best-selling book *The Feminine Mystique*, Betty Friedan has convincingly demonstrated how the media (she focuses on magazine publishing) and educational institutions subtly but incessantly propagandized women back into the home.[11] In techniques varying from neo-Freudian intimidations and motivation research to "functional" education (education in being a "homemaker"), the common denominator was always: CHILD. In brief, the repeated message was this: to be fulfilled as a woman, you must have children, but terrible things (ranging from bad grades through neuroses to juvenile delinquency) happen to children whose mothers work. That is, women need children; children need a full-time mother.

Men, however, were also encouraged to marry earlier. The GI Bill of Rights provided benefits for wives and children as well as for several years of college education. In addition, the liberal credit policies of the Federal Housing Administration, various credit bureaus, and local banks made it possible for the married man to secure "on easy terms" (involving no down payments), homes, furnishings, cars, and other major items previous generations had saved long years to acquire.

And marry earlier they did. By 1950, at a *median* marriage age of twenty for women and twenty-two for men (the *average* for both was about one year higher), young people in America were marrying earlier than they had for at least a hundred years. A median marriage age of twenty means, of course, that half of all girls were married before they reached their twentieth birthday. Birth rates also soared as these couples plunged quickly from "tea for two" to "baby makes three."

Fifties movies featured images of the wholesome wife for a while, but, in general, this proved a not-too-profitable route for the flagging industry. Some of the domestic melodramas like *Little Women, Cheaper by the Dozen, Bells on Their Toes, Life with Father, Stars in My Crown, I Remember Mama,* and *Father of the Bride,* despite their moments of pathos, were cheery tributes to the peace and "rightness" of the happy family. But it is hard to disagree that sobbing June Allyson was really the ideal fifties wife. In movies like *The Glenn Miller Story* (1954) or *Strategic Air Command* (1955) she was always on the fringe of the drama, always waiting, always worrying, eager to cry indiscriminate and indistinguishable tears of joy or sorrow.

The most popular domestic and romantic melodramas gave metaphoric testimony to the sorry, if not sobby, alternatives open to women in the fifties. *Peyton Place* (1957), adapted from Grace Metalious' best-selling novel, described the boredom, lust, and cruel gossip which is the outgrowth of isolated, small town living. The 1950s was one of those decades that relished the memory of the small town and even sought to recreate it in the countless suburbs which sprung up to encase migrants from big city crime and congestion. However, as Betty Friedan discovered when she talked to suburbanites, life in these small communities proved lonely, boring, and very frustrating to the many women who found their worlds constrained by cars and children, while their husbands spent long hours in the city to minimize commuting trips.

But according to the movies, moving back to the city is no alternative either, especially for the woman alone. *The Best of Everything* (1959), in turn based on a best seller by Rona Jaffe, is the story of career girls who go to New York City to seek their fortunes. By the end of the movie, however, the only one of the original group left alive and sane is planning to quit her job to get married.

Among the fifties movies which starred women, catching-the-man was the most popular theme. Such movies, of course, carefully steered clear of questions about what would happen *after* the marriage. Movies like *Three Coins in the Fountain, Gentlemen Prefer Blondes, How to Marry a Millionaire,* and *Seven Brides for Seven Brothers* all focused on a cadre of females in search of the right man—whether they wanted to admit it or not.

Like their more wholesome-appearing sisters, the fifties sexual bombshells were really only seeking a good marriage and kiddies as well, as Marjorie Rosen has pointed out. Judy Holliday was a forerunner of the fifties blond bombshells, but she played roles that would realistically fall to an uneducated, but sexy blonde—such as early marriage in *Adam's Rib* and

The Marrying Kind or a low-status job in *Bells Are Ringing*. Among fifties sex-bombs, Jayne Mansfield (*The Girl Can't Help It*), Kim Novak, and Brigitte Bardot were all head-liners. But Marilyn Monroe, of course, in such movies as *Gentlemen Prefer Blondes, Some Like it Hot*, and *There's No Business Like Show Business*, was the ultimate.

Unlike Mansfield, Monroe wanted to play better parts, or at least she always claimed she did. She battled hard to achieve star status, however, and this was apparently satisfying in itself since she was willing to accept stardom over diversity and development in her roles. She claimed her childhood was tragic, leaving deep wounds of insecurity which never healed, and, unfortunately, those she chose to depend on gave her conflicting images of herself. Her dramatic coaches convinced her she could do great dramatic roles; on the other hand, Arthur Miller, the man she married to help realize this dream, considered her a child.

The public, of course, liked Marilyn just as she was. The male public that is. With audiences down and the industry uncertain as to how to revive them, it seemed only common sense to Darryl Zanuck, chief of Twentieth Century-Fox (Marilyn's studio) to keep Monroe's sexy image intact. Zanuck may well have been a notorious womanizer, but certainly economic considerations entered in as well, since industry-wide there was a growing awareness during the 1950s that not only were audiences getting smaller, but that the composition of the audiences was changing as well.

Most importantly, the female clientele had dropped off at a sharply disproportionate rate. Largely reflected by the dwindling size of matinee audiences, the total percentage of female movie-goers dropped from 67 per cent in 1944 (more than two thirds of all audiences) to 52 per cent in 1951 (barely more than half).[12] Instead of attending the afternoon weepies, women stayed home and watched soap operas on television. In addition, the evening family crowd was also staying home more and more to watch Lucy and Uncle Milty. Who was left to go to the movies? Teen-agers, singles, the dating crowd, young marrieds—in other words, an audience increasingly dominated by the young and the restless—and by men.

Women could not identify with any of the sex goddesses of the fifties. Monroe has become a tragic symbol of male and institutional oppression since her death, but women were not her fans while she was alive. Unlike Elizabeth Taylor, who was also a "man's woman," Monroe was not threatening to women; she was only mildly contemptible. Taylor, on the other hand, while still slim and relatively innocuous-looking in the early fifties, starred in sweet young bride roles in *Father of the Bride* and *Father's Little Dividend*. She blossomed into a sex cat by the middle fifties however, whereupon her appeal to women was lost. So it was with the other big-busted blondes and brunettes including Mansfield, Bardot, Turner, Grable, Hayworth, and Jane Russell. Men loved them; women found them intimidating, or else comical.

The shifting orientation of the movie industry toward males was also revealed in the large number of fifties movies which contained no women at all, or women in bit parts only. Some of these movies were among the best of the decade, including *The Caine Mutiny, The Bridge on the River Kwai, Shane, High Noon, The Wild One, Twelve Angry Men, The Last Angry Man, The Defiant Ones, Stalag 17, No Time for Sergeants,* and so on. These movies have largely been passed over critically as "war movies" or as "Westerns," but in moving beyond pat formulas and standard sensationalism to consider the relationships between the men involved, they foreshadowed the trends that moviemaking would take in the sixties and seventies.

In 1958, the New York *Times* published the results of a nationwide survey conducted by Opinion Research Corporation which confirmed suspicions that audiences were also getting younger. It was revealed that 52 per cent of all moviegoers was under twenty and that an astounding 75 per cent was under thirty years of age.[13]

To further capitalize on the youth market, musicals of the

late fifties went top forty, and the title songs of such hits as Elvis Presley's *Love Me Tender, Loving You,* and *Jailhouse Rock,* Pat Boone's *April Love,* Debbie Reynolds' *Tammy,* and "Theme from *A Summer Place,*" became big hits in themselves. Due to the adolescent youthfulness of audiences, in the Elvis movies, as in the bikini beach movies which followed in the sixties, visions of "going steady" with a "heavy" like Elvis replaced visions of marriage. Elvis asks his gal in one film, "Won't You Wear My Ring?"—on a chain around your neck, of course.

Late fifties movies with a female lead also implied that catching-the-man didn't necessarily mean that marriage was just around the corner. Debbie Reynolds was a huge success as the croony, syrupy-sweet, near-martyr of *Tammy* in 1957. As the movie ends, she has won the love of her rich host away from his snobbish girlfriend. This is it, we think. Wedding bells will ring. But, no. In 1961, a curvier and more self-confident Tammy is back (this time played by Sandra Dee). She's reconsidered her previous choice and has decided to set her cap for schoolteacher John Gavin. Now, we think. This is it. But it isn't. In 1963, Tammy/Dee is back again as a working girl. By the end of the movie, she and Peter Fonda have smooched and made promises, but the audience is doubtful. There are no more sequels, but by this time, it is hard to picture Tammy happily married and settled in a vine-covered cottage. Divorced and working out at an exercise parlor seems more likely.

In the early 1950s, Doris Day played teen-agers, but she grew up into young matron roles in the late fifties. The Day image had much in common with the big-busted blondes, but her freshness and common-sense control of life effectively neutralized her sexuality. In fact, in her young matron movies, she is sometimes directly juxtaposed against a Monroe-type actress. In *Please Don't Eat the Daisies,* for instance, Doris plays a housewife living with husband and four boys in a New York City apartment. Despite a life full of cultural events, parties, and good restaurants (her husband is a drama critic), Day longs to take her brood to the suburbs. This she does, leaving hubby to spend long days and evenings in the city alone. He is tempted to dally with sizzling actress Janice Paige, but the infatuation never really takes hold. Wholesome Doris, who now spends her days dancing around the school playground with community children and directing a community play, wins his heart anew.

In the early sixties, in movies like *Pillow Talk, Lover, Come Back,* and *That Touch of Mink,* Day played a fortyish career girl whose professional contacts led her unwittingly into the hands of a playboy bachelor. She responds to the bachelor's charm while radiating a naïve, no-arguments-please philosophy that sex belongs in marriage only. The bachelor is disarmed by her lack of subtlety and, eventually, marriage results.

Most movie critics have tried to explain Day's popularity. Dwight Macdonald, in his book *On Movies,* claims that Doris is appealing to the female audience because she is wholesome, not too glamorous, and therefore not viewed as competition.[14] Haskell disagrees. Although a fan of Day's, she believes that the actress made women uncomfortable because she had to work so hard (even in her noncareer girl roles, Day is always working at *something*) and because her happiness seemed to hang by a narrow thread. Day may indeed have made women feel at least mildly uncomfortable, but her insistence on sexual chastity and on trust as the basis of relationships must have made men in the swinging sixties *really* uncomfortable.

By the early 1960s, almost every home (including poor as well as affluent) had at least one television set, while movie attendance continued to decline. In 1945, there had been over twenty thousand operating movie theaters in this country; by the early sixties, the number of indoor operating theaters was about half that number. The total number of theaters was pushed up close to the twenty-thousand mark again by the middle sixties, however, by the rapid growth of the drive-in theater business. "B" movies of the sex, crime, violence, and horror variety were given a big boost by the growth of drive-ins, though they were always prominent in movie output.[15]

Although the Production Code was still technically in effect, by the late fifties, TV was clearly the most popular "family" medium, which freed movies to explore more controversial themes. In 1959, Sandra Dee and Troy Donahue created a sensation in their roles as sensuous teen-age lovers and unwed parents in *A Summer Place*. The movie created a mild stir; some children and teens were forbidden to see it, but the reels kept on rolling to ever greater profits. On the one hand, *A Summer Place* inspired a number of variations on the theme of unwed motherhood, including *Parrish* with Connie Stevens, *Two for the Seesaw* with Shirley MacLaine, and *Love with the Proper Stranger*, starring Natalie Wood and Steve McQueen in one of his few romantic roles.

On the other hand, *A Summer Place* fed into the teen emphasis which was already taking over the screen. Also in 1959, Sandra Dee made *Gidget*, which, like *Tammy*, spawned several sequels. Dee, however, who was too ripe and mature-looking to succeed herself as the tomboy surfer (and therefore went to the Tammy roles instead) was replaced by elfin and sleek-legged Debora Walley. Soon, Annette Funicello, fresh from her Mickey Mouse Club role, joined in, and a number of B-quality movies featuring near-nude teen-agers on the beach resulted. Despite the subtle suggestions of swinging-singles resorts (which were soon to appear in quantity in the late sixties), the overt story line was like a second-grade playground drama—she-hates-him-he-hates-her-they-hit-each-other-throw-sand-in-each-other's-hair—till everybody eventually recognizes that they are boyfriend and girlfriend.

Few sixties movies presented marriage and family life as a happy affair. More typically, actresses like Deborah Kerr and Debbie Reynolds, who were virgins or widows in the fifties, played divorcees or near divorcees in the sixties. Even the decade's American-applepie mother image, portrayed by Julie Andrews in such musicals as *Mary Poppins* and *The Sound of Music*, was a supernanny singleton. She married the aloof Baron Von Trapp near the conclusion of *Sound of Music*, but one suspects that her duties as single parent will continue.

During the 1960s, the widescreen, color spectacular ceased to bring in large profits. Expensively produced movies like *Spartacus*, *West Side Story*, and *Lawrence of Arabia* were box office disappointments; *Cleopatra*, released in 1926, actually lost money. Again, television was mainly to blame. For one thing, color TV was coming into its own in the sixties; for another, television had reduced the attention span of viewers. Nothing was good enough to command the undivided unattention of TV buffs for three hours.

Spectacle, then, gave way, and moviemakers relied more and more on violence and sex, or a combination of these, to lure their audiences. In such movies, the theme was more important than the quality of the acting, so producers often saved money by hiring unknowns. Mass ladykillers killed a string of anonymous women in such movies as *No Way to Treat a Lady*, *10 Rillington Place*, and *Pretty Maids All in a Row*. In addition aging actresses were hired to play psychotics in pictures like Crawford's *Strait Jacket*, Davis and Crawford's *What Ever Happened to Baby Jane?*, Davis and De Havilland's *Hush, Hush, Sweet Charlotte*, Zsa Zsa Gabor's *Picture Mommy Dead*, and Tallullah Bankhead's *Die! Die! My Darling*. Lesbian relationships were also explored for their sensationalism in such movies as *The Fox* and *X, Y and Zee*. Critics point out that even without unnecessary sensational scenes depicting breast suckling and masturbation, such themes were premature, since heterosexual love has yet to be explored sensitively in movies.

As American directors grew less and less interested in portraying women, European directors like Fellini, Bergman, Antonioni, Godard, and Truffaut gained popularity while focusing on women's themes. By the middle 1960s, European and particularly English films were providing some of the most memorable images of women. Julie Christie won an Oscar for her performance in *Darling*, a story about a modern, sexually liberated woman who lives the beautiful-people life, which she ultimately finds unsatisfying. Lynn Redgrave created a stir in her role as the fat-girl heroine of *Georgy Girl*, who adopts the baby of her flower-child friend and marries her mother's wealthy employer. Gradually, stars like Glenda Jackson, Catherine Deneuve, Jeanne Moreau, and Liv Ulmann, in addition to Redgrave, Christie, and Julie Andrews, moved in to fill the gap created by the lack of American female stars.

Even in the face of severe competition from television, a reduced output of movies, and the indifference of directors toward starring roles for women, a few strong images were created by American stars in the 1960s. One thinks especially of Anne Bancroft and Patty Duke in *The Miracle Worker*, of Elizabeth Taylor in *Who's Afraid of Virginia Woolf?* and of Ann-Margret in *Carnal Knowledge*. The latter role is especially significant, since it is perhaps the only attempt to deal honestly with the thirtyish singleton who desperately wants to be married, not especially for love or security, but as a symbol of her full acceptance into the existing social order. Both Sandy Dennis and Mia Farrow looked like flower children, and had they been cast as confused runaways or youthful idealists they might have provided poignantly strong and revealing images of the sixties youth culture. By the time kooky Goldie Hawn played these roles, however, their timeliness was lost.

In the main, 1960s trends in movie production continued into the 1970s. These included: fewer movies; more "B" movies of the sex, crime, and horror variety in which unknowns comprised most of the cast; an emphasis in "A" movies on violence, sensationalism, and male/male relationships; and a sparse array of "A" movies starring strong actresses as sexual and social misfits.

The all-black films, which appeared in the early 1970s, tied in to the sensationalism and violence theme as a way of capitalizing simultaneously on a proven movie formula and of linking it to the black-power theme. Two sensitive portrayals of black women followed in 1972, including popular singer Diana Ross as Billie Holiday in *Lady Sings the Blues* and Cecily Tyson as the wife of a poor black sharecropper in *Sounder*. Both performances earned Academy Award nominations.

The Tyson, Ross nominations are especially interesting from the standpoint of the status of black women in the movies. In their 1972 films both played roles generally suggested by previous stereotypes of black women in the movies, but each transcend the stereotypes of these roles. In his book *Toms, Coons, Mulattoes, Mammies and Bucks*, Donald Bogle identifies two dominant images into which black actresses have been compressed since the beginnings of movies in America.[16] One is the "Mammy"—a "desexed, overweight, dowdy *dark* black woman" (emphasis Bogle's), and the other is the "tragic mulatto"—striving, materialistic, and ultimately torn apart by her inability to enter the "white" world of success or be content with the black world and the good black man who loves her. Although mulattoes were allowed to be sexy (unlike mammies), they were highly demeaned sex objects depersonalized by such epithets as "that cinnamon-colored gal" or "high yeller."

In some respects, Tyson's character in *Sounder* is a continuation of the mammy image. Rebecca is a strong, tough, enduring, dark black mother figure. But she is also slender, soft-spoken, and beautiful despite her toil. Most important, it is her own nuclear family that she mothers and her own beloved husband whose strength she bolsters during the time of great need.

By contrast, mammies of the past, like Louise Beavers, Hattie McDaniel, and Ethel Waters were portrayed as the mainstay and support of white people. McDaniel's famous performance as Scarlett O'Hara's Mammy in *Gone With the Wind* won her an Oscar for Best Supporting Actress, and Waters' roles in *Pinky* and *The Member of the Wedding* lent a dignity to black characterizations that made her a folk hero among black people everywhere. Nonetheless, as Bogle has recognized, these roles personified the spirit of endurance "during the hard times of slavery." Rebecca and the rest of her sharecropping family, by contrast, personified the spirit of black independence. They were making it on their own, and through love and perseverance, they prevailed.

Likewise, Diana Ross's role in *Lady Sings the Blues* is in part a rerun of the mulatto theme. Previous tragic mulattoes, played by Nina Mae McKinney in the 1920s, Fredi Washington in the 1930s, white actress Jeanne Craine in the 1940s, and Dorothy Dandridge in the 1950s merely desired to escape the poverty and suffering of the black community, usually by moving up North, "passing" for white, or both. These women had no purpose in life once separated from their black roots, however, so ultimately they met with a tragic end at the hands of their would-be saviors or else reunited with the black community in a spirit of service.

Lady Sings the Blues transcends this theme, however, and the mulatto stereotype along with it. In this regard, it is important that the movie is based on the actual tragedy of singer-turned-drug-addict Billie Holiday. Unlike previous screen mulattoes, Holiday had a purpose in life beyond mere escape of her poverty upbringings. She wanted to develop and use her great singing talent. But the musicians world was its own lonely ghetto, and the difficulties of success were too great. Her failure was more universal than black.

Lady Sings the Blues also transcended another stereotype Bogle discusses in his book—the stereotype of the "entertainer" who appears without role in movies, as herself. According to Bogle, using blacks strictly as entertainers in movies, usually in a contrived night club scene, fed into the myth that Negroes are "rhythmic" and "natural born" entertainers. Black dramatic actresses sometimes sang in their movies, but in addition, some musicians, like pianist Hazel Scott and the legendary Lena Horne, did nothing but perform musically. (Late in her career, Horne had two dramatic roles.) In *Lady Sings the Blues*, the audience never loses sight of the fact that Diana Ross is a musician, but as the leading lady, it is her dramatic acting ability that matters most.

Recently, new black actresses and actors are gaining wide audiences, especially among black teen-agers. *Sweet Sweetback's Baadasssss Song* (1971) kicked off the trend toward separatist, militant films, and *Shaft, Shaft's Big Score, Black Jesus, Super Fly,* and a host of others followed literally as fast as writers and producers could spin them out. Inevitably, a female version of the hard-boiled superbuck emerged in the person of actress Pam Grier. Beautiful, athletic, and sexy, the Grier character is always desired by men both black and white, but her head is not turned. Instead, in such movies as *Black Mama, White Mama, Coffy, Foxy,* and *Sheba, Baby* Grier avenges evil against the black community by shooting off heads, castrating villains, or gorging their guts with a speargun. Villains are male, of course, and often white as well.

Oddly enough, in 1972, the year in which Ross and Tyson were nominees for best actress, two of the other nominees were children—nine-year-old Tatum O'Neill, who costarred with her father in a saga called *Paper Moon* about a 1920s con artist, and twelve-year-old Linda Blair who starred in the Gothic thriller *The Exorcist.* Although the relatively experienced actress Liza Minelli won the award for her performance in *Cabaret,* it is significant that four of the nominees were newcomers to the screen.

Who are the female stars of the 1970s? Probably the biggest box-office draw has been Barbra Streisand whose immensely popular musicals have included *Funny Girl, Hello, Dolly!* and *On a Clear Day You Can See Forever.* Public acceptance of her distinctly Jewish good looks has coincided with a nationwide consciousness of Jewish nationalism; Streisand is also a refreshing antidote to the Jewish-mother image in movies like *Portnoy's Complaint.* In addition, sex-studded Raquel Welch continued to crank out "B" movies which exploit her body but fail to illustrate her acting ability. For a while at least, Ali MacGraw (*Love Story*) portrayed a more sophisticated successor to the sixties teen queens, but after her all-beige role in *The Getaway*, she faded completely.

Several films of the late 1960s and early 1970s have ostensibly had a feminist orientation, but, in fact, these movies are about traditional male/female relationships—a theme which used to permeate the screen! Heroines in such movies as *Klute*, *Diary of a Mad Housewife*, *Such Good Friends*, *Thank You All Very Much*, *Sunday Bloody Sunday*, *Play It As It Lays*, and *Alice Doesn't Live Here Any More* develop a certain self-consciousness regarding themselves and their relationship to men and society, but their goals remain the traditional ones—monogamy and a stable family life.

Nonetheless, strong actresses like Jane Fonda, Diana Ross, Glenda Jackson, Cloris Leachman, Ellen Burstyn, Cecily Tyson, and Elizabeth Taylor are available to portray challenging new images should directors and producers decide to commission or select screen plays with their talents in mind. Several obstacles seem to stand in the way of this development, however. For one thing, fewer than one in ten screenwriters have been women and no female director has achieved enough status to exert an influence on screen images comparable to that of Griffith, De Mille or Capra. Women seem doomed to be viewed through the perspective of men, even if it is a sympathetic one, as is sometimes the case with European directors. Since this is a period when women are questioning traditional sex roles, however, men may prefer not to venture any portrayals at all. Why? Because the movie industry is profit oriented. Since violence, sensationalism, and male/male relationships are big box office, there is every incentive to proceed as before—and that leaves women out.

4.

Images of Women
in Women's Magazines
and Magazine Advertising

Strange things have been happening to women's magazines lately. Through the early 1960s, the magazine racks in grocery and drugstores looked much as they had for nearly one hundred years. Out from the cover of such magazines as *Ladies' Home Journal*, *Woman's Day*, *McCall's*, *Good Housekeeping*, and *Family Circle* beamed a wholesome young woman, usually in her thirties, with "housewife" written all over her smiling, well-groomed countenance. The contents promised articles on fashions, home decorating, cooking, child care, taking the ho-hums out of a marriage, an article or two on famous personalities, an article or two on timely issues involving women (such as juvenile delinquency, venereal disease, or birth control), and maybe a selection of short stories. In addition, readers knew to expect numerous pages of advertising featuring facsimiles of the cover lady calling attention to the latest in clothing, cosmetics, and household items of every type.

Then in 1966, *Cosmopolitan* magazine got a new editor—Helen Gurley Brown, author of *Sex and the Single Girl* and *Sex and the Office*. Though Brown has denied the association, she essentially went about creating a magazine to espouse a female version of the successful *Playboy* philosophy. Most of the features traditionally popular with women were retained except that now "men" replaced "husbands" and everything from fashions to interior decorating to body hygiene was laced with a somewhat manipulative brand of sexuality. So, the new *Cosmopolitan* covers, displaying the cleavage of a voluptuously attractive young woman, joined the sea of more wholesome images making their bid each month for the shopper's choice at the supermarket. Before long, less successful imitators of *Cosmo* (as editor Brown calls it) appeared.

The next new face which beamed radiantly out from the women's magazine racks was a black one. Despite the fact that black women and their families comprise better than 10 per cent of the United States population, they have been traditionally overlooked by magazines and the print media in general. Even after civil rights became a major national issue in the 1960s and black men like Martin Luther King, Jr., Julian Bond, and Muhammad Ali had captured considerable media interest, black women remained barely visible. In 1969, however, four black businessmen sensed that many of the overlooked black women were advancing economically and professionally and developing increased pride and self-awareness. These more image-conscious women would be a prime market for a magazine edited especially for black women. As of January 1977, *Essence* magazine had a respectable circulation of 550,000, a pass-along readership of over two million, and a reputation as one of the fastest-growing magazines in the country.

Editor Marcia Ann Gillespie (since 1971) has defined *Essence* as a service magazine for a large audience of black women who are, on the average, eighteen to thirty-four years old, single, well educated, and employed in skilled clerical, professional, or business occupations.

Such a description could fit the predominantly white readers of *Cosmopolitan* as well. The editorial billing of the two magazines also contains similarities since both regularly feature careers, beauty, fashion, health, food, fiction, celebrity

Left, Mary Pickford in
*Rebecca of
Sunnybrook Farm*

Below, Lillian and
Dorothy Gish in
D. W. Griffith's
Orphans of the Storm

Joan Crawford in *Untamed*

Marlene Dietrich in *Blonde Venus*

Left, Jean Harlow with
director George Cukor
between scenes of
Dinner at Eight

Below, Greta Garbo and
John Gilbert in
Queen Christina

Above,
Katharine Hepburn
and Cary Grant

Right,
Mae West

Bette Davis and Joan Crawford in *Whatever Happened to Baby Jane?*

Katharine Hepburn and Spencer Tracy in *Adam's Rib*

Rita Hayworth

Marilyn Monroe in
Some Like It Hot

Below, Doris Day in
*Please Don't Eat
the Daisies*

Sandra Dee and Troy Donahue
in *A Summer Place*

Diana Ross in *Lady Sings the Blues*

interviews, contemporary issues, and articles about men. But *Essence* also emphasizes child care, and though men are portrayed warmly in *Essence*, there is little of the "catching him and keeping him" type advice so prevalent in *Cosmopolitan*. The *Essence* woman is self-confident, independent, and, as the "Simply Voluptuous" feature emphasizes, she can be beautiful no matter what her size.

For a group of primarily white, middle-class women just gaining a self-conscious identity in the late 1960s, the revamped *Cosmopolitan*, as well as the old homemaker magazines, were a source of considerable irritation. Some of these women picketed at the 1968 and 1969 Miss America pageants, carrying signs which said things like "Cattle Parades Are Degrading to Human Beings" and "All Women Are Beautiful." Other members of the new "women's liberation movement" staged a protest at the offices of one of the leading conservative women's magazines, *Ladies' Home Journal*, demanding that equal time be given to new ideas about women. Associate editor Lenore Hershey conducted negotiations between the feminists and the *Journal* which resulted in a special nine-page section on the movement in the August 1970 issue. Eight sympathetic articles were carried, including titles like "Should This Marriage Be Saved?" (a take-off on a regular *Journal* column called "*Can* This Marriage Be Saved?"), "How Appearance Divides Women," and "Help Wanted: Female, 99.6 Hours a Week, No Pay, Bed and Bored, Must Be Good with Children."

Having done their duty by running this women's liberationist supplement, however, *Ladies' Home Journal* recommenced its regular fare. But the new feminists got much better than a "reformed" old leader; they got an entirely new magazine, geared specifically to the feminist viewpoint—*Ms*. After the spring of 1973, then, yet another style of cover graced the shelves. As opposed to the nameless, every-woman charmers on the traditional covers, the cover of *Ms*. magazine featured female achievers from all walks of life. Newsmaking athletes, actresses, writers, politicians—each has gotten the spotlight.

But will the more diversified images set forth by *Cosmopolitan, Essence, and Ms.* proliferate in the years to come, or are they only transient variations on the wholesome, housewifely, and passive images which have been firmly entrenched in women's magazines since the end of the nineteenth century? In part, this question can be answered by looking more closely at the decade which spawned them—the 1960s.

By far, the most important thing that happened to women during the 1960s was the birth control pill. The fact that pregnancy could not be completely controlled has always been the bottom-line argument against both premarital sex for women and against advancing married women into top-level jobs. In the era before women had rudimentary knowledge about the female ovulation cycle, girls like Charlotte Temple discovered that the wages for a brief sexual interlude could be dear indeed. But even during the first half of the twentieth century, when fairly sophisticated mechanical birth control devices could boast an 85 per cent chance of safety, engaging in premarital sexual activity carried the taint of irresponsibility, since in fact, there was still a chance of pregnancy.

But the birth control pill changed the odds considerably. During the early sixties, results of controlled experiments with users revealed a 99 per cent safety record, and though the pill's detractors have repeatedly tried to link it to cancer, arteriosclerosis, and a series of other deadly illnesses, significant correlations have yet to be established. Once pregnancy could reliably be prevented, the decision as to whether to have sex outside of marriage became a matter of personal and/or religious philosophy, since the practical issue of social irresponsiblity could now be circumvented.

Helen Gurley Brown's best-selling *Sex and the Single Girl,* then, really only pinpointed for discussion what was fact of life for an increasing number of women. During the 1960s, the divorce rate continued to escalate as the age at first marriage started to climb after the all-time lows of the 1950s. With the pill to prevent pregnancy, more and more of the women who found themselves single in mature, young womanhood started asking themselves, "Why not?"

If *Sex and the Single Girl* made a statement by its very title, *Cosmopolitan* turned that statement into an ongoing institution. There was never any reason for Brown to doubt that *Cosmopolitan*'s new formula would be a success, since reader surveys indicated that women were already reading *Playboy* in large numbers. But to make the magazine more respectable and more practical for female readers, Brown retained a fair share of the traditional women's magazine images, varying them slightly to fit the sexier *Cosmo* image. Like the housewifely reader of *McCall's*, for instance, the *Cosmo* reader is also a great entertainer and clever at interior decorating. And studies done as late as 1971 indicate that she is also just as passive in her relationships with men (more on this later).

To the extent that obtaining sexual free will is a part of the liberation of women advocated by feminists, *Cosmopolitan* and *Ms.* have something in common. Until recently, however, most of the nation's black women have been forced to combine work with motherhood in order to guarantee the survival of their families. But both *Essence* and *Ms.* have deeper roots than the sexual revolution of the 1960s.

Black civil rights was the first big issue of the 1960s, although it was really a carry-out from the decade before. But in 1964, a massive and long-overdue Civil Rights Act was drawn up, and, almost by fluke, the word "sex" was added to Title VII, which dealt with employment discrimination. From the outset, the real impetus of the act was toward eliminating job discrimination against black males. So-called "affirmative action" followed, which set up minority quotas for businesses dependent upon federal funds. It wasn't long before black men picked up the ball themselves and began running with it. At a euphoric "black capitalism" conference geared to brainstorming about attracting more blacks into black businesses, a speaker suggested the idea of a black women's magazine. Ed Lewis, the current publisher of *Essence*, together with three of his friends, decided to start one. The magazine almost flopped at first, but after going through three editors and discarding a one-dimensional focus on fashion and beauty, the magazine began to prosper in 1971 under the current editor, Marcia Ann Gillespie.

Meanwhile, in 1961, President Kennedy had formed the Commission on the Status of Women, initially chaired by Eleanor Roosevelt. The Commission had as its goal to identify in quantitative terms those areas in which discrimination was still practiced against women, both black and white. When the Equal Employment Opportunity Commission (EEOC) was set up to enforce Title VII, therefore, the politically active women who were members of the Commission on the Status of Women hoped that steps would be taken to end job discrimination against females.

There was a blatant lack of effort on the part of the EEOC to enforce the sex provision of Title VII, however. So out of frustration, Betty Friedan, already well known because of her best seller *The Feminine Mystique* (1963), suggested at the Third National Conference of the Commissions on the Status of Women (there were several state commissions working in tandem) that an organization be formed with the explicit purpose of lobbying for enforcement of the sex provision of the Civil Rights Act. Accordingly, the National Organization for Women (NOW) was formed.

But older, politically active women like Betty Friedan were only part of the nucleus of the new women's movement. The other major group came from college campuses. The critical year for the young liberationists was 1967, when the blacks literally kicked the white liberals out of the Civil Rights Movement. White males turned their attention to draft resistance—a clearly all-male activity. This further isolated the young white women from the men and further reduced the status of women in protesting organizations in general. The first groups of young women's righters, then, were formed in rage as a result of discrimination within the larger New Left framework. In Chicago and New York, both centers of radical activity, women talked to other women about the new movement and recruits were gained rapidly.

In 1969, the first protest against the "establishment" was staged when career women, housewives, and college students, calling themselves members of the Radical Women's Liberation Front, picketed the Miss America pageant in Atlantic City, New Jersey. In 1969, there were further demonstrations and still more publicity. By 1970, the phrase "women's liberation" was on the national tongue, and on August 11 of that year the United States House of Representatives, in whirlwind action, passed the Equal Rights Amendment by a vote of 350 to 15.[1]

Widespread interest in the women's liberation movement convinced Betty Friedan, Gloria Steinem, and others that a magazine with a feminist viewpoint could be a viable business concern. So, in the spring of 1973, the first issue of *Ms.* appeared. Since then, the editors of *Ms.* have tred a cautious path, seeking not to compromise the overall feminist viewpoint of the magazine while attracting ever more marginally liberated readers through articles on women's health problems, parenting, female personalities of the past and present (such as Marilyn Monroe and tennis pro Billy Jean King), and the like. In addition, though, there are always hard-core articles on such women's issues as job discrimination, rape, and the role of black women in the movement.

But the decade of the 1970s is more settled than was its predecessor. By the end of the 1960s, almost everyone had done some time in the streets—young people, black people, females, and finally the National Guard. Far from seeking to turn over the system, however, protestors just wanted a bigger share of the pie. Having gotten a few nibbles, though, they

seem content to relax until the hunger pangs build up again.
As a result, although the momentum generated by the reform
movements of the 1960s can be expected to last throughout
the 1970s, a partial reversion to the pre-1960s status quo
seems unavoidable, and with it will no doubt come a renewed
emphasis on the more traditional images of women in magazines.

To fully understand the inertia behind the housewifely,
passive, wholesome, and pretty image of women in the majority of women's magazines, however, some understanding of
the relationship between women's magazines, advertising,
and the United States consumer-based economy is crucial.

Historians of the American magazine take it for granted
that the mass-circulated, so-called "national" magazine grew
up alongside of, and largely as a result of, the growth of mass
advertising and the consumer goods industries. What has *not*
been appreciated fully is the special role that women have
played. Women have been key to the development of both
mass magazines and national advertising because of three assumptions traditionally made by publishers and business people. These include the assumptions that:

—women are the primary magazine readers. In fact, a
  majority of the most successful magazines of the present
  century have been women's magazines.
—women purchase most consumer goods. As a result, a
  majority of advertising is directed to women, even in
  general interest magazines.[2]
—advertising gets results by manipulating the self-image of
  the consumer. Since women are assumed to be the major
  consumers, this means an emphasis on manipulating the
  self-image of females.

First of all, it is important to demonstrate the historical
role that women (and assumptions about women) have
played in the parallel development of the mass magazine,
mass advertising, and the consumer goods industries. After
this historical review, images of women in twentieth-century

advertising can be discussed within the broader context of women's role within the U.S. economy.

Magazines, of course, existed in this country well before the advent of mass advertising. In the pre-Civil War era, however, even the most popular magazines had small circulations by modern standards—usually less than 50,000—since they were aimed mostly at prosperous urbanites who could read, had money for magazines, and could easily be reached by independent distributors. Some, like *The North American Review*, were primarily educational; others, like *Knickerbocker* and *Graham's*, were aimed at a more popular taste and stressed fiction. There was a host of religious weeklies and monthlies and some politically oriented journals as well. There were women's magazines like *Peterson's* and magazines aimed at children such as *Youth's Companion*. *The Saturday Evening Post* carried articles and fiction for the whole family.

The magazine which exercised the greatest impact on American culture as a whole during the first half of the nineteenth century, however, was a women's magazine: *Godey's Lady's Book:* James Playsted Wood claims in *Magazines in the United States* that:

> *Godey's* became an American institution in the nineteenth century. It affected the manners, morals, tastes, fashions in clothes, and diet of generations of American readers. It did much to form the American woman's idea of what she was like, how she should act, and how she should insist that she be treated.[3]

Helen Woodward writes in *Lady Persuaders* that, in the entire history of women's magazines, "there were two able, striking people—only two—whose ideas were fresh enough and strong enough to dominate all those who came after them." One of these two people was Sarah Josepha Hale, long-time editor of *Godey's*. (The other was *Ladies' Home Journal* editor Edward Bok.)[4]

Sarah Hale began her editorial career in Boston with the *Ladies' Magazine*. Louis A. Godey was so impressed with her work, however, that he bought the publication in 1832 in order to get its editor for his own infant publication, and in 1837 Mrs. Hale became editor of the Philadelphia-based *Godey's Lady's Book*. Sarah Hale wanted to make every reader a lady, and material for the magazine was chosen accordingly. The formula for *Godey's* included fashions first, then sentimental, domestic stories (always with a moral), and sentimental, didactic verse. The lesser attractions included recipes, embroidery patterns, and beauty and health hints. The great aesthetic appeal of the magazine was created through hand-colored fashion plates and elaborate illustrations that appeared in every issue. *Godey's* looked more like a modern magazine than others of its time.

Godey's Lady's Book was started in the era before public schooling was nationwide and when half the country's women were illiterate. Its initial readership was an elite group by standards of the time, being prosperous, literate, and largely urban. Historians of magazines and of the women's movement who have considered Sarah Hale a feminist because she believed in female education, however, are in error. It is true she thought women should have knowledge of the arts and sciences, but she was opposed to the franchise and thought that only cultural and creative domestic activities were appropriate for ladies. The content of her magazine, with its emphasis on fashion, fiction, and ethereal household pursuits such as gardening and letter-writing, reflect this. Nonetheless, following the "lady" formula, the circulation of *Godey's* was large from the start and reached 100,000 by the Civil War.[5]

The national magazine, per se, did not exist during the days when *Godey's* was at its height, and neither did advertising as we know it today. Publishers during this period were much more involved in their editorial role than in their role as marketers of advertisers' goods. Since the subscription price had to cover the cost of putting out the magazine, U.S. publishers took much of their material from uncopyrighted British materials and paid domestic contributors as little as possible. When Sarah Hale couldn't get the material she wanted for *Godey's*, she wrote it herself.[6]

After the Civil War, however, the middle class grew vastly in numbers and power with the spread of public education and the growth of business, and magazines born in the 1870s, 1880s, and 1890s were aimed at this broad segment of the population.[7] One indication that the lifestyle of middle-class women hasn't changed much over the past hundred years, moreover, comes from the fact that most of the women's magazines that remained million-copy sellers through the mid-twentieth century were started during this time period, including: *McCall's*, 1870; *Woman's Home Companion*, 1873; *Ladies' Home Journal*, which split from *Farm Journal* in 1883; *Good Housekeeping*, 1885; and *Cosmopolitan*, 1886 (originally started as a general-interest magazine). General interest magazines such as *McClure's* and *Munsey's Magazine* also date from this era, but their period of great popularity was shorter-lived.

Of more direct influence on the development of the mass magazine after the Civil War than either education or the growth of business was the growth of advertising as a distinct link within the business chain. In order to maintain their share of the market after the competition in a given industry narrowed to only a few very large corporations, corporate managers felt compelled to encourage demand for their products among consumers. Many magazines accepted advertising before the 1880s, but the ads were small and confined to back pages of the periodical.

One publisher changed all that. His name was Cyrus H. K. Curtis, and the magazine that set the new pace was *Ladies' Home Journal*. Frank Presbrey says of Curtis in *The History and Development of Advertising* that he was the "one element in the process of building magazine advertising that ex-

ceeded any other in influence."[8] Historian Frederick Lewis
Allen explained that Curtis "developed the magical possibilities of national advertising, and demonstrated more
clearly than anyone else that you could lose millions of dollars on your circulation by selling at a low price yet make
more millions out of your advertising, and build up such a
mammoth enterprise you could pay unprecedented prices to
contributors and thus command the market for writers and
illustrators."[9]

Curtis was by nature both publisher and advertising solicitor, volleying back and forth between the two professions
until he successfully combined them in his work on *Ladies'
Home Journal*. As a thirteen-year-old in Portland, Maine, he
started a publication called *Young America* and sold advertising space in the two-penny paper; as a young adult in Boston, he worked for a time as an advertising solicitor for various papers before cofounding, at the age of twenty-two, a
short-lived magazine called *The People's Ledger*. He finally
settled in Philadelphia, the "magazine city" of the nineteenth century, where he began working as an advertising solicitor for the Philadelphia *Press*. He worked up two pages of
advertising for the horticulture department of the weekly edition and became convinced that there was a market for a separate periodical aimed at farmers. As a result, Curtis quit his
job with the Philadelphia *Press* to cofound *The Tribune and
Farmer* in 1879.[10]

The *Ladies' Home Journal* began as a mere supplement to
The Tribune and Farmer, but it proved so successful that
Curtis again turned with the tide and, in 1883, relinquished
his share of the parent publication to concentrate full efforts
on the woman's magazine. (*The Tribune and Farmer* went
out of business in less than a year.) It was at this juncture
that Curtis began to implement the techniques that revolutionized magazine publishing.

By just about any standard, *Ladies' Home Journal* was the
first mass magazine. In brief, Curtis' strategy with the *Journal* was as follows:[11]

—Advertise the magazine extensively, borrowing when necessary to do so.

—Advertise extensively *within* the magazine, soliciting advertisers eager to reach the female audience.

—Boost subscription by offering special subscription rates, "club rates," college scholarships, and gifts for winners in subscription contests and the like.

—Solicit the best staff possible.

—Solicit the best-known authors of the time.

By 1888, *Ladies' Home Journal* contained three times as many ads as any other women's magazine, and at fifty cents per year, it was also considerably cheaper than old leaders such as *Godey's*, at $3.00 per year, and *Peterson's*, at $1.50 per year. Circulation also increased by leaps and bounds, reaching 500,000 by 1890 and nearly 1,000,000 by 1900. Since Curtis was self-consciously growth oriented, however, most of the early profits were put back into the magazine, and advertisements *for* the *Ladies' Home Journal* reportedly totaled $200,000 for the year 1895 alone.[12]

Cyrus Curtis also exerted an important influence on the other mass magazine leaders of the 1890s. Curtis proved that advertising could pay a magazine's way. Taking the lead from him, the publishers of first *McClure's*, then *Munsey's Magazine* and *Cosmopolitan*, slashed to giveaway prices in order to simultaneously attract mass circulation and a massive advertising revenue. Significantly, it was the success of *Ladies' Home Journal* that convinced S. S. McClure that an inexpensive general interest magazine could succeed.[13] Eventually, though, Curtis was his own best follower when he purchased *The Saturday Evening Post* and made of it a long-lived popular leader.

It soon became apparent, however, that the content of magazines was as important as the low subscription price in attracting loyal readers. It also became apparent that to succeed on the basis of advertising revenue, a magazine needed to specialize in attracting a certain segment of the population which could be predicted to buy a certain type of consumer goods.

Neither *Munsey's* nor *McClure's* survived the years of its first flowering, and *Cosmopolitan* survived by slowly switching its appeal to the female half of its readership. The truly "general interest" formula, which combined fiction, poetry, humor, and illustrations with articles of a human-interest quality for the whole family, was never successful enough with advertisers to support more than one or two major publications at a time.

Over the years, some so-called specialized magazines have maintained a broader mass appeal than others, however. *Life* and *Look* presented picture-book displays of American cultural and political activities which remained immensely popular until television proved its superiority at this type of reporting. *Time* and *Newsweek* continue to provide busy Americans with a comprehensive overview of the nation's news each week. *Reader's Digest*, which provides condensed versions of articles and stories from other periodicals, remains by far the most popular magazine in the country.

It was no coincidence, however, that the first mass magazine was aimed at women. The interests of American men have tended to be less homogeneous than those of women—determined by such factors as occupation and social class and political involvement. Women, on the other hand, have always shared a responsibility for home life, regardless of social class or other job responsibilities. As a result, women form a highly predictable market for advertisers of food, clothing, and domestic products. Curtis recognized that women as a group comprised a lucrative consumer market and successfully exploited that market.

Since women are such dependable consumers of home goods, it is not surprising that the woman's magazine has been the largest and most popular category of magazine throughout the twentieth century. Several general women's magazines, including *Ladies' Home Journal*, *Delineator*,

McCall's, Woman's Home Companion, and *Cosmopolitan* (at first aimed for men as well), were well established at the turn of the century, and Presbrey lists all five as among the nation's eleven top advertising mediums at that time.[14] Other general homemaking magazines appeared later, including *Family Circle, Household, Woman's Day,* and *Everywoman's.* More specialized women's magazines gained momentum as the century progressed. These have included such long-term favorites as *Good Housekeeping* (emphasizing food), *Better Homes and Gardens, Parents' Magazine* (also aimed for men), *Vogue, Harper's Bazaar,* and *Workbasket.* Magazines geared for women in the prehomemaking stage also entered the market, including *Seventeen* for fashion-conscious teen-agers and *Mademoiselle* for college girls and young working women. Finally, a host of "true story" and "personality" magazines gained huge circulations after 1920.

That women have done most of the magazine reading for the past several decades, is only verified by the fact that the number of popular women's magazines has greatly exceeded the number of men's magazines throughout the twentieth century. On a list of magazines with yearly circulations of at least a million compiled at mid-century, nineteen magazines with a combined circulation of 51.8 million were aimed primarily or exclusively for women whereas only eight magazines with a combined circulation of 11.4 million were aimed for men.[15]

Cyrus Curtis understood the strategy whereby advertisers and massive subscriptions were simultaneously attracted. But it was Edward Bok, *Ladies' Home Journal's* second editor, who laid down the formula that was to retain the loyalty of advertisers for a century to follow. In some respects, the *Journal* took over where *Godey's Lady's Book* left off. By 1883, when the *Journal* was founded, the owner of the old Philadelphia leader and its editor, Sarah Hale, were dead. *Godey's* had gone into a marked decline; its illustrations and make-up were poor, and even the quality of the paper was bad. This was true in spite of the support of several advertisers whose wares were hawked on the back pages of each issue.[16]

Although both *Godey's Lady's Book* and *Ladies' Home Journal* were aimed at the housewife, the emphasis of the old and new leaders was markedly different, as symbolized by the names of the two publications. Sarah Hale wanted all women to be ladies; Edward Bok wanted all ladies to concentrate their efforts on their homes.

Remember that *Godey's* emphasized self-development, personal appearance, and the leisure pursuits of the housewife. The assumption was that the reader of *Godey's* could afford to have her clothes made and hire a servant to do the cleaning and everyday cooking. No such assumption was held regarding the middle-class reader of *Ladies' Home Journal.* The era of the domestic servant had passed with the turn of the century; the invention of the sewing machine and the evolution of the department store had changed the procurement of clothing for even moderately well-off families; more and more items previously made in the home were being manufactured merely for use there. As the income base of the country broadened and women ascended into the more prosperous ranks, they became, not Sarah Hale's version of the lady, but Edward Bok's version of the housewife.

The transition from a ladies' book to a housewife's trade manual did not happen all at once, but from the first the *Journal's* advertising indicated the direction that the magazine was taking. Like Curtis, Bok was well aware of the symbolic relationship between his magazine and advertising. Bok took over the editorship of *Ladies' Home Journal* in 1889 (previous to this time, the magazine had been capably edited by Curtis' wife, Louisa Knapp), and in an 1898 editorial he wrote:

> The fact must never be forgotten that no magazine publisher in the United States could give what it is giving to the reader each month if it were not for the revenue which the advertiser brings the magazine. It is the growth

of advertising in this country which, more than any other single element, has brought the American magazine to its present enviable position in points of literary, illustrative, and mechanical excellence. The American advertiser has made the superior American magazine of today possible.[17]

Bok edited shrewdly for thirty years, keeping abreast of his times by involving women in popular issues most likely to concern them and by providing advice on every aspect of homemaking. Curtis had paved the way for him by securing popular authors of the day such as Louisa May Alcott. Bok contributed advice columns for married women and young girls; articles by and about women, such as two series which profiled "Unknown Wives of Well-Known Men" and "Famous Daughters of Famous Men"; issues-oriented series by public figures like Jane Addams; and inside views of variously decorated homes. The idea of photographing the interiors of homes was a brilliant Bok original. It inspired many imitators and has had untold effect on the sale of home furnishings, appliances, and knickknacks.

Edward Bok's most important contribution to the mass magazine in general, however, was his campaign against patent medicines—a move which began the process whereby advertising and the trademarked products it pushes were rendered "respectable" in the public eye.

Patent medicines were among the earliest and most heavily advertised goods in this country. Even before the Civil War, proprietary medicine advertising had reached a volume which constituted more than half the total lineage in many newspapers and magazines. The Civil War made the business enormous, since proprietors took advantage of public consciousness of the wounds and various chronic ailments suffered by soldiers, to make patent-medicine users of veterans and their families. Dealers also capitalized on the known fact that as many as 90 per cent of all Americans had some type of digestive difficulty, encouraging the naïve to confuse the symptoms of overeating or incorrect diet with those of serious diseases. As a result, many Americans regularly took relief-giving preparations in which the "relief" was generated by an alcoholic content of up to 50 per cent.[18]

In 1893, with advertising in the *Ladies' Home Journal* at a record high for any periodical, Bok gave notice that he would no longer accept ads for patent medicines. So respectable and firmly entrenched was the *Journal* by this time, in fact, that he was able to *raise* advertising rates and over the next five years maintain the same level of advertising revenue. Having eliminated the offenders from the pages of his magazine, Bok commenced an attack on the industry itself which only ceased when the Pure Food and Drug Act was passed in 1906. Although Bok claims credit for engineering the crusade that led to the passage of this law, he did have a great deal of help. Other magazines, most notably *Delineator* and *Collier's*, were very helpful in raising the level of public awareness regarding the contents of the medicines and the fraudulent promotional tactics used by various companies. Also of great importance was the lobbying effort staged by women's clubs. Bok and *Ladies' Home Journal* clearly got the ball rolling, however.[19]

In later years, other women's magazines continued to *support* advertised products editorially by purporting to weed out products which were not "safe" or "as advertised." In 1911, *Woman's Home Companion* ran an exposé of the "dirty grocery store" which resulted in increased prestige for packaged, trademarked, and thus advertised products. In 1912, *Good Housekeeping* magazine invented its Seal of Approval, perhaps the most potent device of its type for making the consumer feel good about buying advertised products. *McCall's* went even further than *Good Housekeeping* and based its "Use-Tested" guarantee on how well a product would wear. The new guarantee was put into effect in 1958 as a move to help revive the magazine's flagging advertising revenues and was soon being quoted on TV.[20] By purporting to guarantee their advertising, however, women's magazines have placed an undue halo of credibility around all ads. This has the effect of endorsing not only the product (and the fact that buying it would be a nice, respectable thing to do), but also, more subtly, of endorsing the images of women in the ads.

From the business standpoint, however, Bok's move to eliminate spurious ads was absolutely crucial, since women who were turning to manufactured products needed the assurance that they could trust, often sight unseen, the goods that they bought. During most of the nineteenth century, grocers had bought food items in bulk for resale in smaller quantities. The flour bin, cracker barrel, and candy jar were genuine features in the grocery store. As foodstuffs became packaged for direct sale to the consumer, however, they required advertising to make customers aware of trade names. Among brand-name food products, Royal Baking Powder was the advertising leader in the 1880s, though Dr. Price's Baking Powder, Pillsbury's Flour, Epps's Cocoa, Baker's Cocoa, Ferris Hams, Franco-American Soups, Huckins' Soups, Hires's Root Beer, and Mellin's (baby) Food were all advertised nationally as well, according to Presbrey.[21]

Likewise, after the invention of home-sewing patterns during the 1870s, entire magazines arose to advertise patterns and sewing notions, the best known of which were *McCall's* and *Delineator* (started to publicize Butterick patterns). Though textile mills were common by the 1830s, fabrics themselves were rarely advertised. For one thing, dressmaking in the pre-sewing-machine era was a tedious process and only the really prosperous got a new outfit of clothes more often than every five or ten years.[22] At that time, fabric could be picked leisurely from stocks available to local merchants. However, after the sewing machine came into common use, in the years following the Civil War, the output from commercial and home sewing increased dramatically.

Excepting owners of the pattern magazines, though, both in England and in the United States, soap manufacturers took the lead in national advertising. They found a receptive market, since soapmaking had always been a long, hot, smelly, and tiresome process—a part of the household routine detested by every homemaker. The manufacturers of Sapolio, Ivory, Pears, Lever, and Kirk soaps all advertised in the United States prior to 1900, but the most extensive advertising was done by Procter and Gamble on behalf of Ivory Soap. The Ivory slogans "99 and $44/100$ per cent pure" and "It floats" were watchwords as early as the 1880s.[23]

Frank Presbrey listed the major national advertisers, in 1898 and 1928 respectively, by category of product or service advertised. The changes in the types of goods advertised during the early decades of the twentieth century are illuminating. Increasing urbanization was reflected by the disappearance between 1898 and 1928 of such separate advertising categories as "seed, flowers, trees, etc.," "agricultural, poultry, etc.," and "instruction, teachers, agencies, etc." Also reflected are changes in national modes of transportation, since 1898 ads for bicycles, railroads, steamship lines, and carriages had all been replaced by ads for the automobile by 1928.

Of major importance on both categorical listings of advertisers, however, are the producers of goods marketed for personal and home consumption. Not counting tobacco, these products contributed 781 separate advertisers, or a total of about 30 per cent of all national advertisers in the 1898 sample and a total of better than 55 per cent of all advertisers in the 1928 sample.[24] Furthermore, trends in consumer *spending* for later years, coupled with ever-increasing outlays for advertising in magazines and on television, suggest that food, personal, and home products are still among the most heavily advertised.

It seems safe to assume, then, that the importance of the female consumer has only *increased* during the twentieth century as the industries making food, home, and personal-care products have continued to grow. Furthermore, the relationship between advertising and the mass magazine continues to be a crucial one, since advertising—much of it directed to women—continues to support the most popular magazines.

Having briefly examined the relationship of the female consumer to the symbiotic growth of mass magazines and mass advertising, the next step is to explore the process whereby advertising creates a demand for products—and for magazines—by manipulating the self-image of the female consumer. The present analysis will have to be tentative, but it is hoped that the ideas presented here will suggest many of the major trends since the turn of the century and will, in addition, provide ideas for further research.

Few people are so naïve as to think that advertisers only wish to acquaint or "remind" the public about their products. As early as 1903, Walter Dill Scott, in his article "Psychology of Advertising," urged businessmen to create demand for their products by making ads as appealing to the senses as possible. How many advertisements, he asked,

> describe the piano so vividly that the reader can hear it; How many food products are so described that the reader can taste the food? . . . How many describe an undergarment so that the reader can feel the pleasant contact with his body?[25]

Although advertising has increased greatly in sophistication during the present century, the basic techniques used to encourage demand have changed very little. Almost all advertisements seem to contain four basic layers of meaning aimed at the consumer, only one of which contains any information about the particular product advertised.

The two most subliminal (or best disguised) messages include 1) a prodding to "buy!" period, and 2) an encouragement to believe that buying will assuage emotional insecurities. Both of these images are aimed at all consumers regardless of sex. At a level above these subliminal messages, there are the specific images which describe, or more properly stereotype, the person pictured using or recommending the product. As discussed above, in the case of women, the images are the standard housewifely, passive, wholesome, and pretty, so prevalent in other popular media as well. Only at

the most surface level of the advertising copy is there sometimes given a rational reason as to why one brand or product
is superior to another.

At the lowest, or most subliminal level, there is simply the
message, "Buy." The shear volume of advertising helps to in-
still this message. It is aimed indiscriminately at both sexes,
but in combination with the "housewifely" image, it may
have a special impact on women who are doubly encouraged
to accept as natural the housewife/household consumer role.

Although advertising has always sought to convince people
to buy, the problem of adequate consumer spending and
therefore of demand creation has become more acute since
World War Two. In the post-Maynard Keynes era of American economics, politicians and business people have commonly assumed that great and unlimited economic growth is
vital to full employment and American prosperity. In *The
Affluent Society*, John Kenneth Galbraith documents the
process whereby this assumption has led to widespread government financial support of industry and of middle-class
spending power.[26]

The editors of *Fortune* magazine expressed concern in
1953 that Americans might tend to save too much if their in-
comes continued to rise as fast as they had since 1947.[27] As a
result of this fear, several new techniques were developed during the 1950s to convince consumers that "buying" is
inherently desirable. According to Vance Packard's at first
controversial best seller *The Waste Makers* (1960), one of
the most important was a general encouragement toward hedonistic spending. Giving people moral "permission" to
enjoy their prosperity became a major goal of advertising.
Packard reports a study by a Stanford University historian
who concluded that advertising in the late fifties was seeking
to discredit thrift and to encourage the acquisitive impulse.[28]
In the credit card era, such a hypothesis no longer seems to
need debate.

Closely related to the promotion of hedonism on the part of advertisers, according to Packard, has been the increased tendency to glorify change. "Make people discover for themselves that there's fun and pleasure in changing their decor," he quotes a marketing expert as saying. "Establish a standard based on changeability and not on permanence." In the 1950s, advertising also began teaching Americans that they deserved the fruits of life "instantly," says Packard. The "instant" motif has of course been subsequently applied to everything from food to hair curlers to "Di-Gel."

As of 1960, however, Packard thought that the most impressive proof of the tendency toward hedonistic spending came out of a study on three classes of housewives in the Chicago suburbs. The study was conducted by the Chicago *Tribune*, whose director of research and marketing summed up the findings as follows:

> There has been a shift from the philosophy of security and saving to a philosophy of spending and immediate satisfaction. . . . more self-indulgent spending, a tendency to equate standard of living with possession of material goods. . . .[29]

In another Packard best seller, *The Hidden Persuaders*, he documents the use of "motivation research," a psychological tool designed to encourage consumer spending. Of special importance here is Packard's finding that a major portion of this research has been directed toward better understanding and manipulating the female/housewife consumer. He quotes the head of one research firm who defines motivation research as "the type of research that seeks to learn what motivates people in making choices. It employs techniques designed to reach the unconscious or subconscious mind because preferences generally are determined by factors of which the individual is not conscious. . . ."[30]

Significantly, it is the working-class woman who motivation research seeks especially to understand and motivate. Called "the darling of the advertiser," she interests advertisers most because she is assumed to make up to 80 per cent of the purchasing decisions for her large middle-income social class.[31]

Strange by Marxian predictions, the greatest increase in middle-income families has come not from the petty bourgeoisie but from among craftsmen, operatives, and laborers of various types. "The fact is that America's booming new middle-income class consists, to a startling extent, of groups hitherto identified as proletarians," reported *Fortune* in the mid 1950s.[32] According to Lloyd Warner's *Social Class in America* (1948), wives of the large "lower middle" and "upper lower" classes (these classes contain white-collar workers, tradesmen, skilled and semiskilled laborers—per Warner's classification, a total of about 65 per cent of the total U.S. population) have a highly restricted and repressed emotional life and are guided by a strong moral code. As a result, such women reject sexuality themes in advertising if they become too overt, preferring to see themselves as wholesome housewives and mothers.[33]

As late as 1964, Warner's analysis of working-class women was supported by Mirra Komarovsky's *Blue-Collar Marriage*.[34] Komarovsky and her assistants interviewed a large sample of working-class women in one metropolitan area and found them to be oriented almost exclusively to their roles as housewives and mothers, even if they worked. They married soon after high school and set up homemaking immediately, often having one or more children before the age of twenty. Except for occasional meals with relatives and Saturday afternoons with girlfriends, social life was almost nonexistent. Unrelated couples rarely fraternized and dinner parties were unheard of. These women took considerable pride in their homes, however. Komarovsky supports the finding reported by Packard that working-class kitchens tend to be "a lot nicer than an upper-class kitchen in terms of objects there."

Studies also indicate that housewives, and particularly working-class housewives, view shopping itself as a leisure activity. The Chicago *Tribune* study reported that while one third of the shoppers they studied were economy-minded, fully another third saw shopping as "fundamentally social."

Komarovsky reported that the highlight of the working-class wife's day was a trip to the supermarket, often with children in tow. Except for trips to the park in nice weather, this was generally the only daily activity which took her outside the home.

Even given the increased purchasing power of the expanding middle class and the tendency for middle-class women to buy products for home use, how do business people and advertisers convince these consumers to purchase ever more goods *each year* when they are already well-fed, well-clothed, and their homes are already well-equipped? In *The Waste Makers* Packard claims that there are three basic ways to sell to a saturated market: (1) sell a new or improved product, (2) convince consumers that they need more than one of a given product, or (3) sell replacements for used products.

Although technology continues to facilitate improvements in certain products, there has been no really new product designed for consumer use since the late forties. The automobile, vacuum cleaner, radio, refrigerator, electric stove, automatic washing machine, air conditioner, and television were all invented before mid-century. Improvements have been made on early models of each of these devices, but only a few, including the microwave oven and the pocket-sized electronic calculator, have been of such magnitude as to seriously outdate previous editions. New products in the nondurable market continue to appear, but all of these are clearly nonnecessities for which approval and demand must be generated. (One thinks, for instance, of the home permanent wave, false eyelashes, TV dinners, synthetic fabrics, and so forth.)

Of more importance in generating demand for goods has been the strategy of convincing consumers to "buy more than one" of a product already obtained. The strategy was first implemented in the soft goods markets, mostly aimed at "style" conscious women. Given the proper pitch, American women can usually be induced to buy more clothing, even if they are well stocked with stylish items. In recent years, women have become owners of multiple copies of even such traditionally one-to-a-person items as bathing suits, bathrobes, and sunglasses.

As Packard cleverly notes, the ultimate of the two-or-more-of-a-kind concept, however, has become the promotion of the idea of two homes for every family. At the time *The waste Makers* was published the two-home concept was just burgeoning, but it has proliferated widely in the past fifteen years, coming to incorporate a host of summer and winter bungalows, cabins "up North" and "down South," and a wide variety of homes-on-wheels. Since purchasing homes is directly linked to the purchase of such other goods as building materials, cars, appliances, furniture, and household miscellany of all types, business people view the formation of new households and the building of new homes as crucial for the economy. The editors of *Fortune* were elated at the fact that there were 50 per cent more households in the mid-1950s than in the prewar decades. They attributed this largely to the earlier age of marriage of young people after 1947.[35] It is possible that furnishing and stocking a *second* home may symbolically allow a woman to become a bride again. Ironically, if new households are equipped in the process, divorce also becomes "good" for the economy.

Packard believes, however, that "planned product obsolescence" is the most important means whereby demand for new products is generated. Again, the female consumer is particularly important, since advertising executives believe that the fashion industry has long conditioned women to accept obsolescence on the basis of changing styles. As a result, these executives believe that women (and through them, men) are relatively easy targets for advertising campaigns designed to convince them that other items are out of style, including cars and such expensive home durables as refrigerators, ranges, televisions, and major pieces of furniture.

One level up from the "buy" message is the message, contained in a vast majority of advertising aimed at both sexes, that consuming meets basic emotional needs. Women in the ads are continually portrayed as insecure and as needing approval from men and children. By contrast, men are portrayed as desiring approval not only from women, but also from other men, most particularly work superiors. Advertisements in the 1920s, 1930s, and 1940s often featured situations in which failure to use a particular soap or breath freshener resulted in some personal disaster. In such ads, women most commonly lost a husband or boyfriend's approval, but men lost their jobs! After 1950, human-interest situations in ads began to be replaced by single-image or iconographic ads, which relied little if at all on the copy to convey their message. In modern ads, however, women are still dressed, made-up, and posed to suggest an appeal for male approval. Men, on the other hand, are often portrayed in business suits, with straight-front, analytical stares, or in he-man garb and pose. The clear implication in both types of ads is that the man pictured is a success in the world of men. Success with the opposite sex may be an implied by-product but it is not focal as it is in ads picturing a woman.

Interestingly, motivation research discovered in the 1950s that women want more than merely to "get their man"; they want "to be accepted and respected by men as *partners.* . . ." As a result, the Institute for Motivation Research advised the cosmetic industry that it needed "more subtle and more passive sex symbols than was the case a generation ago, with careful emphasis on such ingredients as poetry, fantasy, whimsey, and a distinct soft-pedaling of pure sex."[36] In the past twenty years, this type of cosmetic advertising has been fully implemented.

Sex as an eye-stopper, of course, has gotten bolder as the society has gotten more sexually permissive. The technique goes way back, however. The advertising trade journal *Tide* related a story about an eye-stopping ad in 1932. Lehn & Fink, a cosmetic company, bought a picture of a draped nude to personify "creamy fragrant perfection." Too late they learned that the holders of the negative had previously sold

the nude's services as an eye-stopper to the East Texas
Refining Company, a manufacturer of champagne corks, a
lithographer (who put her on a calendar), a manufacturer of
water wings, a college president (presumably for use in advertising classes), and a New York attorney, who wanted her
for his private files.[37]

In a larger sense, persuasion itself serves as a form of emotional reassurance since it gives people permission to do what
they desire to do. Most generally, ads give people permission
to buy, as discussed above. But more specifically, ads create a
climate of approval for products or services which have a
stigma of fear or guilt attached to them, such as airplane
travel, or the use of labor-saving devices by housewives who
already do less than they remember their mothers doing.

Of course, entire product lines have been built up and
marketed around insecurities and the need for approval. Predominant among these are antiodor products of various sorts
and cosmetics. In their desire to make odor more sensually
alive and repulsive, advertisers have popularized such terms as
"halitosis" (Listerine), B.O. (Lifebuoy soap), and "undie
odor" (Lux). In 1932, Haley's M-O laxative came up with
"sulphide breath" as the most obnoxious by-product of con-
stipation. Each of these odors, of course, is billed as socially
offensive and bound to lead toward peer rejection. Only eliminating the odor will guarantee peer approval.

The way in which the insecurity theme is manipulated to
exploit prevailing fears, moreover, is illustrated by the case of
Listerine. In the pre-antibiotic era when mothers lived in fear
of childhood illnesses, Listerine was marketed as a disin-
fectant and germ killer, guaranteed to keep the little ones
"safe" from harm. In the 1920s, though, advertising people
learned that, as a cure for bad breath, it sold much better.
Likewise, Lysol (not fit for internal consumption) was advertised alternately during the 1920s and 1930s as a general dis-
infectant and as a "feminine hygiene" product. The an-
tifemale-odor theme made for better sales.[38] Colgate
University Psychologist Donald A. Laird capitalized an odor

mania by injecting aromatic substances into offensive or otherwise odorless products, thus initiating the "scented" appeal.[39] He first tried the trick on silk stockings in 1932, but other manufacturers were quick to jump on the bandwagon, scenting various household, clothing, and toilet articles.

The cosmetic industry has grown rich by exploiting female insecurities regarding youth and glamour. Theodore Peterson states in *Magazines in the Twentieth Century* that by midcentury, ads for cosmetics totaled 11 per cent of all national advertising in magazines.[40] This advertising is concentrated in women's magazines, of course, with cosmetic advertising being the largest single source of ads in movie magazines.

Since many women self-consciously use toiletries to make up for inadequacies, advertising has made much of the theme. According to this rationale, cosmetics merely bring out and highlight one's own inner beauty, as opposed to creating an entirely new external image. Cosmetic ads throughout the years have stressed the "natural" or nonmade-up look to be gained by using their brand. Tangee lipstick ads in the 1920s, for instance, stressed the nonpainted look as preferred by discriminating husbands. This theme is echoed in a host of modern ads which claim their brand provides the "sheer, sheerist" coverage possible. No doubt the emphasis on the natural look in make-up derives in part from the fact that during most of the religious nineteenth century "good women" did not wear make-up. Apart from the association with "painted" (or sexually "tainted") women, wearing make-up was simply considered a sign of vanity. As such, it was viewed as un-Christian.

Closely related to the subliminal messages conveyed by ads are the specific images used to personify products. Ads in the popular women's magazines most commonly portray women as housewifely, passive, wholesome, and pretty. In addition, though, a sexier image of women has begun to emerge in some newer magazines and advertisements, most notably in

Cosmopolitan among women's magazines as well as in a number of magazines with a male target audience.

The most consistently used image of women in magazines and magazine advertising, however, is the housewife image—and there are sound, practical reasons for this from the business point of view. As many students of American culture have noted, the fact that at the turn of the century fewer than a quarter of the nation's females were employed outside their homes is to be wondered at, considering the phenomenal rate of American industrial expansion after the Civil War.[41] Even now, when half of all women work, productivity to the society is apparently considered an optional matter by many women. A "wife" may opt to stay home whether or not she has children or other home or civic responsibilities of any type. Clearly, the ideal of the American housewife is firmly embedded in the norms of our culture.

In part, the birth in the 1870s and 1880s of the women's service magazines like *Ladies' Home Journal* derived from and stole much of the thunder of domestic fiction of *The Wide, Wide World* variety. For one thing, the magazines could do a far better job of describing the housekeeping routine than the novels could. Furthermore, these magazines not only provided pictures and articles about good eating, pretty clothes, attractive furnishings, and the like but provided recipes, patterns, and advice on buying and making household and garden needs of all types. Some magazines specialized in one aspect of the household routine, such as sewing or cooking, and others, like the *Journal*, stuck to a more general formula.

Though the number of outright housewives has declined steadily during the past century, studies indicate that even many women who work still see their homes as their primary responsibility. (The situation is complicated, of course, by the fact that women tend to be demanded for jobs with lower status and pay than most men's jobs.) Many feminists argue, however, that advertising which completely overlooks working women is unrealistic and denies dignity to a significant proportion of the female population. Some feminists, most notably Betty Friedan, go further and claim that advertisers very self-consciously and self-interestedly promote the housewife image.

In *The Feminine Mystique*, Friedan says about advertising's use of the housewife image:

> There are certain facts of life so obvious and mundane that one never talks about them. . . . Why is it never said that the really crucial function, the really important role that women serve as housewives *is to buy more things for the house?* In all the talk of femininity and woman's role, one forgets that the real business of America is Business. But the perpetuation of housewifery, the growth of the feminine mystique, makes sense (and dollars) when one realizes that women are the chief customers of American business.[42]

After delving into the records of one large motivation research firm, Friedan became convinced that advertisers consciously attempt to manipulate women to remain housewives in order to keep them purchasing the flood of new home products that saturate the market each year.[43]

Economist John Kenneth Galbraith also sees woman's primary economic function as consuming, a function he sees as essentially menial. If it were not for the services of housewives, he writes:

> all forms of household consumption would be limited by the time required to manage such consumption—to select, transport, prepare, repair, maintain, clean, service, store, protect, and otherwise perform the tasks that are associated with the consumption of goods. *The servant role of women is critical for the expansion of consumption in the modern economy.*[44] (Emphasis mine.)

Although Galbraith believes that most women are happy in their roles as consumers, he believes that the menial nature of their function is shielded from them beneath rhetoric glorifying women as equals in the household. In fact, he claims, most women do *not* make major decisions regarding the household—such as where the household shall live, or what type of schedule the household members shall maintain; they merely implement these decisions by buying the trappings necessary for the predetermined lifestyle.

A debate on whether household consuming is, or is not, a menial function is beside the point here. It does seem obvious, however, that the housewife image is in the best interest of both advertisers and magazine publishers, since most women's magazines are idea books for the home. Strictly speaking, this image no longer applies to 50 per cent of the female population, but if advertisers can keep women *identifying* with their homes (in preference to their jobs?), then these women will continue to fill their leisure hours with home-consumption activities.

It is worth noting at this point that even the women's magazines outside the "trade magazine" category, including the love story pulps such as *True Story* and *True Confessions* and the movie magazines like *Photoplay* and *Modern Screen*, portray housewife images. The love story pulps are really descendants of the nineteenth-century domestic melodrama, and significantly, they began to appear in 1919 just as the domestic novels were becoming more complex and phasing away from their highly formulaic period. Since the *True Story*-type magazine is aimed specifically for working-class women and specializes in descriptive details drawn from the blue-collar lifestyle, the TV soap opera, which portrays men and women in the professional class, is no competition.

Recall from the chapter on fiction that, according to critic John Cawelti's scheme of classification, the moral fantasy of the melodrama is a reassurance that the forces of the universe are benevolent and that good ultimately triumphs over evil, no matter how bad or meaningless things may seem on the surface. Like the domestic novels, the love pulps focus on a heroine, and sometimes a hero, who is beset by unexpected tragedy but who rises to the occasion. Either by assuming a "better" attitude, by seeking professional help or by taking a different job or the like, she manages to recoup her losses.

Likewise, the movie magazines, with all their promise of sex and scandal, rarely offer more than the trivial, daily dealings in the stars' lives. Since women in these magazines are never dealt with as serious professionals, the impression is left that the actresses *really* care most about their interpersonal relationships—just like the housewife reader.

The *passive* image personified by women in magazines and magazine advertising is perhaps the most insidious in the opinion of many feminists. In a 1971 study reported in the *Journal of Marketing Research*, passivity was the underlying image in two of the four stereotypes of women found most commonly in advertising. According to the researchers, these stereotypes were: "women do not make important decisions or do important things," and "women are dependent and need men's protection." (The other most common stereotypes found by the researchers were: "a woman's place is in the home" and "men regard women primarily as sexual objects; they are not interested in women as people.")[45]

One way in which women personify passivity in ads is by appearing eternally receptive to the dictums of an authority figure. Women are shown accepting commands to use various breath fresheners, cleaning products, food products, appliances and so forth from husbands, children, "professional" experts, even from "Mr. Clean." The clear implication is that women need to be given directions in the most mundane aspects of buying and life.

In addition, however, women are rarely shown engaged in any activity requiring physical or mental prowess. This form of the passive image has undergone the greatest change in the wake of the Women's Liberation Movement, but still male athletes far outnumber female athletes in ads; men usually drive and women ride; men are shown bustling about in offices while women sit demurely at typewriters; and more male than female children play so hard that their clothes need Tide to get them clean.

Over the years, fiction has decreased in importance in the women's trade magazines, but a study done as late as 1971 indicates that fiction in both the *True Story*-type magazines, which are aimed for working-class women, and the trade magazines, aimed for middle-class readers, portrays a majority of females as dependent, ineffectual, unemployed, or underemployed, and as unable to achieve economic or social mobility through their own efforts. Women tended to be somewhat less passive, using these measures, in the working-class magazines. But even when women themselves took action to resolve the plot, they tended to do so by cementing a dependency relationship. If single, they decided to get married (often giving up a job, in the process); if married, they resolved to be a "better" (translate, "more subordinate") wife.[46]

Since *Cosmopolitan* magazine adopted its new sex-and-the-single-girl philosophy in the middle 1960s, it is significant that it was one of the two "middle class" magazines used in this 1971 study of passivity in magazine fiction. *Cosmo* and *Redbook* were chosen because the relatively young age of their readers more closely paralleled the age of the readers of the love story pulps. It appears, then, that *Cosmo*'s new philosophy has not disturbed the dominant passive (and housewifely) image of women, since females are still portrayed seeking traditional, dependent relationships with men.

In the August 1971 issue, editor Helen Gurley Brown, herself, attested to the magazine's more dependent and passive images of women in her column "Step Into My Parlor":

> People often ask if *Cosmopolitan* is a female *Playboy*. (More often they tell us it is!) Actually we are not. *Playboy*, by its own definition, is a magazine of entertainment for men. . . . The *Playboy* man is depicted as handsome, affluent, successful, discriminating (he likes his girls nubile, his cars sleek, his wines mellow, his yachts leather-lavished), and he hasn't an emotional hangup to his name. *Cosmo*, on the other hand, is for a girl who does not necessarily "have it made" . . . who wants a great

deal more out of life than she is now getting. Monthly . . . hourly we pour into her loving advice and, hopefully, inspiration on how to find someone to love, keeping him once she's found him, coping with parents, bosses, jealousy, rage, envy, insecurity . . . all the goblins.

In a broader sense, however, Marshall McLuhan believes that picture magazines as a medium encourage passivity on the part of readers. Significantly, women's magazines are picture magazines, with advertisements supplying most of the illustrated matter. "Whereas the spectator of a picture magazine is passive, the reader of a news magazine becomes much involved in the making of meanings for the corporate image," McLuhan writes. McLuhan believes that the mosaic form of magazines demands "deep participation" on the part of readers—inducing a near-hypnotic state. He further believes that ads are not meant for conscious consumption on the part of readers, but are instead intended to be subliminally absorbed in the context of other content.[47] McLuhan's thesis seems logical since editors deliberately integrate editorial matter with the advertisements. If magazine reading, like TV-watching, is truly a passive "activity," then the passivity of the medium reinforces all the passive images of women in the articles, stories, and advertising, making them doubly effective.

The *wholesome* image personified by women in magazines has deep roots in American culture, specifically in the American religious tradition. The United States was originally settled by people with religious concerns and as new immigrants came, transferring their churches to the New World was a major way of transplanting a part of the former culture. Throughout the nineteenth century, preachers held the highest status and credibility in American society, and many of the old, elite colleges in this country were started as theological seminaries.

Even after it was conceded that men had become sullied by the necessity of making a living in capitalist America, however, women were expected to be pure and to transfer religious values to their children. As magazines, sermons, newspaper editorials, and Congressional debates reveal only too clearly, the major opposition to the nineteenth-century women's rights movement stemmed from the belief (held less sincerely by some than others) that involvement in politics would strip women of their purity and Christian innocence, as men had presumably already been stripped.[48]

Women's magazines prior to the Civil War stressed religion just like the domestic novels did. *Godey's Lady's Book* and the other ladies magazines featured short stories and poems in every issue, always with didactic, religious messages. In her article "The Cult of True Womanhood: 1820–1860," Barbara Welter claims that "pious" was in fact the key image of women in the early magazines, and that religious rhetoric was used to rationalize acceptance of the other dominant images, including, according to Welter, "purity (sexual chastity), submissiveness, and domesticity."[49] Shortly after the first women's rights convention was held at Seneca Falls, New York, for example, the *Ladies Wreath* ran the following poem titled *What Are the Rights of Women?*

> *The right to love whom others scorn,*
> *The right to comfort and to mourn,*
> *The right to shed new joy on earth,*
> *The right to feel the soul's high worth. . . .*
> *Such women's rights, and God will bless*
> *And crown their champions with success.*

In place of the religious sentimentality of the early women's magazines, the women's service magazines like *Ladies' Home Journal* substituted an intimate relationship with their readers. Edward Bok and other editors of mass-circulated magazines after the 1870s were less interested in moralizing than in finding out what the readers wanted out of life and helping them obtain it. Bok initiated the fad for "advice columns," first for married women and girls, and later for boys, but the emphasis was on practical application of the prevailing moral code with the goal of earthly happiness as opposed to other-earthly rewards.

The image of women in the service magazines retained its "wholesome" quality, however, but increasingly the emphasis fell on helping others as opposed to religion, per se. This stands to reason since by the 1890s, women across the country had moved out from their homes and churches to become involved in clubwork on behalf of various social reforms.[50] Articles and stories in the *Ladies' Home Journal* and the other trade magazines, however, have traditionally stressed helpfulness in the domestic situation, and advertising has pictured wholesome mother/child combinations with mothers continually providing nutritious breakfasts, soft clothes, and clean surroundings for their offspring.

Throughout the years advertising has implied that cleanliness is, in itself, a virtue, as is clearly suggested by the well-known cliché "Cleanliness is next to Godliness." The success of ads in the 1880s focusing on Ivory "purity" ("99 and 44/100 per cent pure"), usually personified as a mother-daughter combination, spawned many imitations. Another early soap product which made use of the wholesome theme was Sapolio. A series of popular jingles during the 1890s personified Sapolio as the residents of "Spotless Town." Since lack of proper sanitation, political corruption, and prostitution were all heavily associated with city life in the 1890s, the Sapolio ads for Spotless Town suggested a community that was both physically and morally clean.[51] Later ads have also done much to suggest that the "clean" person can be expected to be chaste, responsible, reliable, and meticulous in details, and that in buying cleanliness one purchases this entire package of images. Recently, the ads for Cover Girl make-up have been proclaiming that "clean is sexy." (Cover Girl is billed as the "clean make-up.") But as personified by the wide-eyed young model, clean is a very wholesome kind of sexy.

No one would debate the fact that ads in women's magazines personify women as *pretty*. But since "pretty" has connotations different from such descriptive words as beautiful, glamorous, or interesting, some explanation of this image is required. The fact is that women in most ads are *not* beautiful or unusual-looking in any way. More attractive than heroines in a woman's Gothic or Harlequin romance, women in advertisements are slim and have regular features, but in other respects, they are merely pretty. They also all look alike. One would rarely recognize an ad model on the street; she would look like any other well-dressed woman.

Portraying women as merely "pretty" reinforces the other predominant images of women in ads. A wholesome woman cannot be overly sexy or glamorous; a housewife must not appear unique or frivolously attractive; a passive woman may look receptive to sexual advances, but she should not appear ready to instigate them. In short, most females in advertisements look like the all-American girl/woman—sweet and undefiled and ever ready to subvert her own needs and judgments to those of others.

Only the most surface layer of advertising meaning conveys a specific message about the particular product. This is the ad copy which tells the consumer why Brand X is better than its competitors, and not all products have a "consumer plus" feature to brag about. Examples of products with a consumer plus would include a cereal with added vitamins, an article of clothing made out of a wash-and-wear fabric, a prerust-proofed automobile, or more dubiously, a skin cream with "added emollients" or a "pH balanced" shampoo.

As one might expect, a consumer plus is an important feature in generating demand for a new product. In fact, an A. C. Nielsen project (the same company that does television ratings) studied thirty-four new brand-name products to determine the effect of advertising on gaining a share of an established market. One finding was that products with a distinct consumer plus tended to gain a share of the market relatively rapidly and in fairly direct proportion to the amount of advertising expenditure made.[52]

It is clear, then, women have played an important role in the development of mass advertising and the mass magazine because they comprise a rich market for consumer goods. Cyrus H. K. Curtis was the first to recognize the potential of the female market and his genius produced the first mass magazine, *Ladies' Home Journal*. Under the editorship of Edward Bok, the *Journal* evolved a formula that has remained popular with advertisers to this day.

But old leaders like *Ladies' Home Journal* and *McCall's* are beginning to flag now, their advertising revenues drawn off by ever-specialized periodicals, television, and magazines like *Cosmopolitan*, *Ms.*, and *Essence*. Even some of the stockholders of long-time advertising leader Proctor & Gamble (makers of Ivory soap) are protesting the housewife image of women in advertising, but advertisers have no new images with which to replace those that have served so well for so long such as the earlier transition from Sarah Hale's image of the lady to Edward Bok's image of the housewife/consumer. Women today have a hard time thinking of themselves as either of these outdated images. Accordingly, the time is ripe for the enterprising publisher—or advertiser—who can come up with the new, "right," image for the late-twentieth-century woman.

5.

Images of the
Fashionable Woman

During the early sixties, girls were periodically sent home from my high school for wearing blue jeans to school. The dress code at C. E. Donart High was unofficial, of course, but all of us knew that it was unacceptable to wear "pants." Boys wore jeans; girls wore dresses. It seemed that the mothers of boys had it so much easier. Girls wore pants and shorts for casual wear, of course—that's been the case since the 1920s, although housewives didn't wear pants at home until the 1950s. In the past fifteen years, however, there has been a revolution in women's dress, such that, now, well-dressed and conservative girls and women wear pants, and everyone is suspect of the motives of a female dressed in a short skirt.

Over the years, numerous theories have been developed to explain the shifting trends in women's fashions. Fashion analysts of the nineteenth and early twentieth centuries tended to take a historical approach, claiming that styles were cyclical, with the fashions of past eras serving as inspiration for future designs. Other analysts viewed fashion as sculpture, and then compared it to the architecture of its period.

One twentieth-century anthropologist, Alfred L. Kroeber, measured six dimensions of dress for the time period 1823 to 1934 and then figured the ratio of each of these measurements to the height of models wearing the clothes. He found remarkably predictable cycles with a mean wavelength of ninety-eight years. This led him to conclude that fashions follow an invariant cycle which is independent of other forces of social change.[1]

Most twentieth-century fashion analysts, however, have tended to emphasize the sexual aspects of women's clothing. Some of their theories started with fairly mild assumptions, such as "the subject of fashion is the female body," "women's clothes are designed to be sexually attractive," or "fashion follows the erotic ideal of the day." Other theories are more extreme. For example, J. C. Flugel's theory of "shifting erogenous zones" argues that fashions change to keep humans continually erotic. Without clothes, according to the theory, we would mate seasonally like the rest of the animal kingdom. Edmund Bergler, by contrast, believes that homosexual designers take out their secret frustrations against women by deliberately designing *ugly* clothes.[2]

All of these theorists have failed to ask the central question about fashions, however. The question is: Why have women's styles changed so rapidly over the past century and a half when men's styles have remained essentially stable since the 1830s? Before the nineteenth century, men's fashions had all the characteristics attributed to women's fashions of the nineteenth and twentieth century. They were cyclical; they depicted the status of the wearer; and they were used for sex display (think of tight breeches and cod pieces). In the early nineteenth century, however, men's clothing, especially the "business suit," became the standardized, tailored, and reasonably comfortable uniform it has remained ever since. Only in the second half of the twentieth century has women's clothing taken on these characteristics.

The disparity in comfort and ornamentation between men's and women's clothes is perhaps the most direct reflection of the vast separation in male and female roles that came in with the Industrial Revolution. The Industrial Revolution created a large middle class of men, wealthy by all previous standards. Since one function of the wives of wealthy men has always been to display their wealth, wives, like furniture, became increasingly ornamented and stuffed-looking during the nineteenth century.

Middle-class men were prevented from displaying their wealth on their own persons by the real need to work and by the work ethic itself. Several "virtues" were adopted by the middle-class man because they were viewed as practical tools of business success, including industriousness, efficiency, punctuality, sobriety, chastity (or the avoidance of early marriage and unwanted dependents), and—plain dress. In his *Autobiography*, Benjamin Franklin conveyed the spirit of the new bourgeois male when he wrote: "In order to secure my credit and character as a tradesman, I took care not only to be in reality industrious and frugal, but to avoid all appearance to the contrary. *I drest plainly.*"[3]

Women, on the other hand, barred from property ownership or direct participation in business, became instead the prize showpieces in their own well-appointed middle-class homes. Unfortunately, the image of idleness and powerlessness suggested by women's fashions became destiny as well. The heavy, cumbersome styles upheld by undergarments so tight, contorting and constricting as to be virtually unimaginable to the "braless" generation, inhibited breathing and circulation, contributed to digestive difficulties, and rendered healthy exercise an impossibility. Household management was tiring and difficult for the fashionable woman and even the inevitable work of childbearing was dangerous, often deadly. Though women now outlive men in all civilized countries, throughout the nineteenth century, men typically outlived their mates. A "sickly constitution," poor health, early death—these were the rule for middle-class women. Even so, their lot was superior to immigrant and other "lower class" women who worked at domestic service or in factories.

But although "dress reform" always had a small, vocal number of proponents, most nineteenth-century women who could afford to do so embraced each new and increasingly confining style as it appeared. And though men's dress took on a comfortable and uncluttered look in America before spreading to Europe, American women looked to the greater sophistication of Europe for fashion directives throughout the nineteenth century. Not until middle-class women were demanded in large numbers in the American labor market did clothing styles simplify and American women begin developing fashion preferences all their own.

After the French Revolution, it was considered patriotic to copy French styles and by 1795, the so-called "classical look," symbolizing traditional order and meaning within the context of a democracy, had become popular.[4] Straight sheaths of thin material and even sheer muslin were worn, often with only a colored ribbon beneath the bust. The wearer's shape was revealed, and before the fashion had run its course, fake bosoms had come into vogue in Europe to disguise a lean physique. Napoleon retained the classical look when he came to power in 1804 since the image of ancient empires suited his own political aspirations. During the first two decades of the nineteenth century, then, the "Empire line" was the height of fashion—in America as well as France.

Full skirts and the infamous leg-of-mutton sleeves erupted in the 1830s as a symbolic release from the tensions of wars and revolutions and as a sign of optimism and prosperity. In 1930, Louis Philippe became constitutional monarch of France, and Andrew Jackson began his first full year in the White House. In 1837, Victoria became queen of England and the era of respectability, prosperity, and rapid expansion of the middle classes was fully under way. Initially, the high waistline was preserved along with the fuller skirts, but the cinched waist was not far behind the new style change.

In fact, the tightly cinched waist became the most important symbol of female status during the nineteenth century. Like their well-upholstered furniture, wives were required to be passive and to subordinate themselves to their husbands.

1810–20

This glorified subservience was not only displayed symbolically but enforced literally by the corset and by the series of complex and confining fashions that the corset made possible. Comparing women to furniture may seem farfetched, but accounts of nineteenth-century house fires reveal that women occasionally went up in flames with the household goods because of immobilizing corsets and skirts too full or too tight to run in.[5]

Unlike the rigid upper-body image created by eighteenth-century corsets, the corsets of the nineteenth century presented a more erotic image of curves flowing out in both directions from a tiny waist. The precious little waist had special erotic significance due to the potent suggestions of idleness, fragility, dependence, and, more perversely, bondage. Indeed, the image of the proud husband completely circling his wife's fashionable waistline in his broad hands has become folklore.

Roundness was given to the bust and hips by fabric inserts called gussets. A broad piece of whalebone, or later steel, called a busk, was inserted as a shaping device up the center front of the corset. Up the center back and sometimes in various positions along the sides, narrow pieces of whalebone were inserted. The corset was usually laced tightly up the back to avoid disturbing the dress line in the front.

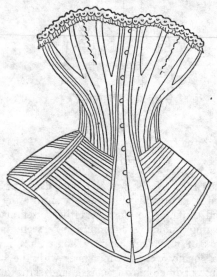

1860–70 (corset)

When full skirts were introduced in the 1840s, the narrow-waisted look was achieved partially by the exterior design of the garments, and lacings were not as tight. Trimmings on the bodice were designed to create a "V" effect in order to emphasize the smallness of the waist in contrast with the width of the shoulders. The waistline was in a fairly normal position, and the moderately full skirts were straight fronted and bustled slightly in back and at the sides. Some stiffened petticoats were worn, but the bustled effect was created mainly through deep gathering at the sides and back of the skirt.

As skirts got wider and wider during the 1850s, however, the fashionable woman's discomfort grew along with them. The collapsible steel-cage hoop was not invented until 1856, and before it came into general use, the additional fullness was created by increasing the flouncy underlayers of heavy, stiffened petticoats, called crinolines. In addition, lavish amounts of material were gathered into the plainest of skirts, and elaborate ones were often layered to create a tiered effect. The layered motif was often repeated in bell sleeves which hung loosely over lace or other ornamental lingerie. Such exorbitant use of material for both under and outer garments loudly proclaimed the affluence of the wearer, who could afford not only the piece goods but also the hours of dress-making labor required to construct each garment.

Oddly enough, the flowing crinoline skirts have been idolized by subsequent generations of middle-class young women who never had to wear them. A particularly romantic image for American girls has been the Scarlett O'Hara-type heroine in her flowing crinoline skirts, waltzing across a giant ballroom in the arms of a romantically domineering young captain. But the South was predominantly rural at the time of the Civil War, and fashion information spread very slowly there. The original model for the "southern belle" type heroine came not from the American South, in fact, but from the court of Emperor Napoleon III of France. That model was the Emperor's wife, the Empress Eugenie.

Born Dona Eugenia de Montijo, Louis Napoleon fell in love with her while he was prince regent of France and she was the Spanish countess of Teba. Like many an American girl who has married into higher professional and economic circles, the Empress Eugenie brought beauty, social graciousness, and a flair for fashion to her marriage with Napoleon III. Fashion historian Anny Latour reports that numerous memoirs of the period record Eugenie's self-conscious beauty, her social gaiety, and her love of clothes. Latour writes,

> From the outset clothes had been the focal point of her life. In the Tuileries life-sized dolls had been installed, on which the Empress's clothes were put when she did not wear them lest they receive the slightest crease. She held real conferences with dressmakers and milliners, modistes and jewellers. On her table lay a list of Marie Antoinette's dresses; it had been found in the archives and she considered it one of her greatest treasures.[6]

Eugenie and her wardrobe were much publicized in America. In May of 1853 *Godey's Lady's Book* published an account of her marriage, complete with descriptions of the dresses she wore in both cathedral and civil ceremonies and an item-by-item account of the dresses in her large trousseau. During her seventeen-year reign as empress of France, most of Eugenie's formal gowns were open throated or off the shoulder with a lace or fabric drape accentuating the bustline and falling delicately over the shoulders. Her waistline was always tightly corseted, and, typically, she wore a long "basque," which was a tight bodice with a V-shaped tab extending below the waistline in front, behind, or both. Eugenie wore full skirts, often layered in several tiers, puffed out at first with crinolines and later with the steel-cage hoop. Her gowns were noted for their variety of ornamentation, including lace, tulle, velvet, ribbons, feathers, and jewels. Eugenie's figure was the model for her era, as well. Small boned and slim waisted, she nonetheless possessed the abun-

1850s

dant curves above the waist that fashionable clothes were designed to in part display.

French prosperity was mirrored in the gaiety of court life
during Napoleon III's reign. Accounts of the formal and costume balls at which Eugenie presided filtered all the way
across the Atlantic. At such occasions, Eugenie, who was always on the lookout for novel and attractive clothing styles,
was fond of asking well-dressed ladies for the names of their
dressmakers. More than once during the 1850s, she heard the
name of an Englishman working in Paris: Charles Frederick
Worth.

Though Empress Eugenie could not have known it, with her help Worth would establish a fashion dynasty which would long outlive the political reign of Napoleon III. Worth began his career in fashion at the age of twelve when he left his poor family in Lincolnshire to get a job in London. He was hired by the firm of Lewis and Allenby, which sold fabrics, shawls, and cloaks. In 1845, at the age of twenty, Worth moved to the world's fashion capitol, despite the fact that he didn't speak French, and eventually found work at the Maison Gangelin, one of the most important Parisian fashion firms of the day. In the finest traditions of the bourgeois dream, Worth rose from employee to partner, married an attractive shopgirl and finally, in the early months of 1858, set up a firm of his own.

Although design experts disagree about Worth's talents as a designer, based on the samples of his work which remain, it is certain that he was a genius at recognizing and using fine fabrics. Even more important, however, Worth was a shrewd businessman who saw the possibilities for high fashion to become big business.

The founding father of Parisian haute couture knew that it was in the best interests of Paris as a high fashion center to create a demand for fabrics and fashion accessories originating from France, as well as for the finished garments themselves. As a result, after securing Empress Eugenie as his customer in 1860, Worth's first goal was to convince her to wear dresses made of silk fabrics produced by the looms in Lyons, France. Largely owing to Worth's influence, the number of looms doubled between 1860 and 1871.

Worth was also the first to display dresses on beautiful young models. His first model was apparently his wife for whom he designed many clothes while still in the employ of the Maison Gangelin. Later, Worth hired young girls especially for this purpose. Like the women who labored at garment construction in the giant workrooms, these models usually came from slum or poverty backgrounds, but Worth gave them English names such as "Miss Kitty" or "Miss Mary" to generate snob appeal for his customers. Initially, models were chosen to approximate the body proportions of individual clients. Accordingly, some were fat and some were thin. By the turn of the century, however, the increased sale of designs for industrial purposes forced a standardization of the mannequin shape, which evolved gradually into the pencil-thin figure we know today.

Worth inherited, so to speak, the flowing skirts and crinolines of the 1850s. (He has credited Empress Eugenie's influence with the widespread adoption of this style.) But because of the great prestige he earned as a result of dressing not only the empress but also a host of other queens, royalty, and wealthy women, Worth is himself accredited with most of the major style changes during the latter half of the nineteenth century.

In sum, the trend in styles initiated by Worth extended the binding around women's waists to include hips, thighs, and legs as well. After abandoning the crinoline skirt in the late 1860s, Worth and the other Paris designers embarked on a series of experiments involving a tubular skirt with bustle and full train. Worth led the way in these experiments. In 1866, he added a train to one of his models; in 1868, he is attributed with introducing the tunic or overskirt. In 1870 came the Franco-Prussian War which deposed Napoleon III and effectively ended the fashion influence of his exiled empress. After a few months in exile himself, Worth returned to Paris, resurrected the eighteenth-century bustle, and introduced it to fashionable society.

Historian Latour reports that Princess Metternich, the wife of the famous Austrian ambassador to Paris from 1859, was Worth's ally in outmoding the crinoline. She was slim and wanted an end to the styles which flattered women with voluptuous curves. As such she gladly wore the first bustled look to the races, fashion's primary showplace during the nineteenth century. The first bustles were variations on Worth's tunic and train ideas. A partial overskirt which fell over the back of the dress, often in pleats, was padded out with material and lengthened below into a broad train.

Styles of the 1870s and 1880s have been considered, in retrospect, to be the most garish and least comfortable in recent history. The garish effect was produced not only by the bustled silhouette but also by the use of multicolors and textures, often inexpertly. It was not uncommon for garments to be constructed in three or four different colors out of five or six different materials, including one with a shiny surface,

1870s

several varieties of lace, ruchings, or tulle, perhaps a velvet ribbon or printed or brocaded inserts, and various vertical and horizontal trimmings. Samples from this era remain to reveal that occasionally the result was a true work of art; more often, it was grotesque.

By the end of the 1870s, Worth had abandoned the bustle, but his clothes were so tight that women of fashion who adopted the style could barely walk in them. According to

1880s

Norah Waugh, who has studied the actual undergarments worn by women over the past two centuries, the new slim line of the seventies was too drastic a change for the average woman, who was used to hiding her plump hips under wide skirts. Most women, she claims, never entirely discarded the bustle (now called a *tournure*).[7]

In 1880, Worth introduced a new undergarment designed to help women achieve the sleek line. Called a "crinolette," it was a short steel cage worn over the hips and concealing them, creating a tubelike silhouette. During the 1880s, crosswise draperies, usually extending from waist to knee, became fashionable, again in an attempt to conceal the hips. To the eye distanced by time and objectivity, these drapings present a very contrived image. They resemble an ornamental fig leaf or chastity belt—an obvious highlighting of the parts they were designed to cover.

It was when skirts became narrow, furthermore, that the corset became a true strait jacket, since the entire trunk had to be molded, as opposed to just the waist area. The corsets were so long and tight that it was difficult to prevent riding up and wrinkling and to keep the whalebone stays from breaking at the waist. Waugh reports that whalebone was in such demand that it became scarce and steel boning began to be widely used. Other elements of torture were soon added. In 1873, the "spoon busk" appeared. (Remember that the busk is the piece of boning that runs up and down the center front of the corset.) The spoon busk was narrow at the top, turned in at the waist and widened out into a pear-shaped base. Steam molding was also used to reduce the pliability of the already stiff corset fabric. When finished, the corset was heavily starched and dried to shape on a metal mannequin mold. Unbelievably, a host of women were so eager to maintain fashion's image that they endured torturously confining corsets for over three decades.

Even though Parisian designers, led by the House of Worth, continued to prescribe cumbersome and confining styles past the turn of the century, the bicycle craze of the

1880s and 1890s made women seriously question the practicality of restrictive clothing. Women had participated in sports before the 1890s, but the games were adapted to prevailing fashions rather than the reverse. Women played tennis, for example, by standing in one position and batting the ball back and forth across the net when it could conveniently be reached. Similarly, women played croquet by taking delicate side swings at the ball. It being unthinkably immodest to do otherwise, women went swimming fully clothed.

But in America no previous sport had attracted masses of female participants like bicycling did. Frank Presbrey provided one indication of the extent of the bicycle craze when he reported in *The History and Development of Advertising* that during the 1880s and 1890s advertisements for bicycles and bicycle sundries comprised the sixth largest category of national advertising, including ads by 133 different nationwide companies.[8] The cost of the early bicycles was high, usually around $100, but the benefits of owning one were great as well. In the preautomobile era when even trains traveled at a speed of only about forty miles per hour, bicycle travel seemed fast indeed. On a bicycle one could ride into the countryside, picnic, hike or lounge in the afternoon sun, and still be home by nightfall.

Such freedom and mobility had great appeal for people of all ages, but it was especially appealing for young people of courting age. The strict nineteenth-century courting etiquette had allowed young people very little privacy, but they soon learned that even if parents, teachers, or chaperones were brave enough to mount the two-wheeled contraptions, they could not for long keep pace with the younger cyclers.

At first "bicycles" were either unicycles or tricycles. Since unicycles were precarious and required bifurcated garments (like pants) for agility and safety, most women rode the safer, if less exciting, tricycles. Neither was as fast or maneuverable as the "safety bicycle," or standard two-wheeler, which was invented in the late 1880s. The safety bike clinched the popularity of bicycling and made riders of the masses of women as well as men.

Several fashion changes followed close on the wheels of the bicycle. To begin with, a generation of young women used to the pleasures of bicycling found the bustle impractical for everyday use and discarded it. In addition, skirts in this country were first raised completely off the ground for the express purpose of bicycling. This in itself aroused no opposition from conservatives until proponents of the shortened styles advocated their use for walking as well.[9] It was too late, how-

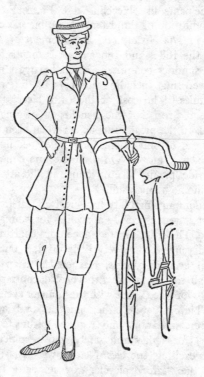

1890s

ever; the practicality and comfort of the shorter skirts were all too apparent. After a brief reactionary period when high fashion again dictated sweeping skirts in the early 1900s, women raised their skirts aboveground in 1908 and kept them there.

Bicycling also gave women their first excuse to wear pants since the collapse of the feminist bloomer movement in the 1850s. College girls, who were especially fond of the new sport, wore pants suits in which jacket tops embodying the prevailing fashion motifs were co-ordinated with fullish knee breeches. A variation of this costume, called knickers, became the rage with women when automobiling became the national pastime in the 1920s.

Other social changes around the turn of the century also contributed to simplifying women's dress and making it more comfortable. Beginning in the 1890s, the demand for female white-collar labor began to rise significantly. This made it possible, even desirable, for thousands of middle-class girls to work who would never have considered it before. During most of the nineteenth century, all but a negligible number of nonfarm female workers were employed in factory or domestic work. Until business opened its doors to women, teaching was the only occupation which a respectable middle-class girl could consider. Since the ultimate goal for all young working girls remained marriage, a job as a typist, a clerk, or a telephone receptionist was viewed as a much better opportunity to meet eligible young men.

At first, including women in a business office was a very controversial proposition. Businessmen favored the idea because women were willing to work for less than men. In addition, many liked the novelty of having a female face and form to gaze upon now and again. It was this second benefit to hiring a woman that the wives of the employers feared.

Since women in business were controversial at first, they followed Benjamin Franklin's credo and dressed as inconspicuously as possible. As a result the tailored ensemble became important for the first time, although versions of it had been available since the 1860s. In the 1890s, women's tailoring became a large business since the garb worn by the young working women was imitated for street wear by nonworking women as well. The ready-to-wear clothing business as a whole (started with men's suits after the Civil War) was boosted by increased sales to women after the 1890s, and in order to tap the trade of ruralites, catalogue houses like Montgomery Ward and Sears and Roebuck sprung up. In addition, pattern magazines like *McCall's* and *The Delineator* provided assistance for the home seamstress while at the same time encouraging standardization in styles and sizes.

The "shirtwaist," or equivalent of the modern-day blouse, was an American innovation which was also popularized by the working girl. In no other country has the "separates" look, consisting of interchangeable skirts, blouses, sweaters, jackets, and the like been as enduringly popular. Some historians have attributed this fact to the more casual lifestyle of Americans; others have stressed the practicality of Americans. Probably another factor responsible for the popularity of the separate look in this country, however, is the general American fetish for cleanliness and neatness, since interchangeable parts can be laundered "as often as needed" without the necessity of cleaning the entire ensemble.

Women were also going to college in ever greater numbers. College girls, like young working women, wanted stylish clothes that were also practical. In particular, it was these younger women with their firmer figures who felt freest to respond with indignity to reports that corsets were damaging to the health. Corsets were banned in most college gymnasium classes; they were uncomfortable for the new sporting activities and impossible to study or work in. Corsets ran contrary to an active life and young women wanted rid of them.

Despite the fact that working girls, college girls, and fitness-conscious women of all ages were rebelling against restrictive styles, the high-fashion silhouette of the 1890s was as confining as ever. It was this silhouette for which the term "hourglass figure" was coined, although strictly speaking,

1890s

some version of the hourglass figure had been mandatory during most of the nineteenth century. During the nineties,
however, the image was least clouded. On the one hand, the
dress lines were less complicated and the visual image more
free-looking than had been the case since the early years of
the century. Sans bustles and drapings, skirts fell gracefully
over the hips and slanted out to the hemline; bodices were
cut and trimmed with a self-conscious simplicity; and the emphasis on the puffed sleeves created a light, butterfly image.
On the other hand, the waistline had never been more tightly

cinched; skirts were excessively long and tight around the
hips and the full sleeves partially immobilized the arms.

Many women who would not have considered abandoning
their corsets altogether, nonetheless wished there were a
healthier means of molding the body into fashion's shape.
These women temporarily got their wish in 1900 when a
"reform" corset was introduced. It was designed by Mme.
Gaches-Surraute of Paris who had studied medicine. Its chief
characteristics were a straight-fronted busk and a pair of
suspenders attached to the point of the busk. The pressure
from the suspenders kept the figure line taut to the knees
and supported the abdomen without interfering much with
breathing.[10]

For a while it seemed that fashion design would accommo-
date to the new corset. The fashionable waist was allowed to
expand somewhat while the simple skirt and bodice lines of
the 1890s were retained. Then, exaggeration crept in, and the
infamous "S curve" was born. This style was also called the
"wasp waist," since it made the female body look like a wasp.
In 1904, a researcher reported that monkeys laced up in
these corsets moped, became excessively irritable, and within
weeks sickened and died.[11]

When worn on a woman, the bust billowed out over the
low-fronted corset; the waist was tightly laced, and the superfluous abdominal flesh, pressed flat by the heavy front
busk, swelled out at the sides and back in behind. Norah
Waugh says that the corset engineered to facilitate the S-
curve "was a miracle of cutting and shaping; never before or
since has it been quite so complicated. It was constructed
from numerous curved pieces—as many as ten to fifteen each
side, plus gussets—all expertly joined together and traversed
by a quantity of whalebone and steel of varying degrees of
thickness and weight. . . . 'butterfly' blue was the favourite
color."

At this time the "bust bodice" or antecedent of the modern brassiere first appeared. Since the corset began below the
bust, full-busted women lost the support provided by earlier

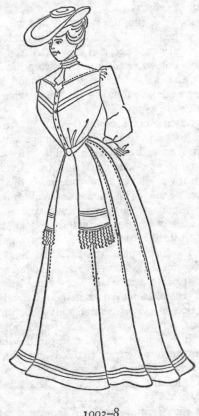

1903–8

styles of corsets; small-busted women lost the uplifting quality which tended to define and accentuate smaller curves.
Styles of the bust bodice made for the full figure were fitted
and lightly boned to provide the needed support. Styles designed for the thin woman were made looser and decorated
with ruffles and other flounces to provide the illusion of a

larger bust. When made looser and decorated, the bust bodice was called a camisole.

Blouses designed during the S-curve period were loose, lacy,
and flouncy to highlight the fashionably pendulous bustline.
Skirts were circular or gored and were fitted tightly over the
hips but swung out below the knees to sweep the floor. Often
trimmings in the bodice were repeated around the edge of
the skirt. As an additional aid to the flouncy image, parasols
and large hats were worn.

The exaggerated S-curve silhouette only served to emphasize the fact that the female fashion image was in serious
conflict with female lifestyles. In addition to the growing
number of women who were working outside the home, middle-class women were doing more work *inside* their homes. As
the great wave of foreign immigrants waned after the 1880s,
middle-class women could find fewer young immigrant
women who were willing to live in and do domestic work for
small wages. Instead, immigrant women and girls went to
work in the factories where wages, low as they were, were
higher than for domestic labor. In 1870, about 60 per cent of
all employed women worked as domestics. By 1900, only
about 30 per cent of employed women did domestic work.

This reduction in available immigrant labor produced the
much-vaunted "servant problem" of the 1890s and early
1900s. Ironic in retrospect, women active in the suffrage campaigns during the teens were chagrined by editors of magazines and newspapers for not finding a solution to this more
pressing problem before moving on to "less substantial" issues, like the vote.

Because of the "servant problem," however, even women
of moderate means were required to do more and more of
their own housework. Fortunately, technological advancement which made work in the home more palatable came
along at a rapid pace. In 1879, Thomas A. Edison's incan-
descent lamp turned night into day. This not only eliminated
the mess and bother of kerosene lighting devices and added
hours to the housewife's working day, but it also gave inspira-

tion for the invention of a host of other household devices, including the electric flatiron, the electric stove, the electric vacuum cleaner, and the electric sewing machine. Although mechanical versions of the refrigerator and washing machine had both been invented in 1858, more efficient electrical versions appeared after the turn of the century.

By the turn of the century, change was everywhere in the air. The telephone, with its initially erratic reception, was evaporating distance and increasing the speed of communication between businesses and private individuals. It was also providing jobs for thousands of female telephone operators and receptionists. Likewise, the sputtering automobile, at first a toy for the wealthy, made travelers out of masses of Americans when inexpensive, mass-produced models became available. President Taft rode to his inauguration in 1908 in a horse and buggy; Woodrow Wilson rode in a car in 1912. In 1903, Orville and Wilbur Wright invented the airplane and took the first short, bumpy ride. Meanwhile, still-life photography was giving way to the motion picture.

And then there was the tango. Even more than the telephone, the automobile and the motion picture, the tango symbolized the coming together of men and women, both for work and pleasure, after the hundred-year separation of the nineteenth century. No sooner had the waltz given way to the two-step when the "tango fever," as it was called, erupted and seemed to enflame the Western world. Men and women of all ages experienced an adolescent joy in holding each other closely and swaying to the sensuous rhythms of the Latin melodies. Before the dance craze had frenetically spun itself out in the two years before World War I, several other dances, including the fox trot, the turkey trot, the bunny hug, and the grizzly bear, were introduced in addition to the tango. In the United States a married dance team, Vernon and Irene Castle, made a name for themselves by going around the country and teaching dance-crazed students of all ages how to do the new steps. They even invented a version of their own, called appropriately the Castle Walk.

Parisian designer Paul Poiret caught the spirit of the early years of the twentieth century and translated it into dress. Though in the long span of the century, he has proved to be only a transitional figure, his styles represented a radical departure from respectable, that is "fashionable," designs of the times. He gleaned his inspiration from the Orient which (as a result of Western colonization, the Sino-Japanese War of 1894–95, and the American-inspired "Open Door" economic policy in China) had aroused Western curiosity at the turn of the century.

Under the guise of oriental elegance, Poiret's fashions revealed the form of the female body as it had not been revealed since the years immediately following the French Revolution. Having served unhappy apprenticeships with both the House of Worth and one of its leading competitors, the House of Doucet, Poiret branched out into his own business in 1904. At first, his customers came mainly from the demimonde, the class of women on the fringe of respectable French society who were supported by wealthy lovers. Bit by bit, however, elements of the Poiret look were adapted to the more conventional styles until by the end of the new century's first decade, he was the established leader of Parisian haute couture.

Being a self-conscious chauvinist, moreover, it is perhaps no coincidence that Poiret chose to articulate these styles using the oriental motif. Poiret said of his apprenticeships at the houses of Worth and Doucet: "What I saw there convinced me that one must dominate women unless one wishes to be delivered to them body and soul." Although he discouraged women from wearing the corset, he was proud of the fact that the narrow skirts he introduced shackled women's legs. Here again, it is impossible not to think of the oriental tradition of binding the feet, since the immobilizing and therefore subjugating effect is the same regardless of whether it is the midriff, legs, or feet that get bound.

In 1906, when the wasp-waisted S-curve was at its height of popularity, Poiret raised the waist on some of his models almost to the Empire line and introduced the fundamentals of his oriental look. This consisted of a straight skirt, usually single colored, below a high-waisted tunic. His famous "lamp-shade tunic" ended at the knees, but some versions fell low like a cloak and reached nearly to the hem of the skirt.

In 1907, dresses in general began to lose fullness. Skirts in the United States were moderately full between 1908 and

1914

1910, but cut straight and ending about two to four inches from the floor. Wide, cummerbund waistlines, suggestive of the oriental motif, were popular, along with kimono sleeves. Between 1910 and 1915, skirts became very narrow until a slit up the front or at the sides was imperative to allow the wearer to walk. These narrow "hobble skirts" were perfect for the clinging undulations of the tango, however.

When dresses lost all fullness, it was no longer possible to corset away excess fat, although, at first, extreme efforts were made to do so. Corset-makers were quick to develop a long corset—sometimes seventeen inches from the waist—to facilitate the new slim look. Wearing such a garment was pure torture, however, and most historians agree that by about 1919 the corset had ceased to be an item of fashion and had become instead a corrective device. Women did as little corseting as they could get away with.

Not only the exotic and impractical contours of the Poirot look, but all the restrictive, ornamental styles of the nineteenth century suddenly seemed embarrassingly outmoded to women confronted with the austere realities of living in a world at war. During the war years, then, first in Europe, then in the United States, women adopted a natural waistline and fuller, somewhat shorter skirts.

More than any other designer, however, it was Gabrielle "Coco" Chanel who understood how the burdens, responsibilities, and liberties of the World War One experience had affected the self-image of women. Chanel, who had worn a convent uniform during her childhood and who had avoided wearing the fancy "uniform" of the cocotte she later became, knew well the psychological meaning of dress. And the styles she chose to express her own independence and equality became the birthmarks of the New Woman everywhere.

Only recently have the true details of Chanel's ironically successful career begun to emerge. In 1975 a thoroughly documented biography was released in which most of the myths of Chanel's life, carefully fabricated by the designer herself, were dispelled. The miraculous thing, however, is that at least from the vantage point of the 1970s, the truth as biographer Edmonde Charles-Roux tells it in *Chanel* is every bit as fascinating as the fabrications appeared to be.[12]

Chanel used to tell interviewers that she was the daughter of a wealthy landowner and that after her parents' death, she was raised by two aunts. She openly acknowledged her series of wealthy lovers, claiming that each in his turn begged a marriage which she declined. One oft-told story involved an alleged proposal by the duke of Westminster, who once gave Chanel pearls valued at $69,000. According to the designer, she declined his offer of marriage by saying, "There have been many duchesses of Westminster, but there is only one Chanel." Though she always claimed she was unwilling to marry (she didn't want to weigh more heavily than a bird on any man), Chanel could not deny that she had frequently used her lovers' money as a springboard for her own creativity.

Biographer Charles-Roux is now claiming, however, that Chanel used far more than her lovers' money in her work; rather, she claims Chanel copied the very clothes in their closets. Previously concealed facts about the designer's life also had profound effects upon her art. According to Charles-Roux the two most important ones were her teen years in a convent orphanage (where she was left by an itinerant father) and her adult life, not as the courted beloved of a string of nobility, but rather as a repeatedly jilted mistress— or "cocotte."

Chanel used to claim that she wasn't much of a seamstress, but in fact she learned to sew to perfection in the convent orphanage where she lived between the ages of twelve and nineteen. After leaving the convent, she took a job as a seamstress, moonlighting at a music hall by night. There the raven-haired, sparkly-eyed Coco met her first paramour, horseman Étienne Balsan, with whose money she set up a small hat shop in Paris. Chanel migrated to Deauville during the war, however, where her second lover, polo star Arthur "Boy" Capel, set her up in an elegant shop in 1914.

From her earliest postconvent days, Chanel had herself worn the simple, tomboy designs that she would introduce as "fashion" to the postwar world. According to Charles-Roux, Chanel cultivated the look of transvestitism in open rebellion against the corseted, plumped-out look expected of the French cocotte. Chanel was humiliated by her status as Balsan's mistress and wished to avoid every overt association with it. She first marketed the famous jersey sailor jackets, copied from military uniforms, in Deauville, however, and their huge success resulted largely from the fact that Chanel wore the modish jackets conspicuously in public herself.

Back in Paris after the war, Chanel did her first major fashion show in 1920, again with "Boy's" backing. Here she introduced the classic Chanel suit, copied from the basic uniform at the convent orphanage and spiced up only slightly with functional, military-type trimmings like braids, buttons, and pockets intended for use. In sharp contrast to the ornately trimmed oriental styles still being shown by Poirot, Chanel's first suit consisted of a simple wool jersey jacket, a lightweight pullover sweater and a short accordion-pleated skirt. Another Chanel classic, the knitted black jumper, usually trimmed in white (suggestive of the habit of convent nuns), also became a staple item in most women's wardrobes beginning in the 1920s.

Charles-Roux claims that Chanel's relationship with her famous fourth paramour, the immensely wealthy duke of Westminster, was responsible for the costume jewelry fad initiated by the designer. (The third lover had been responsible for her "Slavic" period.) The duke gave Chanel elegant real jewels and it was these she copied in plastic and cut-glass models. Her personal preference was always for pearls, and she popularized the wearing of fake pearls, claiming at the time that people always stare at the real thing and that the great lady should be inconspicuous. Of course, the long string of pearls became a flapper trademark.

In its several variations, the Chanel look became the 1920s standard. Though she is often given credit for innovating the bobbed-hair style as well, in fact many women had been wearing their hair bobbed throughout the teens. Among the first was the dancer Irene Castle of "Castle Walk" fame, who bobbed her hair in 1914. The cloche hat, on the other hand, may have evolved in part from the exotic turbans which Poirot popularized.

Brassieres as we know them were first worn in the twenties, but their object was to flatten, not support the bust, since the goal of the twenties woman was to look young and boyish. Trousers became an accepted item of women's wear during this decade, though Poirot had paved the way with his harem pants. Besides traveling, however, pants were only acceptable for lounging at home, for sports, and for beach wear.

In the late 1920s, another woman, Italian-born Elsa Schiaparelli captured a growing mood for a more feminine and decorative style in clothing. After spending several years in poverty, she turned to the trade when friends admired a black sweater she had designed for herself. Like other female designers, Schiaparelli took to dress designing when a divorce forced her to earn her own living. Her first successes came with co-ordinated sweaters and skirts which were purchased by an American buyer, and by 1935, she was ranked among the top five in her profession.

Schiaparelli and Chanel created side by side in Paris for nearly a decade, viewing each other as competitors. Although "Schiap," as she was called, specialized in knitted fabrics which Chanel had made the vogue, the newcomer incorporated highly ornate cubist and surrealist patterns into her designs. Her forte was less the line of the garment itself than the novelty of the decorations. Schiaparelli had fabric printed in patterns of newspaper cutouts. She also designed clothing and accessories which featured a range of gimmicks—some of them functional and some not. For instance, she designed handbags which played melodies, collapsible hats which could be conveniently packed for travel, and jewelry which lit up at night. She also designed clothing for special purposes such as skiing and flying.

Schiaparelli's active clientele would today be considered jet setters. Most were wealthy society women or movie stars with abundant time and money for leisure pursuits. Since her speciality was novelty, however, it was inevitable that her own standards would one day rise up to judge her old-fashioned.*

The third woman to have a profound impact on the course of fashion during the twenties and thirties was Madeleine Vionnet. Even from the vantage point of the middle seventies, Vionnet is still considered one of the greatest technicians of all haute couture. Chanel worked with line to create simple styles that made all women look at ease and youthful. Vionnet worked with the cut of the material to develop styles that flattered the body in the same manner.

In the 1920s, Vionnet invented the bias cut, the diagonal crosscut now standardly employed when a moderately pliable or draped effect is desired. Cutting fabric on the bias allows it at once to cling more closely to the natural curves and to stretch gently in response to pressure from movement. Paradoxically, then, the bias cut has the effect of revealing the body form while concealing its excesses. Even the long gown when cut along the bias can be very comfortable to wear.

In addition to the bias cut, Vionnet also invented the cowl neckline, and did pioneering work with halters (the backless look), handkerchief hems, petal skirts, and caftans. All her innovations stemmed from her dual principles that the drape of the fabric should be fundamental to the design of a garment and that dresses should follow the body's lines, not conceal them.

*In 1947, Christian Dior introduced his "New Look," a long, full-skirted style in women's clothing which not only required more material per garment than any style for over fifty years, but which also called for a complete wardrobe change for the truly stylish woman. On the eve of the great showing, Schiaparelli authored an article for The American Magazine which asked the question, "Do you give your wife too much (money for clothes)?" The purpose of the ill-timed article was to praise the versatility of the basic black sheath, so easy to vary with the right (translate "Schiaparelli") accessories. Schiaparelli's day was over.

1920S

In 1929, the major Paris designers lowered hemlines to mid-calf. In order to re-establish a flattering proportion between the bodice and skirt, natural waistlines soon followed. Women in the United States, however, resisted the new longer styles for two years. Fashion historian James Laver credits the Great Depression with the ultimate success of the longer look. Skirt lengths, he believes, reflected a new sense of social responsibility engendered by hard times.[13] The Depression wiped out the flapper image, which had come to be associated with youth and irresponsibility, and in its place appeared styles which favored older women, but without making them dowdy.

Although Paris won the "hemline battle" of 1929–31, the institution of haute couture lost much prestige with American women in the process. It was clear that even the wealthy style setters would be responsive to a change in fashion leadership, and New York designers, led by Elizabeth Hawks and others, set out to assume this role.

New York's ally in taking the fashion reigns from Paris was Hollywood. Every fashion business needs models. Worth

19308

knew this when he paraded his wife in his early designs and, later, when he initiated the use of live mannequins. Chanel, of course, was her own best model. Between the two world wars, however, stars like Joan Crawford, Gloria Swanson, Norma Shearer, Jean Harlow, Greta Garbo, Ginger Rogers, and Vivien Leigh created a new type of fashion excitement which rapidly caught on with American women.

Fashion commentator Winifred Raushenbush articulated the difference between the Paris and Hollywood fashion principles in 1945. Paris fashions, she said, have traditionally been designed to startle; clothing selected by Hollywood stars, on the other hand, is expected to flatter.[14] Key to the image of most Hollywood superstars was their irresistibility to the opposite sex. And in major part, of course, sex appeal was created by make-up, hairdos, and flattering clothes.

The link between movies and fashion probably officially began during the 1920s when Cecil B. De Mille ordained that his stars would change clothes for every scene. In addition, De Mille movies emphasized clothing by showing women dressing and undressing, and by including the "shopping spree" as a movie staple. Certain stars also had a special appeal for youthful, fashion-conscious audiences, however. Joan Crawford's make-up, Jean Harlow's platinum-blond hair, the short-shorts Ruby Keeler and Joan Blondell wore in *Gold Diggers of 1933*—all were imitated by teen-agers everywhere. In addition to the fashion looks which became fads, however, female movie-goers were quick to copy more subtle distinguishing features of hairdos and clothes worn by stars with body types similar to their own. In this way, Hollywood expanded the concept of "fashion" while further stimulating American designers.

American designers, most of whom worked for the ready-to-wear industries, were also given an extra boost during World War Two when a temporary moratorium was imposed on Parisian haute couture fashions. The American-born Mainbocher, who was establishing himself in Paris when the war broke out, was commissioned by the armed forces to design

Early 1940s

an economical and chic uniform for the women's forces. The
style which he developed was widely copied for civilian wear
as well.

Rationing of cloth during wartime necessitated short skirts
made with skimpy amounts of material. Overall, then, the
early forties style was austere and masculine, with variety of
design achieved by small details like tucking or appliqué. The
hairdos of the period were shoulder-length "page boys," or
featured a sausage-shaped roll of hair which swept backward
from the forehead and circled the entire head. Shoulders
were padded, midriffs had a sunken look, and the knee-length

skirts were cut straight or slightly flared, often with a kick pleat. Practical shoes were worn since walking had taken the place of riding in cars in many cities. Shoulder bags, again suggested by military uniform, and Robin Hood or wide-brimmed sailor hats completed the look.

As never before, the female work force was mobilized during World War Two, and the requirement that women wear safety garb in factories led directly to the acceptance of slacks as work clothes for women as well as men. During the war, women began adapting men's clothing for their own use, wearing such items as slacks, loose sweaters, crew shirts, moccasins, and raincoats for work and play. Sporty garments such as T-shirts, playsuits, trousers, and shorts all originated in America, but they quickly spread to Europe during the postwar years. Fashion historian Jane Dormer reports that girls in Los Angeles wore fancy blouses with blue jeans as early as 1945.[15] This practice of dressing up the top half while dressing down the bottom has become a standard part of the 1970s style.

During World War Two, many commentators predicted a permanent end to Parisian-based haute couture. The important designers of the prewar years had retired or faded, and no shining stars seemed to be on the horizon to take their places. More importantly, however, haute couture had long ceased to compete financially with the American ready-to-wear giants. Most of the great couturières, including Chanel and Schiaparelli were supported by the sale of their perfumes. Prices for couture fashions remained well beyond the means of all but the very wealthy, and even including sales to retail distributors, profits per item were small since so much time and labor were required to produce a single creation.

Furthermore, the average woman seemed indifferent to the dictates of high fashion. Only with a great struggle had Paris designers managed to lower hemlines in the early thirties and no major coup had been accomplished up through the mid-forties.

So imagine the utter shock when Christian Dior splattered

the fashion ho-hum with his genuinely New Look in 1947. The excitement was so great at the Dior showing that many buyers went racing to the fitting rooms before the show was over, to make sure they got their orders in first. Buyers who had already purchased at the more established houses knew they had made a great mistake. Indeed, one American buyer allegedly remarked, "God help the buyers who bought before they saw this. It changes everything."

Christian Dior was a shy man who wore a look of perpetual surprise. Surely the greatest surprise of all to this modest, sensitive artist must have been his own fame, achieved so unexpectedly in the late middle years of an otherwise uneventful and unambitious life. When Dior abruptly died in 1957, still at the pinnacle of the quaky fashion business, it was said he had saved haute couture.

Dior set a frenetic pace of fashion change in the postwar decade, paralleled by his own frenetic, uncertain life, fraught with ulcers, emotional outbursts, and chronic dependence on spiritual mediums for reassurance that the ever-upcoming showings would be a success. Until textile magnate Marcel Boussac created his fashion kingdom for him in 1946, Dior led an unambitious and unsuccessful life. His father wanted him to be a diplomat but when the young man finally rebelled, the elder Dior set his son up with an art dealership. Dior's business sense was not good, however, and when his father lost his money in the Depression of the early 1930s, Dior was thrust on the charity of friends. He was refused work as an insurance salesman, a baker, and an office boy, and after two years of unemployment and poverty, he suffered a physical breakdown. Amazingly, the twenty-nine-year-old bounced back from this collapse and began sketching and sewing tapestries. This led him into couture. He first worked as a salaried designer for Robert Piquet, then after the war briefly for Lucien Lelong, both highly renown in the profession.

The immensely wealthy Marcel Boussac picked Dior the way he picked his race horses—he wanted a winner. For ten long and tedious years, Dior did not disappoint him. In 1955 alone, Dior Enterprises grossed over $15,000,000, almost all of which went to Boussac who retained ownership of the business. Dior's take for 1955 was only about $100,000, mostly in salary.[16] Some have said, however, that Boussac's control of finances gave Dior a great advantage over other couturiers, especially since the designer had proved to be inept at business.

The mammoth size of the Dior operation no doubt contributed to Dior's incessant fear of failure—a failure he feared not only for himself but also for the huge staff in several countries for whose paychecks he was responsible. In addition to the couture establishment in Paris, Dior outlets also fanned out into England, Chile, Cuba, Mexico, Canada, Australia, and Venezuela. In the United States, Dior Enterprises established its own factory. Besides clothing, the Dior label also appeared on furs, hosiery, countless accessories including sunglasses, and the inevitable perfume.

Friends claim that Dior fretted and worried up to the last minute over every semiannual collection and that when plans were finally complete for the showing, he would break into sobs and lament passionately that there was "nothing new" and that all the designs were worthless. It is tempting to tread gently with this sensitive soul who judged his own work so harshly. But the truth is that even though the Dior line changed hectically from year to year, encompassing almost the entire panorama of historically suggested silhouettes, nothing really new emerged after 1947.

Dior's best and most innovative designs appeared in his first collection—the fashion showing in 1947 which so electrified the static fashion world. His "New Look" put haute couture back on the fashion map. It demolished the old look, born of wartime austerity, cloth rationing, and the enforced masculinization of women. It even did away with the philosophy of the old look—practicality. After 1947, women's dresses no longer had to be practical. Now clothing could be "fun."

1947 ("New Look")

The design metaphor for Dior's initial New Look was the inverted flower. The best known of the early models was black with plunge neckline, natural waist, flared, calf-length skirt, and batwing sleeves. The flower, with its sweet smell and delicacy, symbolized the aspects of femininity which women in the postwar decade wanted for themselves. The mass media and male business establishment may have had other things in mind for women—that they leave their jobs and become full-time wives and mothers, for instance. But women themselves just wanted to be sweet, soft, and appealing for the men who had been away for so long. Dior captured that mood.

Also at the 1947 showing, Dior introduced, or more properly, resurrected from nineteenth-century couture, the "figure 8." It was this silhouette that he chose to play around with for the next six years, introducing a series of low-necked, corseted sheaths, Empress Eugenie-style ball gowns, bustles, bells, and so forth. To further emphasize the waistline, Dior advocated wearing a small corset which would take two inches off the waist; some styles had boning built right into the bodice.

During the years after his initial triumph, the architect of the New Look came increasingly to be referred to as "the dictator of the hemlines," as loyalty to his fashion decrees remained absolute despite the lack of innovation. Hemlines, by the way, remained at mid or upper calf.

Then in 1954 an almost unheard of thing happened—Gabrielle Chanel, out of the business since 1938, made a comeback. Not only did Chanel herself make a comeback but so did the "Chanel look," featuring boxy suits, low waists—simple, comfortable styles. Chanel's biographer has revealed that her "retirement" in Switzerland after 1945 was in fact an exile from a country which had not yet forgiven its German collaborators. Charles-Roux's book deals extensively with what she believes was a "principled" defection to Naziism on Chanel's part. Chanel's fashion comeback in 1954 was not marred by political backbiting, however, and as usual the designer had a number of tales ready to cover her return. One story had it that the owner of Chanel No. 5 perfume, Pierre Wertheimer, asked her to resume designing to boost lagging perfume sales—also Chanel's major source of income. Chanel herself once said she did it because, "One night at dinner Christian Dior said a woman could never be a great couturier."

Chanel's showing, in February 1954, was scorned as disappointingly old hat, but by the following July, all the major designers were incorporating elements of her look—including Dior. At his July showing Dior introduced his H-line, the first radical departure from the New Look. The following year, Dior followed with his A-line.

After 1955, a series of waistless styles were introduced, the most extreme new design becoming a temporary rage each season. Dior's A-line held its own until Christobel Balenciaga stole the limelight in 1957 with his chemise, or sack dress. The chemise wore itself out after a mere eighteen months, only to be replaced by Yves St. Laurent's "trapeze," a style based on the shape of a trapezoid which flared out from bust to hem in a line suggestive of advanced pregnancy. In fact, this style introduced a vogue for one-piece maternity dresses.

It is surely no coincidence that during the 1950s, when the birth rate was soaring and young people were marrying at ever earlier ages, the look of expectant motherhood became high fashion. It is perhaps also no coincidence that these styles were designed with the full figure in mind—especially the full bustline. What has been coined the "mammary madness" of the 1950s applied both to sex and motherhood. Evening gowns during the later fifties continued to be tight-waisted, very décolletage, and either extremely tight or extremely full. That way, the 1950s supermom, clad demurely by day in garb overtly suggestive of maternity, could blossom by night into the decade's alternative image—the sexpot.

Paralleling the trend toward earlier marriage and larger families during the 1950s was the trend in the United States toward suburban migration. A major appeal of suburbia, of course, has been the opportunity to spend one's nonworking hours in more casual, family-oriented pursuits. The suburban theme has emphasized do-it-yourself home, lawn, and garden maintenance; barbecuing and various other family lawn activities; and participation in sports activities at community clubs and schools. This outdoors, sports-oriented lifestyle has caused a great increase in the demand for casual clothing such as shorts, slacks, knit tops, sweaters, bathing suits, ten-

1950s

1960s

1970s

nis shoes, and the like. Because suburbia's influence extends far beyond its boundaries, even nonsuburbanites have begun to dress more casually, with the result that fashion itself has become ever more casual over the past quarter century.

The casual influence has also spread to nonsports-style clothes. One example of this trend is the popularity after 1955 of the looser silhouette, to a great extent patterned after the casual look introduced by Chanel in the 1920s. Another is the increasing popularity of separates for all occasions, including work, general daytime wear, and formal evening attire. In fact, the waistless silhouette of the late fifties and sixties may in part have been pushed by designers in an effort to revive the flagging dress industry and to stem a growing preference for the more casual skirt-and-blouse fashion. Dior's New Look, for example, was conceived as a one-piece, usually monocolored costume, but American women discovered it could be achieved more cheaply and casually by combining separate skirts and blouses. *Fortune* magazine reported in the mid-fifties that production of skirts alone had jumped from 24 million in 1947 to 53 million in 1949 (more than double) to 75 million in 1953.[17]

After 1960, the most successful designers specialized in casual, youthful, and increasingly androgynous or bisexual designs. In the early sixties a group of young British designers, including most notably Mary Quant, inaugurated a number of very youthful variations on the tubular-shift silhouette which became known as the Chelsea Look. Quant claims she went into dress designing because she hated the way adults looked and hated the fact that young people were compelled to adopt this look to symbolize their release from childhood. As a teen-ager she decided that the young should look like the young, that the old could look young if they wanted to, but that the young must never look old. An art school dropout in the forefront of the generation gap revolt, Quant logged up two firsts in the early sixties—she opened the first boutique in London and then became the first English person to design clothes directly for mass production. Quant kept her prices conspicuously low so as to be affordable by the broad range of the youth market; nonetheless, Mary Quant, Ltd. was a multimillion-dollar concern by the time Quant was thirty.

The Quant image was decidedly childish. She is credited with initiating the fads for high boots, colored tights, above-the-knee skirts, and shiny plastic raincoats. Other designers rounded out the look by introducing little-girl shoes, hats, and purses.

On first consideration, there might seem to be a conflict between the "little girl" look created by Quant and the swinging sixties decade in which she created it. But in fact, Quant's styles fed right into the movement for sexual liberation that was fermenting in the early 1960s. Not only had Helen Gurley Brown's *Sex and the Single Girl* made it clear that women of all ages, protected by the pill, were indulging in the pleasures of premarital and postdivorce sex, but movies like *A Summer Place*, *Parrish*, and the host of popular bikini beach flicks lent potent support to the worst fears of parents everywhere—that their teen-age daughters were "turning on" to more sexual images of themselves as well.

Quant thinly disguised the sexuality of her short-skirted, revealing dresses by incorporating motifs of childhood into her designs, including such features as short puffy sleeves, sailor collars, or oversize stripes or polka dots. Quant also claimed that the colored tights she designed and sold made her styles more "decent." And in fact, short skirts, worn with tights or with the panty hose they inspired, *felt* more decent than they looked. But the childish decorations on her dresses also had another psychological effect on the wearer; they encouraged a fun-loving sense of irresponsibility. To the male eye, however, short short skirts were just plain sexy. It was a dynamite combination.

Mary Quant's clothes were intended for the teens and twenties set; French designer André Courrèges, however, demanded that mature women leap to one or the other side in fashion's generation gap when he introduced the miniskirt to Parisian haute couture. At first Courrèges was branded as "the lord of the space ladies," because his short costumes, all precisely miniskirted at four inches above the knee, were cut along sharp, angular lines; seams were striped over in dark contrast fabrics; and the recommended accessories included white calf-high boots and slit-eyed sun goggles. Courrèges also introduced tight pants in a woven-ribbon fabric that suggested space suit mobility and insulation. His flat-chested and hipless styles were designed to be worn sans jewelry and, insofar as possible, sans underwear. In 1965, Courrèges predicted bras would be as outmoded ten years later as whalebone corsets. (He proved prophetic to the extent that the "no-bra look" has taken over.)

By 1965, the space age metaphor had been dropped and Courrèges was being lauded or damned, depending on the point of view, as the inventor of the Little-girl Look. To those with their sights on Paris, it made no difference that

Mary Quant and the other British designers had already popularized this look.

Courrèges' designs, however, became even sexier as the sixties waned. Just as the bikini was becoming the most popular fashion item at resort areas across the world, Courrèges also bared the navel by featuring halter tops, bra tops, hip-hugger pants, and bouncy dresses with cutouts.

As one fashion commentator remarked about the miniskirt revolution of the late sixties: everyone who could wear one did; everyone who couldn't suddenly felt old. The majority of mature women who found themselves left out by the new style remained true to the semitailored shifts, shirtwaists, and casual suits which dated back to the late fifties and early sixties. Especially enduring were the high-necked, semifitted A-line shifts, suits, and coat dresses popularized by Jacqueline Kennedy Onassis when she was First Lady. The former First Lady herself switched to miniskirts and pants suits when these became high fashion, but the styles she preferred while performing her public role outlived her interest in them.

It is worth noting that styles became sexier in the late sixties without sacrificing the androgynous look. For one thing, fashion's female image remained unnaturally straight hipped. In addition, men's clothing, beginning with the styles started by the so-called flower children, became ever more eccentrically colored and decorated during the same period.

In 1970, however, designers and retailers tried to reintroduce calf-length skirts called midis as an alternative to short skirts and pants. Despite the fact that the midi campaign was pushed feverishly in this country by the clothing industry's influential trade magazine, Women's Wear Daily, women of all ages refused to buy the new styles. Those who were unable or unwilling to wear the ultrashort minis, popular with the young and the very thin, stuck with their knee-length styles, preferring no change over a return to the encumbrance of long skirts.

By about 1972, however, women of all ages and lifestyles had made the transition to the decade's dominant fashion, the pants suit. College girls and young women had become disillusioned with the miniskirt in part because of its adoption by Parisian designers. No longer was a short skirt a sign of youth, as Quant and the Chelsea set had intended. Other factors contributed to make pants, and especially jeans, seem just right for the young woman of the 1970s, however. For one thing, women were swarming the ranks of Vietnam war protesters. Just as women wore more masculine styles with military trimmings during the first and second world wars as a symbol of support for men in the service, so they adopted more masculine garb during the late sixties and early seventies in part to symbolize unity in protest. In fact, "high fashion" hip-hugger pants were copied from men's blue jeans. In addition, though, the Women's Liberation Movement was picking up converts fast by 1970, and from the first, its leaders stressed the importance of "the image" to equality—thus the picketing at the Miss America pageants of 1968 and 1969. And finally, the practicality of blue jeans was as apparent and appealing to young women who did their own laundry as it had long been to the mothers of young boys.

For more mature women, the pants suit offered a logical and comfortable compromise between the modish and unflattering mini and longer but less comfortable midis. The perfection of wash-and-wear polyester double knit fabrics made it possible to construct pants which stretched out in sitting but bounced back wrinkle and sag free when the standing position was resumed. Like a standard suit, the two-piece styling facilitated greater freedom in arm and upper-body movement. Waist-to-toe stretch hosiery also allowed great freedom and comfort. In fact, the transition from short skirts to pants can easily be considered an extension of pantyhose outward to include the clothing style with the comfortable coverup look and feel.

Although some women proclaimed the pants suit as the new style-for-a-century, change already seemed on the forefront by the middle 1970s. The disastrous 1970 midi campaign notwithstanding, undaunted American designers had some success with below-the-knee skirts during 1975 and 1976, especially when a comfortable flared skirt or "bib overall" styling was combined with casual blue jean or denim-look fabrics. Cleverly, designers are aiming their efforts at style change on the group that, throughout the twentieth century, has shown the greatest fashion free will—the young. The success of the blue jean skirts, moreover, suggests that young women are interested in a new (more feminine?) image, a new expression of themselves. But significantly, too, they are reluctant to relinquish comfort and the tough, independent image suggested by jeans. For, American women in the 1970s plainly want the right, freedom, and mobility to do what they want to do and go where they want to go. Our clothing, the closest extension of ourselves, speaks this message loud and clear.

Epilogue

As the preceding chapters have shown, women have been portrayed primarily in domestic roles by popular culture over the past century and a half. In a retrospective review, therefore, it seems appropriate to attempt some generalizations about the reason for this consistent image, despite the continuing shift of middle-class women toward the labor market beginning in about the 1870s.

In this regard, a conversation that I recently had with a man in the educational consulting business was illuminating. The man complained that writing children's stories had become "dull pablum" for him because state laws were increasingly requiring that women and female children be equally represented with men and male children. He went on to complain that he could no longer portray women as housewives "despite the fact that that's what most women do" but now had to put them in unusual jobs—"such as a truck driver." "The worst part of it is," he continued, "you can't show a female truck driver as a butch, which she'd be, but you have to show her as *normal*-looking," he said, moaning. At first I was angry. Writing about a female truck driver sounded like anything but pablum to me. Then I realized: he was serious. He wasn't leveling a personal indictment at me or my feminist principles. From his perspective and experience, writing about working women (maybe about women at all) was just plain dull.

And I think therein lies the clue. It's true that over the years many women have created and consumed the traditional passive, domestic female images with relish. But it also seems true that the greater the control women have exerted over popular culture images, the *less* passive and domestic they have been and the more reflective of women's work and commitments outside the home. Conversely, the greater the influence of men over a particular medium at a particular time, the more traditional and outdated the images have been.

As an example of this principle, consider women's fashions. Of the media covered in this book, fashions have without doubt kept pace best with changing female lifestyles. But women have exerted more control over this medium than any of the others as well. Especially in recent decades, the most important control has been exerted by the consumer herself. As the long "hemline battle" of 1929–31 and the disastrous midi campaign of 1970 have displayed, women just won't buy what they don't like. They will sew instead—or wear last year's clothes. Dating back to the 1880s, moreover, American women have demanded and sometimes created their own fashions to meet their changing needs. Think of the shirtwaist craze started by working women, of knickers worn for bicycling and later for automobile travel, of pants worn in factories during World War Two and later for work at home, and most recently, of blue jean skirts made from cut-up blue jeans (and later copied by designers). In addition, female fashion designers from Chanel to Quant have been a trendsetting force, simplifying women's clothes and making them more comfortable and more functional.

Movies at times also portrayed many strong, definitely "unhousewifely" images of women, especially during the 1930s and 1940s. But again, women disproportionately dominated movie audiences during these decades; they were always the mainstay of the matinee audience and, during the war years, they provided the bulk of the evening audience as well. It was women, and not men, who thrilled to the successes of the independent, strong-willed characters played by Bette Davis, Joan Crawford, or Katharine Hepburn. Furthermore, the occasional female screen writer, such as Mae West (who wrote her own movies) or Ruth Gordon of the husband and wife writing team of Gordon and Kanin, gave notable strength and depth to the female characters they scripted. By contrast, movie heroines in the postwar era, with larger male audiences and dominated by male writers and producers, have tended to be far more superficial than male protagonists.

Popular fiction presents a special case. On the one hand, the two formulas which have been enduringly popular with women—the romance and the sentimental domestic tale—are as eagerly read today as they were in the middle eighteenth century, though I suspect that the primary audience for the modern versions of these formulas consists of adolescents and working-class housewives. On the other hand, best-selling female writers from E. D. E. N. Southworth to Erica Jong have used fiction as a vehicle for expressing their grievances and uncertainties about the male role. In either case, the fact that women have been avid readers has guaranteed a market for female writers who have featured female images in their books.

Overall, magazine and television images of women have been most conservative and most consistently locked into the passive, wholesome housewife theme. As the chapter on magazine images suggests, advertisers, most of whom are male, of consumer goods, most of which are used in the home, believe that it is crucial to the continued profit of their products for women to identify with (and thus feel responsible for) the care and appearance of their homes, even if their primary job is elsewhere.

Since men have the controlling positions in most popular arts today, it seems safe to conclude that they will continue to portray women in the manner that's easiest, most profitable, and maybe most interesting for them—as the opposite of, and refuge from, the power struggle in the world of work, that is, as domestic and compliant to the point of self-sacrifice. Meanwhile, the protagonists of the "raised consciousness" best sellers continue to "wake up in the empty trough of marriage and leave in search of their identity," and a few hard-working, competitive, unself-sacrificing women are working their way into prominence in television and starting magazines like Ms. These women are facing setbacks and even backlash, but in broadly drawn metaphors from lives and events of the past and present, they are telling a different story—their own.

Notes

CHAPTER 1

1. John G. Cawelti, *Adventure, Mystery and Romance* (Chicago: University of Chicago Press, 1976).

2. Herbert Ross Brown, *The Sentimental Novel in America, 1789–1860* (Durham, North Carolina: Duke University Press, 1940), pp. 204–5.

3. Ian Watt, *The Rise of the Novel: Studies in Defoe, Richardson and Fielding* (Berkeley and Los Angeles: University of California Press, 1957). See especially p. 138ff.

4. A good discussion of Pamela as entrepreneur is contained in the Richardson section of Joseph Wood Krutch's *Five Masters: A Study in the Mutations of the Novel* (New York: Jonathan Cape & Harrison Smith, 1930).

5. Phyllis Chesler, *Women and Madness* (New York: Doubleday, 1972), p. 116. Chesler reports findings of several studies which indicate that married women (both white and nonwhite) are more likely than either single women or married or single men to *report* nervousness, distress, or fear of a mental breakdown. In addition, many more women than men seek the help of a therapist, and many more women are institutionalized for reasons of mental illness.

6. Brown, op. cit., pp. 31, 123. Brown says that nine-

teenth-century U.S. magazines were "embellished" with "female elegiac verse and mortuary art," but that fiction's dying young ladies preferred Young's *Night Thoughts*. In his wide readership of the pre-1860 novels, he concluded that every respectable deathbed scene featured a copy.

7. Helen Waite Papashvily, *All the Happy Endings*, A *Study of the Domestic Novel in America, the Women Who Wrote It, the Women Who Read It, in the Nineteenth Century* (New York: Harper & Brothers, 1956), P. 25.

8. Susanna Rowson, *Charlotte Temple*, A *Tale of Truth* (New Haven: College and University Press, 1964; originally published in London in 1791, (1794—first U.S.); pp. 102–3. Though the novel has gone through more than 200 editions, the editors, Clara M. and Rudolf Kirk, claim that their 1964 edition is the first re-edition to be based on the original 1791 text. The Kirks supply a useful introduction.

9. Papashvily, op. cit., 32–34.

10. Frances Trollope, *Domestic Manners of the Americans* (New York: Dodd, Mead & Company, 1927). Originally published in 1832.

11. James Fenimore Cooper, *The Crater*, II (New York, 1847), p. 89.

12. Gerda Lerner, "The Lady and the Mill Girl: Changes in the Status of Women in the Age of Jackson," in Jean E. Friedman and William G. Shade, eds., *Our American Sisters: Women in American Life and Thought* (Boston: Allyn and Bacon, Inc., 1973), pp. 82–95.

13. Krutch, op. cit., p. 123.

14. Papashvily, op. cit., p. 3.

15. Two excellent works which convincingly theorize that corruption follows when individuals possess excessive power within the domestic situation are John Stuart Mill's famous treatise *The Subjection of Women* (London, 1869) and Ronald V. Sampson's more scholarly *The Psychology of Power* (New York, 1966).

16. E. D. E. N. Southworth, *The Deserted Wife* (Philadelphia, 1855), p. 195.

17. Brown, op. cit., p. 264.

18. Frederick Lewis Allen, "Best-Sellers: 1900–1935," *Saturday Review of Literature*, 13, No. 6 (December 7, 1935), pp. 3–4.

19. Russel B. Nye, *The Unembarrassed Muse: The Popular Arts in America* (New York: The Dial Press, 1970), pp. 36–37.

20. Queenie D. Leavis, *Fiction and the Reading Public* (London: Chatto & Windus, 1965). First published in 1932.

21. John G. Cawelti, *The Six-Gun Mystique* (Bowling Green, Ohio: Bowling Green University Popular Press, circa 1970).

22. Bobbie Ann Mason, *The Girl Sleuth: A Feminist Guide* (Old Westbury, N.Y.: The Feminist Press, 1975).

23. See Kay J. Mussell, "Beautiful and Damned: The Sexual Woman in Gothic Fiction," *Journal of Popular Culture*, 9, No. 1 (Summer 1975), pp. 84–89.

24. Joanna Russ, "Somebody's Trying to Kill Me and I Think It's My Husband: The Modern Gothic," *Journal of Popular Culture*, 6, No. 4 (Spring 1973), pp. 666–91.

CHAPTER 2

1. The figures on the increases in the number of operating TV sets are from Russel B. Nye, *The Unembarrassed Muse: The Popular Arts in America* (New York: The Dial Press, 1970), p. 406. Figures on current set ownership and on average hours spent viewing were reported in *English Journal*, December 1972, p. 1248.

2. Nye, op. cit., p. 396.

3. "Family Fun," *Newsweek*, March 15, 1971, p. 68.

4. John Kenneth Galbraith, "The Economics of the American Housewife," *The Atlantic Monthly*, August 1973, p. 79.

5. See Packard's books *The Hidden Persuaders* (New York: D. McKay Co., 1957) and *The Waste Makers* (New York: D. McKay Co., 1960). See also the chapter on women's magazines and magazine advertising in this book.

6. Nye, op. cit., p. 414.

7. One indication that publicity of the women's movement peaked in 1970–71 is the fact that during these years many more articles were indexed on the topic in the *New York Times Index* and *Reader's Guide to Periodical Literature* than in years preceding or following. In comparison to 1969, for example, when there were less than ten news accounts listed in the *New York Times Index* under the heading "Women's Liberation Movement," there were more than 200 such news accounts indexed in 1970.

8. Horace Newcomb, *TV: The Most Popular Art* (Garden City, New York: Anchor Press, 1974).

9. An in-depth study of the Western formula with some suggestive comparisons to other forms like the detective story is John G. Cawelti, *The Six-Gun Mystique* (Bowling Green, Ohio: Bowling Green University Popular Press, circa 1970). Also see Cawelti's "Notes Toward a Typology of Literary Formulas," *Indiana Social Studies*, 26, No. 3 (Winter 1973–74), pp. 21–34.

10. See *Violence on Television;* Hearings Before the Subcommittee on Communications of the Committee on Commerce, United States Senate, on Department of Health, Education and Welfare's Progress in Developing a Profile on Violence on Television, 93rd Congress, 2nd Session, April 3, 4, and 5, 1974 (Serial No. 93–76; U. S. Government Printing Office, Washington, D.C., 1974). Highlights from this sixth annual report on televised violence are accessibly summarized in Tony Chiu, "The Violent World of the TV Viewer," *Science Digest*, March 1975, pp. 80–83. In addition to the findings that women and minorities comprise most of television's victims, George Gerbner and Larry Gross of the University of Pennsylvania's Annenberg School of Communications presented evidence to the Senate Subcommittee indicating that heavy TV watchers also tend to have a highly distorted view of their own safety from crime. Avid watchers tend to consider themselves far less safe than they actually are.

CHAPTER 3

1. Leslie Fiedler, *Love and Death in the American Novel*, rev. ed. (New York: Stein and Day, 1966). Fiedler's broad, and at first highly controversial, thesis is that American literature in the "elite" tradition has been incapable of dealing with adult heterosexuality, but that it has been pathologically obsessed with death instead. Films of the 1960s and 1970s seem to provide another illustration of Fiedler's thesis. Films of this period correlate better with "elite," as opposed to strictly popular, literature in other respects as well. For one thing, these more recent films are more dominated by the taste of the male portion of the viewing audience. Likewise, male scholars, who dominate in academia and critical circles, have made the decisions as to what works of literature would be accorded "elite" status (and therefore would be studied in schools and universities).

2. Molly Haskell, *From Reverence to Rape: The Treatment of Women in the Movies* (New York: Holt, Rinehart & Winston, 1973).

3. Marjorie Rosen, *Popcorn Venus: Women, Movies and the American Dream* (New York: Avon, 1974).

4. See, for example, Henry F. May, *The End of American Innocence; A Study of the First Years of Our Own Time, 1912–1917* (New York: Alfred A. Knopf, 1959); William L. O'Neill, *The Progressive Years: America Comes of Age* (New York: Dodd, Mead & Company, 1975); and Robert H. Wiebe, *Search for Order, 1877–1920* (New York: Hill and Wang, 1967).

5. William L. O'Neill, *Divorce in the Progressive Era* (New Haven: Yale University Press, 1967).

6. Rosen, op. cit., p. 103.

7. Russel Nye, *The Unembarrassed Muse: The Popular Arts in America* (New York: The Dial Press, 1970), pp. 377–78.

8. Gary Carey, *Katharine Hepburn* (New York: Pocket Books, 1975), pp. 111–12. Carey reports that, in 1938, the president of the Independent Theatre Owners of America published a list of stars branded as "box-office poison," which included Hepburn, along with Joan Crawford, Marlene Dietrich, Greta Garbo, Mae West, Kay Francis, and (strangely) Fred Astaire. The strong, invincible heroine had apparently lost her appeal for Depression audiences.

9. See National Manpower Council, Hon. James D. Zellerbach, Chairman, *Womanpower: A Statement By the National Manpower Council* (New York: Columbia University Press, 1957), pp. 161–62. The Council reported that a 1944–45 Woman's Bureau survey of 13,000 employed women (in all occupations except domestic service) revealed that three out of four intended to keep their jobs after the war ended. At the time these findings created an uneasy stir, since it was assumed that female labor would need to be displaced in order to make room for returning servicemen. In fact, the demand for female labor (cf. Valerie Kincade Oppenheimer, *The Female Labor Force in the United States*, Population Monograph Series, No. 5, University of California Institute of International Studies, 1970) increased dramatically after World War Two, however, so that, although only one in four did actually quit their jobs, there was no significant effect on the rate of male employment.

10. Nye, op. cit., pp. 384–85; 406.

11. Betty Friedan, *The Feminine Mystique* (New York: Dell Publishing Co., 1963).

12. Rosen, op. cit., p. 276. Rosen cites a study reported by *Variety* magazine in which 3,000 exhibitors were polled.

13. Nye, op. cit., p. 386.

14. Dwight Macdonald, *On Movies* (New York: Berkley-Medallion Edition, 1971), p. 137.

15. Nye, op. cit., pp. 384–85.

16. Donald Bogle, *Toms, Coons, Mulattoes, Mammies and Bucks: An Interpretive History of Blacks in American Films* (New York: The Viking Press, 1973).

CHAPTER 4

1. See Judith Hole and Ellen Levine, *Rebirth of Feminism* (New York: Quadrangle Books, 1971), and Jo Freeman, "Origins of the Women's Movement," in Joan Huber, ed., *Changing Woman in a Changing Society* (Chicago: University of Chicago Press, 1973).

2. The extent to which advertising is directed to women is indicated by the fact that, over the years, advertisements *for* general interest periodicals (that is, magazines aimed for both men and women) in such advertising trade journals as *Tide* and *Advertising Age* have often stressed the number of female readers the advertisers will be able to reach.

3. James Playsted Wood, *Magazines in the United States,* 2nd ed. (New York: Ronald Press Co., 1956), p. 54.

4. Helen Woodward, *The Lady Persuaders* (New York: Ivan Obolensky, Inc., 1960), p. 5.

5. Circulation statistics in Wood, op. cit., p. 55. In an 1850 editorial, Sarah Hale made the following comment on the budding women's rights movement: "We have said little of the Rights of Women. But her first right is to education in its widest sense, to such education as will give her the full development of all her personal, mental and moral qualities. Having that, there will be no longer any questions about her rights; and rights are liable to be perverted to wrongs when we are incapable of exercising them."

6. For a concise description of the publisher's role in the premass-advertising era, see Theodore Peterson, *Magazines in the Twentieth Century*, 2nd ed. (Urbana: University of Illinois Press, 1964), p. 64. For Hale's view of her editorial role, see Wood, op. cit., p. 56.

7. See Peterson, op. cit., p. 4ff.; Wood, op. cit., p. 103.

8. Frank Presbrey, *The History and Development of Advertising* (Garden City, New York: Doubleday, Doran & Co., 1929), p. 479. Presbrey traces the development of American

advertising from colonial times to 1928. His is the only comprehensive history of advertising, though it is badly dated.

9. Frederick Lewis Allen, "American Magazines 1741–1941," *Bulletin of the New York Public Library*, June 1941. Quoted in Wood, op. cit., p. 104.

10. An interesting biography of Curtis is Edward Bok's, *A Gentleman From Maine* (New York: Charles Scribner's Sons, 1923).

11. Wood, op. cit., pp. 106–7.

12. Ibid.; see also Presbrey, op. cit., p. 480ff.

13. Peterson, op. cit., p. 7.

14. Presbrey, op. cit., p. 437.

15. Peterson, op. cit., p. 82. Men's titles included *Popular Science* (which is no doubt read by some women in the same way that *Better Homes & Gardens* is read by some men), *Popular Mechanics, Mechanix Illustrated, Boy's Life, Scouting, American Legion, Elks Magazine,* and *V. F. W. Magazine.* Such a list compiled in the sixties would doubtless have included *Plabyoy* and *Esquire,* but the balance between women's and men's magazines would not be greatly altered by such inclusions since many new women's magazines have appeared as well.

16. Wood, op. cit., pp. 57, 59.

17. Ibid., p. 112.

18. See Presbrey, op. cit., p. 290ff. See also, Harvey Young, *Toadstool Millionaires* (Princeton, N.J.: Princeton University Press, 1961). Patent medicine advertising was imported from England along with the first settlers. Although the term now refers to medicines patented under U.S. laws but available over the counter without prescription, early products were so labeled if any medicinal claim was made for them whatsoever. In fact, among the earliest "patent medicines" advertised in England were coffee and tea. Patent medicine advertising had elicited public indignation and regulation long before Bok's time, however. Between 1860 and 1880, the names of various curatives were painted indiscriminately on fences, barns, cliffs, rocks, and amid scenic locale every-

where. Legislation in the late 1860s restricted such advertising to areas within sight of the railroad right of way.

Many individual patent medicine dealers became millionaires, and the combined earnings of the industry were mammoth in the post-Civil War decades. Families of the great proprietors weren't quite respectable, but then neither had the medical profession established a semblance of its current standards by the 1890s. Until the American Medical Association became a strong force for upgrading the quality of medical education (between about 1890 and 1910), many doctors were little more than quacks who had no compunctions about endorsing popular patented products.

19. Edward Bok's autobiography, *The Americanization of Edward Bok* (New York: Charles Scribner's Sons, 1922), contains a good account of these events. See also Presbrey, op. cit., pp. 531–35. The women's club movement reached a peak of activity between about 1890 and 1920. Good accounts of their reform efforts appear in William L. O'Neill, *Everyone Was Brave; The Rise and Fall of Feminism in America* (Chicago: Quadrangle Books, 1969); Eleanor Flexner, *Century of Struggle, the Women's Rights Movement in the United States* (Cambridge: Belknap Press of Harvard University Press, 1959); and Aileen Kraditor, *Ideas of the Woman's Suffrage Movement, 1890–1920* (New York: Columbia University Press, 1965).

20. Woodward, op. cit., p. 110; 129–30; 137; 140–41.

21. Presbrey, op. cit., pp. 338–39. The practice of selling from bulk supplies, of course, continued well into the twentieth century in some rural locales.

22. Styles also changed considerably more slowly. See the chapter on fashion images in this book.

23. "Jingles" were particularly popular in America during the late 1880s and the 1890s. The rhyming beer parlor songs, such as "Bicycle Built for Two," date from this era. Advertisers were quick to exploit the trend by inventing slogans and jingles which, it was hoped, would catch the public's ear. Ivory led the pack. Presbrey has a chapter on ad jingles.

24. In 1954, the editors of *Fortune* magazine reported that America's six largest markets were for housing, home goods, food, cars, clothing, and leisure. This is still the case. In 1974, an "intermediate budget" family, earning about $14,000 annually, spent 25 per cent of its total income for food, 23 per cent for housing and home goods, 8 per cent for transportation, 8 per cent for clothing, 2 per cent for personal care, 5 per cent for medical care, and 9 per cent for all "other" consumption. About 20 per cent also goes for taxes. (Source: U. S. Department of Labor, Bureau of Labor Statistics, *News Release*, April 9, 1975.)

25. See Walter Dill Scott, "Psychology of Advertising," *Atlantic Monthly*, 93 (January 1904), pp. 29–36.

26. John Kenneth Galbraith, *The Affluent Society*, rev. ed. (New York: Houghton Mifflin, 1966). The effects on national economic policies (in areas such as defense spending, growth of government, programs to aid the nation's poor, etc.) of the post-World War Two "unlimited-growth-to-maintain-full-employment" philosophy is the topic of Galbraith's book.

27. The Editors of *Fortune*, *The Changing American Market* (Garden City, New York: Hanover House, 1955), pp. 233–34; 241.

28. Vance Packard, *The Waste Makers* (New York: D. McKay Co., 1960), p. 159ff.

29. Ibid., p. 169.

30. Packard, *The Hidden Persuaders* (New York: D. McKay Co., 1957), p. 7.

31. Ibid., p. 116.

32. Editors of *Fortune*, op. cit., pp. 57, 15–21. After 1947, the American "middle" class began growing rapidly. In 1953, the editors of *Fortune* reported that 58 per cent of all family units had a real income of $3,000 to $10,000 as against only 31 per cent of all families in 1929 (using 1953 dollars). Furthermore, nearly 40 of the 52 per cent increase in middle-income families came after 1947.

33. See William Lloyd Warner, *Social Class in America; A Manual of Procedure for the Measurement of Social Status* (New York: Harper & Row, 1949, 1960), Chapter 1. See also, Packard, *The Hidden Persuaders*, pp. 115–17.

34. Mirra Komarovsky, *Blue-Collar Marriage* (New York: Random House, 1964).

35. Editors of *Fortune*, op. cit., p. 23.

36. Packard, op. cit., p. 85.

37. *Tide*, January 1932, p. 19.

38. During the early 1970s, feminine hygiene *deodorants* became big sellers. These products make it possible to bypass germs and go straight to the odor. As of this writing, they are fast on their way to becoming illegal.

39. *Tide*, January 1933, pp. 12–13.

40. Peterson, op. cit., p. 38.

41. See, for example, Alva Myrdal and Viola Klein, *Women's Two Roles: Home and Work* (London: Routledge & Paul, 1956; rev. ed. 1968); and Theodore Caplow, *The Sociology of Work* (Minneapolis: University of Minnesota Press, 1954). More explicitly feminist commentaries on the slow-paced entry of middle-class women into the labor force appear in Caroline Bird, *Born Female; The High Cost of Keeping Women Down* (New York: McKay Publishing Co., 1968); and Betty Friedan, *The Feminine Mystique* (New York: Dell Publishing Co., 1963). A good analysis based on labor market demand is Valerie Kincada Oppenheimer, *The Female Labor Force in the United States; Demographic and Economic Factors Governing Its Growth and Changing Composition*, Population Monograph Series, No. 5 (Berkeley: University of California Institute of International Studies, 1970).

42. Friedan, op. cit., p. 197.

43. See Friedan's chapter on "The Sexual Sell."

44. John Kenneth Galbraith, "The Economics of the American Housewife," *The Atlantic Monthly*, August 1973, p. 79.

45. Alice E. Courtney and Sarah Wernick Lockeretz, "A Woman's Place: An Analysis of the Roles Portrayed by Women in Magazine Advertisements," *Journal of Marketing Research*, VIII (February 1971), p. 93.

46. Cornelia Butler Flora, "The Passive Female: Her Comparative Image by Class and Culture in Women's Magazine Fiction," *Journal of Marriage and the Family*, August 1971, pp. 435–44.

47. Marshall McLuhan, *Understanding Media: The Extensions of Man* (New York: Signet Books, 1964), pp. 183, 202–3.

48. The best account of the nineteenth-century women's movement is still Eleanor Flexner's *Century of Struggle*. O'Neill's *Everyone Was Brave* and Kraditor's *Ideas of the Woman's Suffrage Movement* are also helpful. See note 19 for complete citations. The most comprehensive history is Elizabeth Cady Stanton, et al., *History of Woman Suffrage* (Rochester, New York, 1889).

49. Barbara Welter, "The Cult of True Womanhood: 1820–1860," in Jean E. Friedman and William G. Shade, *Our American Sisters: Women in American Life and Thought* (Boston: Allyn and Bacon, Inc., 1973). Poem from the *Ladies Wreath* quoted on page 114.

50. See note 19.

51. Presbrey, op. cit., gives several examples of Spotless Town jingles on pages 378 and 379. The jingle about the Spotless Town doctor goes as follows:

> This lean M.D. is Dr. Brown,
> Who fares but ill in Spotless Town.
> The town is so confounded clean,
> It is no wonder he is lean,
> He's lost all patients now, you know,
> Because they use SAPOLIO.

52. Steward H. Revoldt, James D. Scott, and Martin R. Warchaw, *Introduction to Marketing Management* (Homewood, Illinois: Richard D. Irwin, Inc., 1969), pp. 432–35.

CHAPTER 5

1. See Alfred L. Kroeber, *Style and Civilizations* (Ithaca, New York: Cornell University Press, 1957), p. 7ff.

2. J. C. Flugel, *Psychology of Clothes* (New York: Robert O. Ballou, 1930). See also Edmund Bergler, *Fashion and the Unconscious* (New York: Basic Books, 1955). Among more generalized theories, British fashion historian James Laver, for example, believes that men have historically chosen their mates on the basis of sexual attractiveness whereas women have chosen their mates on the basis of social status or their ability as providers. His ideas seem unduly influenced by middle-class, industrial-era values, but they lead him to conclude, in *Modesty in Dress; An Inquiry into the Fundamentals of Fashion* (Boston: Houghton Mifflin Company, 1969), that women's clothes have been governed by what he calls the "Seduction Principle" in contrast to men's clothes which he claims are governed by the "Hierarchical Principle."

3. Benjamin Franklin, *The Autobiography and Selections from His Other Writings* (New York: The Illustrated Modern Library, Random House, 1944), p. 75.

4. For a brief period in the early 1790s, following the onset of the French Revolution in 1789, the "peasant style" dresses worn facetiously as costumes by Mme. Pompadour and Marie Antoinette became a sort of national costume. They featured plain, gathered skirts, without hoops, and bodices emphasizing the bust. The more elegant Grecian look became dominant after 1795, however.

5. In her *Reminiscences*, for example, Lady Dorothy Neville related an incident in which her hooped skirts caught on fire in the drawing room when only other ladies were present. She saved herself by rolling in some rugs on the floor, but was appalled at the realization that "None of the other ladies present could of course come to assist me, for their enormous crinolines rendered them almost completely impotent to deal with fire."

6. Anny Latour, *Kings of Fashion*, Mervyn Savill, trans. (London: Weidenfeld and Nicolson, 1958), p. 102.

7. See Norah Waugh, *Corsets and Crinolines* (Boston: Boston Book and Art Shop, 1954).

8. Frank Presbrey, *The History and Development of Advertising* (Garden City, New York: Doubleday, Doran & Co., 1929), pp. 362–63.

9. David L. Cohn, *The Good Old Days; A History of American Morals and Manners As Seen Through the Sears, Roebuck Catalogs, 1905 to Present* (New York: Simon and Schuster, 1940), p. 294.

10. According to James Laver, prior to the 1890s many doctors unscrupulously advocated tight lacing, saying it *supported* the female figure. During the nineties, however, medicine became increasingly professionalized under the influence of the American Medical Association, and doctors became unanimous in urging saner dress for women. In particular, women were warned against tight lacings.

11. Reported in Cohn, op. cit., p. 376. The research was done in London by Dr. Arabella Kenealy, but Cohn cites interesting corroborating studies done in the United States as well.

12. Edmonde Charles-Roux, *Chanel: Her Life, Her World, and the Woman Behind the Legend She Herself Created*, Nancy Amphoux, trans. (New York: Alfred A. Knopf, 1975).

13. See Laver, op. cit.

14. Winifred Raushenbush, "Fashion Goes American," *Harper's Magazine*, December 1941, pp. 75–83.

15. Jane Dormer, *Fashion: the Changing Shape of Fashion Through the Years* (London: Octopus Books, 1974), p. 109.

16. Figures quoted in Richard Donovan, "Dior," *Collier's* 135 (June 10, 1955), pp. 34–39.

17. See The Editors of *Fortune, The Changing American Market* (Garden City, New York: Hanover House, 1955), pp. 175–96.

Index

ABC (TV), 51

Academy Awards, 110, 128–29, 130, 132

Actors, 87, 91, 92, 97, 102, 104, 105, 106, 107, 109–10, 111, 125, 127. *See under* name

Actresses, xv, xix, 43, 44, 82, 84, 85ff., 92, 95, 97, 101, 103, 104, 105, 109–10, 117, 118, 119, 122ff., 129, 130–33, 225; sexuality, 43; strong, 133; "supermoms," xiii. *See also under* name

Adams, Harriet S., 31

Adam's Rib, 92, 113, 116, 122

Addams, Jane, 151

Adolescents, fiction for, 27. *See* Teen-agers *and* Youth

Adultery, xviii

Adversary relationship, 63, 67, 72, 99

Advertising, 142, 189; audience, 142; consumer self-image, 142; cosmetics, 161–63, 171; creating demand, 155–56, 159–60, 172–73; foods, 153; goals, 156; homemaking, xii; images of women, xv, 154–55, 161, 225; "instant motif," 157; "jingles," 235 n. 23, 238 n. 51; magazines, 142ff., 145, 151–54 (*see also under* Magazines); market, 148; motivation research, 157ff., 161; national,

146, 153–54; patent medicine, 151–52, 234 n. 18; "Psychology of," 155; sex, 161–62; soaps, 153–54; stereotypes, 167; techniques, 155–56, 157ff.; trade journals, 233 n. 2

Advertising Age, 233 n. 2

Affluent Society, The, 156

African Queen, The, 92

Alcott, Louisa May, 31, 151; *Little Women*, 31

Alger, Horatio, 3

Alice Doesn't Live Here Anymore, 2

Allen, Frederik Lewis, 25, 146

"All in the Family," 48, 50, 63, 70–72, 75

Allyson, June, 121

Alther, Lisa: *Kinflicks*, 1

America. *See* United States

American Magazine, The, 204 n.

American Medical Association, 235 n. 18; 240 n. 10

American Revolution, 14

Andrews, Julie, xiii, 127–28, 129

Anna Christie, 106

Ann-Margret, 129

Anthropologists, 175

Apartment, The, 92

Arnaz, Desi, 68–69

Arthur, Jean, xv, xix, 109, 111

Arthur, T. S., 16; *Ten Nights in a Barroom*, 21

Arzner, Dorothy, 112

Astaire, Fred, 109, 232 n. 8

"As the World Turns," 56, 61–62
Astor, Mary, 118
Atherton, Gertrude: *Black Oxen*, 27
Australia, 211
Automobile, 191, 197, 224
"Avengers, The," 84–85

Bacall, Lauren, 115
Bain, Barbara, 85
Balenciaga, Christobel, 214
Ball, Lucille, 68–69
Balsan, Étienne, 201, 202
Bancroft, Anne, 92, 129
Bankhead, Tallulah, 128
Bara, Theda, 99
Bardot, Brigitte, 43, 123, 124
Barrymore, John, 110
Beavers, Louise, 130
Beery, Wallace, 107
Bells on Their Toes, 121
Ben Hur, 26
Benny, Jack, 49
Bergler, Edmund, 176
Bergman, Ingmar, 128
Bergman, Ingrid, 118
Bergstein, Eleanor: *Advancing Paul Newman*, 1
Berle, Milton, 49
Better Homes and Gardens, 149
Bicycling, 188–90, 224
"Big Valley," 82
"Bionic Woman, The," 89
Birth control, 8, 10, 60; the Pill, xviii, 138, 139, 217
Birth of a Nation, 112
Birth rate, 121, 214
Blackman, Honor, 85
Blacks, 136, 139–40, 141; job discrimination, 139–40; magazines, 136, 140; media, 136; movies, 129–32; TV, 58, 72, 73, 86, 87
Blair, Linda, 132
Blake, Amanda, 82
Blondell, Joan, 207

Blonde Venus, 105–6
Blue Angel, The, 105
Boardinghouses, 22
"Bob Newhart Show," 65
Bogart, Humphrey, 92, 104, 114–15
Bogle, Donald, 130–31; *Toms, Coons, Mulattoes, Mammies and Bucks*, 130
Bok, Edward, xii, 143, 149, 150–52, 153, 170–71, 173
"Bonanza," 77, 80, 81, 82
Bond, James, 85
Bond, Julian, 136
Books: Clubs, 29; housewife lifestyle, x. *See* Reading
Boone, Pat, 125
Boussac, Marcel, 210–11
Boutiques, 217
Bow, Clara, xv, 102, 103, 104, 112
Boyer, Charles, 110
Brando, Marlon, 91
Bridge on the River Kwai, The, 124
Bringing Up Baby, 110
Broadway, 110. *See* Theater
Brown, Helen Gurley, 135–36, 139, 168–69, 217; *Sex and the Office*, 135. *See Sex and the Single Girl*
Brown, Herbert, 11
Brown, William Hill: *The Power of Sympathy*, 14
Bunker, Archie, 50, 71
Burns and Allen, 49
Burstyn, Ellen, 133
Butch Cassidy and the Sundance Kid, 91

Cabaret, 132
Cagney, James, 104
Caine Mutiny, The, 124
Caldwell, Erskine: *God's Little Acre*, 28
Camille, 106
Canada, 33 *n.*; fashion, 211; TV, 71

Capel, Arthur "Boy," 201, 202

Capra, Frank, 133

Carey, Gary, 110

Carnal Knowledge, 129

Carroll, Diahann, 73

Castle, Irene, 197, 203

Castle, Vernon, 197

Catholic National League of Decency, xviii, 108

Cawelti, John G., 4–5, 24, 30, 43, 80, 166; *Adventure, Mystery and Romance*, 4–5

CBS (TV), 50, 62

Censorship: movies, 107–8; -self (TV), 50

Chanel, Gabrielle "Coco," xvi, 200–3, 204, 209, 216, 224; comeback, 213–14; "look," 213; models, 207

Chaney, Lon, 111

Chaplin, Charlie, 102

Charles-Roux, Edmonde, 201–2, 213

"Charlie's Angels," 88–89

Charlotte Temple: A Tale of Truth, xiv, 12–14, 16, 40

Chastity, x, xvii–xviii

Cheaper by the Dozen, 121

Chicago, 141; *Tribune*, 157, 158

Child, Julia: "The French Chef," 52

Children, 25, 30–31, 49, 51 *n.*, 60, 78, 143

Chile, 211

Christie, Julie, 92, 128–29

Cinemascope, 120

Cinerama, 120

Civil War, 151, 153, 164, 170, 181, 192

Clubs (women's), 152

Colbert, Claudette, xix, 109, 110, 111

Colgate University, 162

Colleges, 169; fashion, 191, 192; women's lib, 140–41

Collier's, 152

Comedians, 49

Commission on the Status of Women, 140; Third National Conference, 140

Como, Perry, 49

Cooper, Gary, 110, 111

Cooper, James Fenimore, 15, 41; *The Leatherstocking Tales*, 41

Cosmopolitan (Cosmo), xii, xviii, 2, 135ff., 139, 145, 147, 148, 149; advertising, 173; editor, 135; image of women, 164, 168; philosophy, 168; readers, 168–69

Costain, Thomas, 26–27; *The Silver Chalice*, 27

Costume jewelry, 202

Cotton, Joseph, 110

Courrèges, André, 218–19

Courting: etiquette, 189

Craine, Jeanne, 131

Crane, Stephen; 26 *n*; *Maggie*, 26 *n.*

Crawford, Joan, xv, 92, 101–2, 104, 111, 112, 118, 128, 207, 225, 232 *n.* 8

Critics, xiv, xxi, 4, 11, 17, 20–21, 28, 29, 38, 80, 108; fiction, 166; movie, 91, 126, 128; TV, 74, 82

Crosby, Bing, 49

Cuba, 211

Culture. *See* Popular culture

Cummins, Maria: *The Lamplighter*, 18

Curtis, Cyrus H. K., 145–47, 148, 149, 173

Curtis, Louisa Knapp, 150

Daisy Kenyon, 118

Dancing, 109, 197; fashion, 200

Dandridge, Dorothy, 131

Daniels, Bebe, 103

Dark Victory, 118

Darling, 92, 129

Daughters of the American Revolution (DAR), xviii, 108

Davies, Marion, 103
Davis, Bette, xv, 92, 111–12, 118, 128, 225
Day, Doris, xiii, xix, 125–26
Days of Wine and Roses, 92
Dee, Sandra, 125, 127
De Havilland, Olivia, 118, 128
Delineator, The, 149, 152, 153, 192
De Mille, Cecil B., xiii, xv, xix, 99–101, 120, 133; fashion, 207
Demimonde, 105–6, 198
Deneuve, Catherine, 129
Dennis, Sandy, 129
Depression, Great, xiii, 101, 104, 109, 110, 210; fashion, 205; movies, xiii, 111, 232 *n.* 8
Designers (fashion), xvi, 176, 183–84, 188, 194, 198, 200, 203, 204 *and n.*, 209ff., 214, 216, 217, 218, 224; American, 206, 207–8, 221; English, 217, 219. *See also under* name
Diamond Jim, 107
Diary of a Mad Housewife, 1, 3
Dickinson, Angie, 88
Dickson, William Kennedy, 93
"Dick Van Dyke Show, The," 66–68
Dietrich, Marlene, xv, xix, 104–6, 232 *n.* 8
Dinner at Eight, 107
Dior, Christian, *xvi*, 204 *n.*, 209–13, 214, 216
Dirty Harry, 91
Disc jockey, 49
Discrimination (Title VII), 139, 140
Divorce, 64, 100, 160, 203; rate, 139
Donahue, Troy, 127
Dormer, Jane, 209
Double Indemnity, 118
Doucet, House of (fashion), 198
Douglas, Lloyd: *The Robe*, 26
Doyle, Conan: *A Study in Scarlet*, 29

"Dragnet," 83
Dreiser, Theodore: *Sister Carrie*, 26 *n.*
Dressler, Marie, 103
Dressmakers, 183. *See* Designers *and* Sewing
Drinking, 21–22
Duke, Patty, 129
Dunne, Irene, xix, 109

Easy Rider, 91
Economy. *See under* United States
Edison, Thomas Alva, 93, 94, 196–97
Editors, xi, xii, 135, 136, 137, 143, 170, 196. *See under* name
Education, xx, 19, 121, 144, 231 *n.* 1, 233 *n.* 5; fashion, 175; magazines, 143; medical, 235 *n.* 18; moral, xi; public, xi, 15, 144, 145; TV, 52; women, 11, 12, 144. *See* Colleges
Elsie Dinsmore series, 31
Emmy awards, 66
Employment, 8, 139–40; women, 196–97; fashion, 178, 208–9, percentage, 164, postwar, 232 *n.* 9; TV portrayal, 65
England, 10–11, 12, 145, 153, 178, 183, 184; advertising, 234 *n.* 18; fashion, 184, 211, 217–18, 239 *n.* 2; Harlequin romances, 33 *and n.*, 37–38 *(see also under* Fiction); Industrial Revolution, 7; movies, 128–29; TV, 84–85
Equal Employment Opportunity Commission (EEOC), 140
Equal Rights Amendment, 141
Ecapism, 4, 38; movies, 111, 113, 118
Essence, 136–37, 138, 139, 140, 173; editor, 136
Eugenie, Empress of France, 181ff., 185
Europe, 105, 200; fashion, 178 *(see* Paris); movies, 128–29

Evans, Augusta Jane: *St. Elmo*, 18
Everywoman's, 149
Exorcist, The, 132

Fabian, Warner: *Flaming Youth*, 2
Fairbanks, Douglas, 97
Family, 71, 74–77; surrogates, 65–66, 74; TV, 49, 50
Family Circle, 135, 149
Farm Journal, 145
Farrow, Mia, 92, 129
Fashion (clothing), xiii–xiv, xvi, xxii, 16, 52, 175, 176–77, 216–17, 220, 239 *n.* 2, 4; affluence, 181; analysts, 176; bikini, 219; capitol, 184 (*see* Paris); catalogue houses, 192; commentators, 207, 219; cost, 209; creating demand, 159–60; cycles, 175–76; designers (*see* Designers); Europe, 178 (*see* France *and* Paris); free will, 221, 224; haute couture, 209–11, 218, as big business, 184 (*see* Designers); historians, 182, 205, 209, 239 *n.* 2; -image, relationship, xvi–xvii; leadership, 206; -lifestyles, relationship, 224; maternity, 214; men's, 176–77, 219; miniskirt, 218, 219, 220; models, 184–85, 206–7; New Look, 204 *n.*, 210, 211–13, 216; Orient, influence, 198–200, 202; pants, 191, 203, 209, 219–21; Paris-Hollywood differences, 207; postwar, xvi; psychological meaning, 200; ready-to-wear industry, 207, 209, 216, 217; separates, 192, 216–17; sex, 176, 180, 217–19; showplaces, 185; sports, 188–90 (*see* Sports); trade magazine, 219; trends, 175ff., 185, -history, relationship, 178. *See* Designers, Fashionable women, Movies *and* Paris
Fashionable women, 177–78, 181,
185, 192–94, 199, 202–3, 218–19; accessories, 203, 204 *n.*, 218; "classical look," 178; costume jewelry, 202; health, 177 (*see* Health); *illustrations*, 179, 180, 183, 186, 187, 190, 193, 195, 199, 205, 206, 208, 212, 215–16; images of, 175ff., 188, 189, 191, 211–13, 214, 218, 219, 221, -lifestyle conflict, 196ff., 200, 217; postwar, 211ff.; ready-to-wear, 191–92; sexpot, 214; style: as reflection of society, 178ff., 191, 205–6, 217ff., 220, -status, relationship, 178. *See* Designers *and* Fashion
Father of the Bride, 121, 124
Fawcett-Majors, Farrah, 88
Fear of Flying, 1
Fellini, Federico, 128
Feminine Mystique, The, 120–21, 140, 165
Feminists, 137, 139, 144, 164–65, 167, 224, 237 *n.* 41; fashion, 191. *See* Women's Liberation Movement
Fiction, xvii, 1, 3, 4–7, 9, 11, 14ff., 27, 28, 41, 99; adventure, 5, 39, 41; best sellers, 1, 2, 3, 4, 12, 16, 25, 26, 27, 28–29, 41; children, 25, 30–31; classification, 166; detective, 3, 4, 5, 29–31, 38, 40–42, 44 (*see* Spillane, Mickey); domestic, 117, 164: melodrama, xii, xiii, 3, 10, 27–28, 49, novel, 14ff.–26, 56, 166, 170; *Elsie* books, 19; formulas, 3, 4–6, 10–11, 28–29, 74 (*see* Richardson, Samuel); Gothic, 14, 27, 32ff., 40; Harlequin, 27, 33 *and n.*–38; heroes, 3, 34ff., 39, 42; heroines, 1–2, 7, 12–13, 14, 17–18, 19, 24–26 *and n.*, 32–33; historical, 26, 33–35, 38; images of women, 1ff., 32, 45, 120, 122, 225; magazines, xii, 143, 168;

moral fantasy, 4–5, 24, 27–28, 44–45; most popular, 5; mystery, 5 (*see also* detective); pornography, 41; ranking system, 28–29; religion, 17, 18, 19, 21, 22, 24–25; romance (*or* courtship), 3, 4, 5–6, 10, 33ff., 40; serialized, 49; sex, 1, 28, 41–44; "social novel," 21–22; themes, 1, 2, 3, 14–15, 19–21, 28, 33; Westerns, 4, 5, 39, 41, 80
Fiedler, Leslie, 91
Fielding, Henry, 6; *Shamela*, 8–9
Fields, W. C., 102
Finley, Martha, 19
Finley, Walter, 65
Fisher, Dorothy Canfield, 27; *The Brimming Cup*, 27–28
Fitzgerald, F. Scott, 27
Flappers, 202, 205
Flugel, J. C., 176
Flying Down to Rio, 109
Fonda, Jane, 92, 133
Fonda, Peter, 125
Fontaine, Joan, 118
Fortune, 156, 158, 160, 216–17
France, 105, 184; fashion, 178, 181–83, 239 *n.* 4. *See* Designers *and* Paris
Francis, Arlene: "Home Show," 52
Francis, Kay, 110, 232 *n.*
Franco-Prussian War, 185
Franklin, Benjamin, 191; *Autobiography*, 177
French Connection, The, 91
French Revolution, 178, 198, 239 *n.* 4
Frenzy, xv
Freud, Sigmund, 39
Friedan, Betty, 120–21, 122, 140, 141; *The Feminine Mystique*, 120–21, 140, 165
Funny Girl, 132
Furness, Betty, 51

Gable, Clark, 107, 110, 112
Gabor, Zsa Zsa, 128
Gaches-Surraute, Mme., 194
Galbraith, John Kenneth, 53–54, 156, 165–66
Garbo, Greta, xv, xviii, xix, 104–5, 106, 207, 232 *n.* 8
Garland, Judy, 109
Gavin, John, 125
Gelman, Judith S.: *Women in Television News*, 51
Gentlemen Prefer Blondes, 122
Georgy Girl, 129
Gerbner, George, 230 *n.* 10
Germany, 105
Gidget, 127
Gillespie, Marcia Ann, 136, 140
Gilman, Caroline Howard, 16
Gish, Dorothy, 112
Gish, Lillian, 98, 112
Glenn Miller Story, The, 121
Glynn, Elinor, 102
Godey, Louis A., 144
Godey's Lady's Book, xi, xiv, 143–45, 147, 149–50; editor, 143 (*see under* name); fashion, 182; influence, 143; religion, 170
Godfather, The, 91
Gold Diggers of 1933, 207
Goldfinger, 85
Gone With The Wind, 26, 120, 130, 181
Good Housekeeping, 135, 145, 149; Seal of Approval, 152
"Good Times," 73
Gordon, Ruth, 116, 225
Grable, Betty, 118–19, 124
Graduate, The, 92
Graham's, 143
Grant, Cary, 106, 110, 114, 115, 118
Grant, Lou, 66
Griffith, D. W., 98–99, 100, 112, 133
Gross, Larry, 230 *n.* 10
"Gunsmoke," 81–82

Hairstyles, 203, 207, 208

Hale, Sarah Josepha, 143, 144–45, 149, 150, 173

Hamill, Dorothy, xx

Hamner, Earl, Jr., 74

Hardy Boys, 30

Harland, Marion: *Alone*, 18

Harlequin Enterprises, 33 *and n.*, 34, 38. *See also under* Fiction

Harlow, Jean, xv, xviii, xix, 104, 106–7, 207

Harper's Bazaar, 149

Hartley, Emily, 65

Haskell, Molly, 102, 106, 108, 109, 111, 118, 126; *From Reverence to Rape*, 92–93

"Hawaii Five-O," 83

Hawks, Elizabeth, 206

Hawks, Howard, 114, 115

Hawn, Goldie, 92, 129

Hawthorne, Nathaniel, 5

Hays Office, 108

Hayworth, Rita, 119, 124

Health (*and* safety): -fashion, relationship, 177, 179, 187, 188–89, 192, 239 *n.* 5, 240 *n.* 10; women vs men, 227 *n.* 5

Hearst, William Randolph, xviii, 108

Heflin, Van, 110

Hello, Dolly!, 132

Hemingway, Ernest, 27, 29, 114

Hepburn, Katharine, xv, 92, 110, 114, 115–17, 225, 232 *n.* 8

Hershey, Lenore, 137

Hidden Persuaders, The, 157

Hijacking, xx

Hill, Grace Livingston, 25

His Girl Friday, 113, 114, 115

Historians, 182, 205, 209, 239 *n.* 2

Holden, William, 112

Holiday, 110

Holiday, Billie, 130, 131

Holliday, Judy, 116, 122–23

Hollywood: -fashion, 206–7. *See* Movies

Homes: two-home concept, 160

Homosexuals, xviii, 128; "cultural," 91; designers, 176

Hope, Bob, 49

Horne, Lena, 131

Housewives, xi, xii–xiii, xiv; fantasy, 60, 69; function, 54; image (*see under* Images of women)

How to Marry a Millionaire, 122

Hudson, Rock, 87

Hull, Edith M.: *The Sheik*, 27

Hutchinson, A. S. M.: *This Freedom*, 2

"I Dream of Jeannie," 69–70

Illiteracy, 144

Illustrators, 146

"I Love Lucy," 64, 68

Images of women: assessment, xx; creators, xxi; deserted wife, xxi; enduring fantasy, 44–45; housewife, ix, x, xii, xvii, 165–66, 223, 224, advertising, 155, 156, 158–59, 163–66, 172, 173, clothing, 175, ideal, 164, magazines, 135, 138, 142, 150, 164, 166–68, 225, TV, xiii, 64–65, 70, 225; passive, ix, x, xiv, xvi, xvii, 224, advertising, 155, 163, 167, 172, fashion, 178, fiction, 12, 13, 225, magazines, xv, 138, 139, 142, 167–68, 225; pretty, x, xix–xx, advertising, xix–xx, 155, 163, 171–172, magazines, xix–xx, 142, 171–72, movies, xix, TV, xix; standard, ix–x; wholesome, ix, x, xvii, advertising, 155, 163, 171, 172, fiction, 7, magazines, 138, 142, 169, 171

Independent Theatre Owners of America, 232 *n.* 8

Industrial Revolution (*and* industrialization), xi, 7–8, 10, 16, 177–78; women's, xi–xii

Institute for Motivation Research, 161

It, 102

Italy, 203

It Happened One Night, 110

Jackson, Andrew, 178

Jackson, Glenda, 92, 129, 133

Jaffe, Rona: *The Best of Everything,* 122

James, Henry, 5

Jaws, 91

Jazz Singer, The, 103

Jet setters, 204

Jewelry (costume), 202

Jews, 132

Jezebel, 92

Johnston, Mary: *To Have and to Hold,* 26

Jolson, Al, 103

Jong, Erica, 1, 225; *Fear of Flying,* 1

Journal of Marketing Research, 167

Juveniles (fiction), 30–31

Kanin, Garson, 116, 225

Kaufman, Sue: *Diary of a Mad Housewife,* 1, 3

Keeler, Ruby, 207

Kennedy, John F., 140

Kerr, Dorothy, 127

Kilgallen, Dorothy, 51

King, Billy Jean, 141

King, Martin Luther, Jr., 136

Kirk, Phyllis, 87

Klute, 2, 92, 133

Knickerbocker, 143

Komarovsky, Mirra, 158–59; *Blue-Collar Marriage,* 158

Kroeber, Alfred L., 175

Laddie, 25

Ladies Home Journal, xii, xiv, 135, 137, 145–48, 149–52, 164, 173; advertising, 150–51; circulation, 147; editors, 137, 143, 149 (*see under* name); formula, 151, 164, 170, 171, 173

Ladies Wreath, 170

Lady in the Dark, 118

Lady Sings the Blues, 130, 131–32

Laird, Donald, 162–63

Last Picture Show, The, 92

Latour, Anny, 182, 185

Laurel and Hardy, 102

Laver, James, 205, 239 *n.* 2, 240 *n.* 10

Lavin, Mary, 2

Law and order, 82–83

Lawford, Peter, 87

Leachman, Cloris, 92, 133

Lear, Norman, 50, 70

Leavis, Queenie D.: *Fiction and the Reading Public,* 28–29

Lee, Hannah F. S., 16

Leigh, Vivien, 207

Leisure, xi, 11, 33

Lelong, Lucien, 210

Lerner, Gerda, 15–16

Lesbians, xviii, 128

Libbey, Laura Jean, x, 25–26

Life (magazine), 148

Lifestyles, 10, 15–16, 21–22, 145; fashion, 214, 216, 224; suburbia, 214, 216

Life with Father, 121

Lillie, Bea, 103

"Little House on the Prairie," 75, 76–77, 81

Little Women, 121

Lombard, Carole, 109

London, 184. *See* England

Look (magazine), 148

Louis Philippe, of France, 178

Lovely, Louise, 95

Love Story, 133

Loy, Myrna, 87

Luce, Clare Booth, 113

Lurie, Alison: *War Between the Tates,* 1

McCall's, 135, 139, 145, 149, 173, 192; patterns, 153; "Use-tested" guarantee, 152

McClure's, 145, 147, 148

McDaniel, Hattie, 130

Macdonald, Dwight: *On Movies*, 126

McDoughall, Ruth Doan: *The Cheerleader*, 1

McGraw, Ali, 133

McKinney, Nina Mae, 131

MacLaine, Shirley, 92, 127

McLuhan, Marshall, 63, 169

McQueen, Steve, 127

Mademoiselle, 149

Magazines, 2, 49, 146, 226, 234 *n.* 15; advertising, 145–47, 150–51, 154, 233 *n.* 2, images of women, 142, 153, 155; advice to women, xiv–xv; circulation, 146, 149; fiction, xii; history, 143; images of women, 153, 155, 169, 225 (*see* Images of women); love story, xii, 166–67, 168; mass, 146, 148, 151, 173; men's, xii; most popular, 148; movie, 166, 167; national, 142, 144; pattern, 153, 192; picture, 169; specialized, 148; trade, 219; types, 143; women's, 135ff., 148–49, 169, 173, advertising, 151–53, 163ff., Blacks, 136, 140, content, x–xii, 147–48, cost, 147, feminist, 141, fiction, 168, history, 143, 144, 147ff., images of women, 135ff., 142, 143, 169, influence, 143, readership, 142, 144, service, 164, 170–71, standards, xvii–xviii. *See also under* name

Magazines in the Twentieth Century, 163

Magazines in the United States, 143

Mainbocher, 207–8

Major, Charles: *When Knighthood Was in Flower*, 26

Maltese Falcon, The, 118

Mansfield, Jayne, 44, 123, 124

"Marcus Welby, M.D.," 78–79

Marriage, x, 9–10, 16, 25, 63, 177, 214, 226; age, 121, 139, 160; *Blue-Collar Marriage*, 158; fiction, 9, 13; as goal, 191; importance, 7–9; media, 120–21; movies, 100–2, 108, 113, 122, 125–26, 127ff.; TV, 64

Marshall, Herbert, 105

Marx Brothers, 102

Mary Poppins, 127

"Mary Tyler Moore Show," 65–66, 72, 73

"M*A*S*H," 66

Mason, Bobbie Ann: *The Girl Sleuth*, 32

"Maude," 63, 65, 72

Media, xi, 1, 48, 80; images of women, 120; influence, xx

"Medical Center," 78, 79

Melville, Herman, 5

Member of the Wedding, The, 130

Men, xx, 8, 9, 15; fashion, 176–77, 219; magazines, xii (*see Playboy*); status, 10, 15. *See* Heroes *under* Fiction, Movies *and* TV

Metalious, Grace: *Peyton Place*, 28, 122

Metternich, Prince, 185

Metternich, Princess, 185

Mexico, 211

Michener, James: *Hawaii*, 27

Middle-class, xi–xii, 26, 30, 117–18, 157–59, 177

Midnight Cowboy, 91

Mildred Pierce, 118

Miller, Arthur, 123

Minelli, Liza, 132

Minorities, xvi, 89. *See* Blacks

Miracle Worker, The, 129

Miss America pageant, 137, 141, 220

"Mission Impossible," 85

Mitchell, Margaret, 26. *See Gone With The Wind*

Models (fashion), 184–85, 206–7

Modern Screen, 166

"Mod Squad," 86, 87

Monroe, Marilyn, 43, 44, 123, 124, 141

Montgomery, Lucy: *Anne of Green Gables,* 25

Montgomery, Robert, 112

Montgomery Ward, 192

Moore, Colleen, 101, 103

Moore, Mary Tyler, 66, 67

Morality, xviii, 101. *See* Values

Moreau, Jeanne, 129

Morgenstern, Rhoda, 65

Motherhood, 8, 139, 171, 214; "supermoms," xiii; unwed, 13, 127

Movies, xviii, 2, 63, 85, 87, 91, 101, 111, 112, 197, 217–18, 231 *n.* 1; attendance, 50, 119, 123, 126; audience, 94–96, 97, 101, 102, 103, 110, 112, 117, 123–25; "B," 126–27, 129, 132; best year, 103; Blacks, 129–32; censors, 107–8; children, 108–9, 132; cinemascope, 120; cinerama, 120; classics, 108, 114; comedy, 102–3, 104, 108–10, 115ff., best, 115; couples, 115; critics, 99; directors, 93, 115, 128–29, 133; drive-ins, 126–27; escapist, 111, 113, 118; fashion, 100, 204, 207; feminist, 2; formulas, 129–30; gangster, 104, 108; heroes, 91, 95, 96, 114, super-, 91; heroines, xviii, xix, 92ff., 101ff., 110–12ff., 118–19, 122ff., 132, 133, 232 *n.* 8, child, 97, *demimonde,* 105–6, goals, 133, sexy, 122–24; history, 91–92, 93ff., 103, 111; horror, 111; images of women, xv, xix, 44, 91ff., 115, 121, 125ff., 133,

224–25, conflicting, 113, "mammary madness," 119, sexpots, 43, 44; industry, 94, 95, 96, 103, symbol, 101; -life, reflection of, 112ff.; magazines, 166, 167; matinees, xiii, 50; melodramas, 110–11, 121–22; musicals, 104, 109, 111, 113, 124–25, 132, wartime, 118–19; orientation, 133; plots, 95, 96–97, 100–1, 102, 104, most popular, 108; postwar, xv, 113, 119; producers, 123; Production Code, xviii, xix, 108–9, 127; productions, number, 119–20; sequels, 127; serialized, 49; sex(uality), xviii, 43, 44, 97, 99–100, 102, 104ff., 118ff., 128, "B," 126–27, 129, 132, censors, 107–9, equality, 116–17, Garbo, 106; silent, 95, 96, 98ff., 102–3, 108; sound, 103ff.; spectaculars, 120, 128; stars, 104, 129, 132–33, 207 "box-office poison," 232 *n.* 8, system, 97, super-, 97, 101, 207; stereotypes, 95–96; teen-agers, 49; theaters, 94–95, 103, number, 126–27; themes, xii–xiii, 28, 32, 110, 120, 122, 124–25, 128, 133, women's, 128–29; trends, 124, 129–30; TV, 48, 49–50, 119–20, 128; "vamp," 95, 96, 99; violence, 128; war, 112ff., 124; "weepies," xvii, 117; Westerns, 95, 109, 124; "women's," 117–18; writers, 93, 116, 133, 225

Mr. Deeds Goes to Town, 111

Ms., 137, 138, 139, 141, 173, 226

Muhammad Ali, 136

Munsey's Magazine, 145, 147, 148

Music(ians), 48, 49, 131–32

Nancy Drew series, 31

National Organization for Women (NOW), 140

Napoleon I, 178
Napoleon III, 181–84, 185
NBC (TV), 59
Nelson, Ozzie, 65
Neville, Lady Dorothy, 239 *n.* 5
Newark *Daily Advertiser,* 17
Newcomb, Horace: *TV: The Most Popular Art,* 74
Newhart, Bob, 65
Newscasters, 51
Newsweek, 148
New York City, 103, 141, 206–7; Broadway, 110
New York *Times,* 124
Nielsen, A. C., 48, 172
Nixon, Richard M., xix
Normand, Mabel, 103
North American Review, 143
No Sad Songs for Me, 117
Notorious, 118
Novak, Kim, 44, 123
Novels, x, xi, xii, xiv, 3, 6, 14, 17, 21–22, 23, 27. *See* Fiction
NOW. *See* National Organization for Women
Nye, Russel, 25, 26, 49, 59, 103; *Unembarrassed Muse, The,* 49

Oates, Joyce Carol, 2
O'Connor, Carroll, 71
Onassis, Jacqueline Kennedy, 219
O'Neill, Tatum, 132
O'Neill, William L., 100
Opinion Research Corporation, 124
Orient, 198–200
Oscars, 128–29, 130. *See* Academy Awards
Our Dancing Daughters, 101, 102

Packard, Vance, 54, 156–57; *The Hidden Persuaders,* 157; *The Waste Makers,* 156, 159, 160
Paige, Janice, 126
Palmer, Betsy, 51
Pamela, xvii, 6, 7, 8–9, 10, 11, 13, 17

Papashvily, Helen, 14–15, 16, 20–21, 24–25; *All the Happy Endings,* 14
Paperbacks, 28, 29
Paper Moon, 132
Parents' Magazine, 149
Paris: fashion, 183–85, 188–89, 194, 198, 201, 203, 205, 206ff., 214, 220, World War II, 207–9; -Hollywood, fashion differences, 207. *See also* Designers
Parrish, 217–18
Passive image. *See under* Images of women
Patent medicine advertising, 234 *n.* 18
Pat Garrett and Billy the Kid, 91
Perfumes, 209, 211, 213
Peterson, Theodore, 163
Peterson's, 143, 147
Peyton Place, 122
Philadelphia, 144, 149; "magazine city," 146; *Press,* 146
Philadelphia Story, The, 110
Photoplay, 166
"Phyllis," 63, 72
Pickford, Mary, 97–98, 103, 104, 107
Pill, The, xviii, 138, 139. *See also* Birth control
Pinky, 130
Pin-up girls, 119
Piquet, Robert, 210
Playboy, 135–36, 139; *-Cosmo,* relationship, 168–69
Poe, Edgar Allan, 5, 29
Poiret, Paul, 198–99, 200, 202, 203
"Police Woman," 88
Pollyanna, The Glad Girl, x, 25
Pope, Alexander, 17
Popular culture, xi–xii, xvii, xx, 2, 39, 103; critics, 80, 108; image, xiv, xxi, 7ff., 223, 224; symbols, 83–84
Pornography, 41

Porter, Eleanor, 25; *Pollyanna, The Glad Girl*, x, 25

Porter, Gene Stratton: *Freckles*, 25; *Girl of the Limberlost*, 25; *Laddie*, 25; *Michael O'Halloran*, 25

Portnoy's Complaint, 132

Possessed, 118

Powell, William, 87

Power, Tyrone, 112

Prejudice, 72. *See also* Discrimination

Presbrey, Frank, 149, 153, 154 189; *History and Development of Advertising*, 145, 189

Presley, Elvis, 125

Pretty, Arline, 95

Pretty image. *See under* Images of women

Private eye, 29. *See* Spillane, Mickey

Procter and Gamble, 154

Professions, 11–12, 16, 19, 225

Prostitutes, 105

Publishers, 140, 144–46, 147, 173

Pure Food and Drug Act, 152

Quant, Mary, 217–18, 219, 220, 224

Rachel, Rachel, 92

Radcliffe, Anne, 38

Radio, 48–49, 52–53, 56; -TV, 48

"Raised consciousness," 1, 2, 3, 4, 226

Raushenbush, Winifred, 207

Reader's Digest, 148

Readers(ing), xi, 11, 30, 44, 168, 225; -TV, 48

Reasoner, Harry, 51

Redbook, xii, 2, 168

Redgrave, Lynn, 129

Reed, Donna, xx

Reiner, Carl, 66

Reiner, Rob, 71

"Relevance movement," 79

Religion, 143, 169–71; fiction, 17, 18, 19, 21, 22, 24–25

Remick, Lee, 92

Reynolds, Debbie, xiii, xix, 125, 127

"Rhoda," 63, 65, 73

Richardson, Samuel, 3, 6, 7, 8, 9, 10–11, 12, 33; *Clarissa*, 6, 7, 8, 10, 11, 13, 49; critics, 11, 17; "moral messages," 11; *Pamela*, xvii, 6, 7, 8–9, 10, 11, 13, 17

Rigg, Diana, 84–85

Robe, The, 120

Robinson, Edward G., 104

Robinson, Jill: *Bed/Time/Story*, 1

Rogers, Ginger, 109, 118, 207

Roiphe, Anne: *Up the Sandbox*, 1

Role-playing, xi–xii, 22, 89, 176. *See* Images

"Rookies, The," 83, 86–87

"Room 222," 79–80

Roosevelt, Eleanor, 140

Rosen, Marjorie, 99, 101, 122; *Popcorn Venus*, 93

Ross, Diana, 130, 131, 132, 133

Rover Boys, 30

Rowson, Susanna Haswell, 12–14; *Charlotte Temple: A Tale of Truth*, xiv, 12–14, 16, 40

Russ, Joanna, xiv, 38, 39

Russell, Jane, 43, 124

Russell, Rosalind, xv, 114, 115

St. James, Susan, 87

St. Laurent, Yves, 214

Saturday Evening Post, The, 143, 147

Schiaparelli, Elsa "Schiap," 203–4 and n., 209

Scott, Hazel, 131

Scott, Sir Walter: *Waverley*, 26

Scott, Walter Dill, 155

Sears and Roebuck, 192

Sedgwick, Anne Douglas: *The Little French Girl*, 28

Sedgwick, Catherine Maria, 16

Serials, 49. *See under* media

Servants, xi, 196

Seventeen, 149

Sewing, 153

Sex, xviii, 82, 83, 102, 138, 139, 207, 214; advertising, 161–62; fashion, 176, 180, 207, 217–19; fiction, 1, 28, 41–44; -marriage, 8; movies (*see under* Movies); premarital, 138, 139, 217; rape, 141; revolution (1960s), 138, 139, 161, 217–18; symbols, 83–84, 88; TV, 54–55, 60, 88

Sex and the Single Girl, 138, 139, 217

Shampoo, 92

Shane, 124

Shearer, Norma, 110, 207

Shore, Dinah, 49; "Dinah's Place," 52

Shulman, Alice Kate: *Memoirs of an Ex-Prom Queen,* 1

Sigourney, Lydia, 16

Sino-Japanese War, 198

Slavery, 22–23

Smith, Kate, 49

Snake Pit, The, 118

Social survival-values, relationship, 9

Songs, 125, 235 *n.* 23

Sorry, Wrong Number, 118

Sounder, 130–31

Sound of Music, The, 127

Southworth, Mrs. E. D. E. N., xxi, 19–20, 24, 225; critics, 20–21; *The Deserted Wife,* 20, 21; *Retribution,* 19–20

Spillane, Mickey, 41–43; heroes, 42–43; *I, The Jury,* 41, 43; *Kiss Me Deadly,* 42, 43; *One Lonely Night,* 42, 43

Sports, -fashion, 188–90, 191, 192, 203, 209, 214, 216

Stalag 17, 124

Standards. *See* Values

Stanford University, 156

Stanwyck, Barbara, 82, 118

Stapleton, Jean, 71

"Star Trek," 85–86

Status, 7–8, 15–16, 18, 20

Steinbeck, John, 27

Steinem, Gloria, 141

Stepford Wives, xv

Stereotypes(ing), xi, 53, 55, 60–61, 62, 95–96, 130, 131, 167; sexual, 82, 83; Victorian, 60

Stevens, Connie, 127

Stewart, James, 110, 112

Sting, The, 91

Stowe, Harriet Beecher: *Uncle Tom's Cabin,* 22–23

Strategic Air Command, 121

Stratemeyer, Edward, 30–31

"Streets of San Francisco," 83

Streisand, Barbra, 132

Struthers, Sally, 71

Suburbia, 214, 216

Suffrage, 15

Suicide, xx

Sullivan, Margaret, 117

Summer Place, A, 125, 127, 217–18

Sunday Bloody Sunday, 92

"Superman," 49

"Supermoms," xiii

Suspicion, 118

Swanson, Gloria, xix, 101, 103, 104, 207

Sweet, Blanche, 95

Switzerland, 213

Taft, William Howard, 197

Tammy, 125, 127

Tarkington, Booth: *Claire Ambler,* 2

Taylor, Elizabeth, 92, 124, 129, 133

Teachers(ing), 16, 19

Technology, 120, 159, 196–97

Teen-agers, x, 31–32, 49, 127, 149, 217–18; Blacks, 132; fashion, 207, 218; movies, 49, 50, 101–2. *See* Youth

Television (TV), xviii, 2, 48, 50, 51, 62–63, 85–86, 88, 148, 152, 226; adversary relationship, 63, 72; audience, xiii, 44, 50, 51ff., 58, 62–63, 73, 169; Blacks, 58, 72, 73, 86, 87; classics, 75; crime drama, 82–83, 84–89; doctors, 78–79; drama, 50, 62, 63, 74, 77–80, 82, 83, 84–86; daytime, 47, 50ff., 62, 89; educational, 52; evening formulas, 47, 50, 74ff., 77ff.; "family" drama, xviii, 74–75, 76–77, 80, audience, 44; formulas, 32, 47–48, 50–51 and n., 74 (see daytime and evening); game shows, xiii, 50, 52, 53–54, 55; heroes, xvi, xix, 47, 63, 71, 78, "super," 48, 76, 80, 83, "Wasp" image, 86; heroines, xviii–xix, 66, 84–89; history, 48ff.; images of women, 47ff., 62, 72–73, 77–78, 82, 89, 225, vs. men, 50ff. (see also stereotypes); imitations, 86–87; influence, xx; issue-oriented programs, 72, 79; -movies, 119–20, 128; prime time: programs, 62–63; quiz programs, 52–53; ratings, 127, 172; -reading, relationship, 48; sets, number of, 119, 126; situation comedy (sitcoms), xiii, xv–xvi, 47, 48, 50, 62–74; soap operas, xiii, xv, xvii, 50, 55–62, 65, 89, 117, 166, audience, 58, 117, 123, themes, 56–58, 60; spin-offs, 73–74; stereotypes, 53, 55, 60–61, 63; structural inequality, 89; values, xviii, 64; victims, xvi, 89, 230 n. 10; violence, 88; watching time, 48; Westerns, 74, 76–77, 80–83; writers, 66
Temple, Charlotte, 138
Temple, Shirley, 108, 111
Ten Commandments, The, 120

Ten Nights in a Barroom, 21
10 Rillington Place, xv
Theater, legitimate, 94, 110
"Thin Man, The," 87
Thompson, Maurice: Alice of Old Vincennes, 26
Three Coins in the Fountain, 122
Tide, 161, 233 n. 2
Time, 148
To Have and Have Not, 113, 114–15
Tom Swift, 30
Towering Inferno, The, 91
Tracy, Spencer, 92, 115–17
Travel, -fashion, 203
Tribune and Farmer, The, 146
Trollope, Anthony, 15
Trollope, Frances, 15
True Confessions, xii, 166
True Story, xii, xvii, xviii, 166
Turner, Lana, 124
TV. See Television
TV Guide, 62, 81, 83
Twentieth Century-Fox, 123
Tyson, Cecily, 130–31, 133

Ulmann, Liv, 129
Uncle Tom's Cabin, 22–23
Unembarrassed Muse, The, 49
United Artists, 107
United States, 11, 14, 15, 122, 136, 161, 178; civil rights, 82, 136, 139, Act, 139, 140; economy, 156, 160, 165–66, 263 n. 24 and 32, -purchasing, relationship, 54, women's role, 142ff.; health, 151–52; middle-income families, 157–59; religious tradition, 169; self-image, 96–97
United States House of Representatives, 141
University of Pennsylvania: Annenberg School of Communications, 230 n. 10
Up the Sandbox, 1

Values, x, xi, xvii, xviii, 9, 26, 64, 96, 117–18, 156–57, 158, 177
"Vamp," 95, 96, 99
Van Dyke, Dick, 66
Vaudeville, 94
Venezuela, 211
Victoria, Queen of England, 178
Vietnam War, 82, 220
Violence, 88, 128
Vionnet, Madeleine, 204
"Virginian, The," 81
Vogue, 149
Von Sternberg, Joseph, 105–6

Wagner, Lindsay, 88
Walker, Alice, 2
Walker, Frank, 119
Wallace, George, 82
Wallace, Lew: Ben Hur, 26
Walters, Barbara, 51; "Not For Women Only," 52
"Waltons, The," 74–76, 77, 80; imitators, 76–77
War Between the Tates, 1
Warner, Lloyd: Social Class in America, 158
Warner, Susan, 16–18; The Wide, Wide World, x, 16–18, 40
Warner Brothers, 103
Washington, Fredi, 131
"Wasp" image, 86
Waste Makers, The, 156, 159, 160
Waters, Ethel, 130–31
Watt, Ian, 7; The Rise of the Novel, 7–8
Waugh, Norah, 188, 194
Wayne, John, 112
Webster, Hannah; The Coquette, 14
Welch, Raquel, 132
Welter, Barbara: Cult of True Womanhood, 170
Wertheimer, Pierre, 213
West, Mae, xv, xviii, xix, 107, 225, 232 n. 8
Westerns, 80–81; fiction, 4, 5, 39,

41, 80; movies, 95, 109, 124; TV, 74, 76–77, 80–83
Westminster, Duke of, 201, 202
Wharton, Edith, 27
"What's My Line?", 52
When Knighthood Was in Flower, 26
Wholesome image. See under Images of women
Who's Afraid of Virginia Woolf?, 92, 129
Wide, Wide World, The, 164
Wiggin, Kate Douglas: Rebecca of Sunnybrook Farm, 25
Wilder, Laura Ingalls: Little House books, 76
Wilson, Woodrow, 197
Woman of the Year, 116
Woman's Day, 135, 149
Woman's Home Companion, 145, 149, 152
Women, 10, 71, 81; images of (see Images of women); "liberated" archetype, 32; life span, 16; lifestyles, 10, 15–16, 22; status, 7–8, 20
Women's Liberation Movement, xx, 1, 2, 72–73, 137, 140–41, 144, 167; "image," 220; nineteenth century, 16, 170, 233 n. 5, 238 n. 48; peak, 72, 230 n. 7
Women's Wear Daily, 219
Wood, James Playsted, 143
Wood, Natalie, 127
Woodward, Helen: Lady Persuaders, 143
Woodward, Joanne, 92
Workbasket, 149
World War I, 94, 96, 97, 197; -fashion, 200
World War II, 40, 112ff., 118, 156, 213; -family life, 113ff.; -fashion, 207–9, 211, 224
Worth, Charles Frederick, 183–88, 198; models, 206–7
Wright Brothers, 197

Writers, 1, 2, 3, 5, 14, 15, 16, 18, 19, 25, 26–27, 29, 146, 151; "elite," 27; movies, 93, 116, 133, 225; popular, 18; stereotypes, xi; TV, 66

Young, Edward: *Night Thoughts*, 11

Youth: -fashion, 217, 218, 221; fiction, 30–31; movies, 101–2, 123–24. *See also* Teen-agers
Youth's Companion, 143

Zanuck, Darryl, 123